Form, Function, and Style in Instructional Design:
Emerging Research and Opportunities

Shalin Hai-Jew
Kansas State University, USA

A volume in the Advances in Educational Technologies and Instructional Design (AETiD) Book Series

Published in the United States of America by
IGI Global
Information Science Reference (an imprint of IGI Global)
701 E. Chocolate Avenue
Hershey PA, USA 17033
Tel: 717-533-8845
Fax: 717-533-8661
E-mail: cust@igi-global.com
Web site: http://www.igi-global.com

Copyright © 2020 by IGI Global. All rights reserved. No part of this publication may be reproduced, stored or distributed in any form or by any means, electronic or mechanical, including photocopying, without written permission from the publisher.
Product or company names used in this set are for identification purposes only. Inclusion of the names of the products or companies does not indicate a claim of ownership by IGI Global of the trademark or registered trademark.

Library of Congress Cataloging-in-Publication Data

Names: Hai-Jew, Shalin, editor.
Title: Form, function, and style in instructional design : emerging research and opportunities / Shalin Hai-Jew, Editor.
Description: Hershey, PA : Information Science Reference, [2020] | Includes bibliographical references.
Identifiers: LCCN 2019010621| ISBN 9781522598336 (hardcover) | ISBN 9781522598343 (paperback) | ISBN 9781522598350 (ebook)
Subjects: LCSH: Instructional systems--Design. | Web-based instruction--Design.
Classification: LCC LB1028.38 .F67 2020 | DDC 371.3--dc23 LC record available at https://lccn.loc.gov/2019010621

This book is published in the IGI Global book series Advances in Educational Technologies and Instructional Design (AETID) (ISSN: 2326-8905; eISSN: 2326-8913)

British Cataloguing in Publication Data
A Cataloguing in Publication record for this book is available from the British Library.

All work contributed to this book is new, previously-unpublished material.
The views expressed in this book are those of the authors, but not necessarily of the publisher.

For electronic access to this publication, please contact: eresources@igi-global.com.

Advances in Educational Technologies and Instructional Design (AETID) Book Series

ISSN:2326-8905
EISSN:2326-8913

Editor-in-Chief: Lawrence A. Tomei, Robert Morris University, USA

MISSION

Education has undergone, and continues to undergo, immense changes in the way it is enacted and distributed to both child and adult learners. In modern education, the traditional classroom learning experience has evolved to include technological resources and to provide online classroom opportunities to students of all ages regardless of their geographical locations. From distance education, Massive-Open-Online-Courses (MOOCs), and electronic tablets in the classroom, technology is now an integral part of learning and is also affecting the way educators communicate information to students.

The **Advances in Educational Technologies & Instructional Design (AETID) Book Series** explores new research and theories for facilitating learning and improving educational performance utilizing technological processes and resources. The series examines technologies that can be integrated into K-12 classrooms to improve skills and learning abilities in all subjects including STEM education and language learning. Additionally, it studies the emergence of fully online classrooms for young and adult learners alike, and the communication and accountability challenges that can arise. Trending topics that are covered include adaptive learning, game-based learning, virtual school environments, and social media effects. School administrators, educators, academicians, researchers, and students will find this series to be an excellent resource for the effective design and implementation of learning technologies in their classes.

COVERAGE

- K-12 Educational Technologies
- E-Learning
- Instructional Design
- Collaboration Tools
- Adaptive Learning
- Virtual School Environments
- Digital Divide in Education
- Bring-Your-Own-Device
- Social Media Effects on Education
- Curriculum Development

IGI Global is currently accepting manuscripts for publication within this series. To submit a proposal for a volume in this series, please contact our Acquisition Editors at Acquisitions@igi-global.com or visit: http://www.igi-global.com/publish/.

The Advances in Educational Technologies and Instructional Design (AETID) Book Series (ISSN 2326-8905) is published by IGI Global, 701 E. Chocolate Avenue, Hershey, PA 17033-1240, USA, www.igi-global.com. This series is composed of titles available for purchase individually; each title is edited to be contextually exclusive from any other title within the series. For pricing and ordering information please visit http://www.igi-global.com/book-series/advances-educational-technologies-instructional-design/73678. Postmaster: Send all address changes to above address. Copyright © 2020 IGI Global. All rights, including translation in other languages reserved by the publisher. No part of this series may be reproduced or used in any form or by any means – graphics, electronic, or mechanical, including photocopying, recording, taping, or information and retrieval systems – without written permission from the publisher, except for non commercial, educational use, including classroom teaching purposes. The views expressed in this series are those of the authors, but not necessarily of IGI Global.

Titles in this Series

For a list of additional titles in this series, please visit:
https://www.igi-global.com/book-series/advances-educational-technologies-instructional-design/73678

Utilizing Educational Data Mining Techniques for Improved Learning Emerging Research and Opportunities
Chintan Bhatt (Charotar University of Science and Technology, India) Priti Srinivas Sajja (Sardar Patel University, India) and Sidath Liyanage (University of Kelaniya, Sri Lanka)
Information Science Reference • copyright 2020 • 250pp • H/C (ISBN: 9781799800101) • US $165.00 (our price)

Claiming Identity Through Redefined Teaching in Construction Programs
Sherif Mostafa (Griffith University, Australia) and Payam Rahnamayiezekavat (Western Sydney University, Australia)
Information Science Reference • copyright 2020 • 259pp • H/C (ISBN: 9781522584520) • US $185.00 (our price)

Global Perspectives on Teaching and Learning Paths in Islamic Education
Miftachul Huda (Universiti Pendidikan Sultan Idris Malaysia, Malaysia) Jimaain Safar (Universiti Teknologi Malaysia, Malaysia) Ahmad Kilani Mohamed (Universiti Teknologi Malaysia, Malaysia) Kamarul Azmi Jasmi (Universiti Teknologi Malaysia, Malaysia) and Bushrah Basiron (Universiti Teknologi Malaysia, Malaysia)
Information Science Reference • copyright 2020 • 341pp • H/C (ISBN: 9781522585282) • US $195.00 (our price)

Social Justice and Putting Theory Into Practice in Schools and Communities
Susan Trostle Brand (University of Rhode Island, USA) and Lori E. Ciccomascolo (University of Rhode Island, USA)
Information Science Reference • copyright 2020 • 359pp • H/C (ISBN: 9781522594345) • US $195.00 (our price)

Handbook of Research on Diverse Teaching Strategies for the Technology-Rich Classroom
Lawrence A. Tomei (Robert Morris University, USA) and David D. Carbonara (Duquesne University, USA)

For an entire list of titles in this series, please visit:
https://www.igi-global.com/book-series/advances-educational-technologies-instructional-design/73678

701 East Chocolate Avenue, Hershey, PA 17033, USA
Tel: 717-533-8845 x100 • Fax: 717-533-8661
E-Mail: cust@igi-global.com • www.igi-global.com

This is for R. Max, Lily, and Asher, into the alluring future.

Table of Contents

Preface viii

Acknowledgment xviii

Section 1
About Building Learning to Learners

Chapter 1
Cognitive Load Theory, Spacing Effect, and Working Memory Resources Depletion: Implications for Instructional Design 1
Ouhao Chen, Nanyang Technological University, Singapore
Slava Kalyuga, University of New South Wales, Australia

Chapter 2
Applying Uses and Gratifications to Promote Cognitive and Affective Learning via Online Instructional Content 27
Rebecca M. L. Curnalia, Youngstown State University, USA
Amber L. Ferris, University of Akron, USA

Chapter 3
Intergenerational Learning Styles, Instructional Design Strategy, and Learning Efficacy 40
Michael G. Strawser, Bellarmine University, USA
Renee Kaufmann, University of Kentucky, USA

Section 2
Form, Function, and Style

Chapter 4
Some Basics to the Initial Setup and Maintenance of Serialized Online Learning 53
Shalin Hai-Jew, Kansas State University, USA

Chapter 5
Designing Integrated Learning Paths for Individual Lifelong Learners and/
or Small Groups: Backwards Curriculum Design From Target Complex-Skill
Capabilities (for Nonformal Informal Learning) 68
    Shalin Hai-Jew, Kansas State University, USA

Chapter 6
Recognizing Curricular Infusions in Extant Online Learning Contents by
Types and at Varying Scales 105
    Shalin Hai-Jew, Kansas State University, USA

Chapter 7
Optimizing Static and Dynamic Visual Expressions of Time-Based Events,
Processes, Procedures, and Future Projections for Instructional Design 134
    Shalin Hai-Jew, Kansas State University, USA

Chapter 8
Defining Salient Features of "Boutique" Instructional Designs and
Implications for Design, Development, and Deployment 151
    Shalin Hai-Jew, Kansas State University, USA

Section 3
Data for Design

Chapter 9
The Respective Roles of Broad and Deep Research in Instructional Design
and Development Work 168
    Shalin Hai-Jew, Kansas State University, USA

Conclusion 183

Related Readings 186

About the Contributors 200

Index 202

Preface

On-ground, instructional design work arrives in various ways. The initial query usually arrives by an email or a phone call from a colleague. Early on, details are usually light and sketchy, but over time, an understanding starts to emerge, and the information asymmetry starts to resolve.

Generally, the initial information involves some light objectives, some general deliverable types (and preferred technologies), the target learners, the available budget, the hard and soft deadlines, and required standards for the learning resources. The early work involves filling in some blanks, such as the learning outcomes, assessments, technologies, teaching and learning methods, acting or voice or other talent, learning contents (based on research), and other aspects. The works are at once standard and also "boutique."

Every participant in the work brings not only serious expertise but insights and observations that inform the work. Also, there may be open-shared resources in the environment that may be used in part of the learning sequence. There is a guaranteed learning experience for instructional designers in every project. The acquisition of new skills enable a larger skill set in future work.

In higher education, the requests may evolve as follows:

- The work is a campus-based project, and the subject matter expert (SME) is also a faculty member, or the teaching team is a group of faculty, and they want review of an online course that they've co-created and will use for co-teaching into the next few years. They want to make sure that their design is conductive to learning, that the technologies are properly used, that the copyright policies are properly adhered to, and that the accessibility is achieved correctly. This is a very common ask.
- Perhaps the principal investigator (PI) of the grant has dropped enough information to start a Google Search about the particular grant funding agency or grant information. Then, the team coalesces and work together to fill in the details of the original vision or ambition. If one has had the privilege of helping to design the work in the grant application form, one should already

Preface

know the learning objectives, the target learners, the planned deliverables, the requisite policy standards (in addition to adhering to intellectual property laws and accessibility laws and policies), the general timelines, and the available resources. What is not documented but still in the forefront of one's mind is what technologies may be used, what talent to bring on board, and how to achieve the work to quality, within the time limits. By the time the work is ready to proceed, the authorizing documents from the grant funding agencies, the raw files, the notes, and other elements help inform the work.

- A grant has gone into its unfunded no-cost extension because the original team was unable to actualize the promised work within the original time span. Over the multiple years of the grant, the employees have changed, and while the local co-PI has a sense of what she wants, she has not been able to advance the work. The technologies used are wholly original with a co-PI handling the technology in another state, and another co-PI is a content expert. The local co-PI has some funds left over to hire an instructional designer. This moment is do-or-die, and the work is required quickly and to standard. Not following through on the work would leave a black eye to the university, and the government funding agency has a long memory.
- Or the work is a local inspiration by an administrator who is infamous for wrangling free work with her "woo" and sense of self-entitlement. The informational wiki that will showcase online teaching and learning at the university. She will acquire as much free work as possible from others and then place her organizational unit's stamp on the work and claim credit and use the projects to win awards from a professional organization. Still, because of the political ties on a campus, this work has to be taken on. The faculty who have promised to contribute mostly will not come through because they are so busy and because they expect to be paid extra. This method of the political ask is not uncommon. Universities are known for faculty and administrators trading on their "celebrity" for free (but expensive and risky) work, with others taking on the costs. These projects tend to be open-ended, with participants "on call" for years. However these are handled, finesse is required. While "rate cards" for services help limit such asks, the economy of a campus encourages such outreaches, sweetened with over-politeness and professions of friendship.

In a publicly traded corporation, the instructional design work may be as follows:

- The publicly traded corporation has commissioned a particular online learning module about how to teach and learn online. They have a global workforce, and they need the learning to be accessible across geographical regions and cultures and languages. They want the optimal designs based on the known-knowns from the educational research literature. Access to others' services within the corporation is expensive. The animation artwork is expensive, in the five figures, for something that would be fairly simple today. Talent within the corporation is unavailable without a lot of political wrangling and expenditure. There is a sense that the team has to do-it-yourself (DIY).

Then, once there is clarity, the work begins. Research of secondary-source data is conducted. In some cases, primary research may be necessary. Scripts and slideshows are drafted, critiqued, revised. Changes made in one area have knock-on effects on others. Learning objects are drafted, and they are reviewed through in-house alpha-testing for functionalities and alignment with standards. There is beta-testing for learner experiences with the learning resources. The test phases are critical to ensure that the designed learning is efficacious. For grant funding organizations, they may add additional layers of review and revision. The respective digital learning objects are revised. Throughout, if a grant funding agency is involved, they are kept in the loop. Also, raw files are maintained and kept for easy reference by the team, so that retrofitting of the learning resources may be easily achieved. Project documentation is maintained throughout to ensure that hand-offs are smooth. In general, the work is achieved as efficiently as possible, and technology is harnessed for the most efficient outcomes. An instructional design project has a lot of moving parts. Finally, the deliverables are conveyed to the grant funder, and the team disbands and moves on to other projects.

In reviewing some of my experiences with instructional design in a number of contexts, I notice that while designs are important, serendipity and available resources also play important roles. For the same work prompts, different designers and developers…and different teams…may come up with very different deliverables and for different reasons. There is no "equifinality"; the individuals and teams do not necessarily arrive at the same designs. Different instructional designers may have different "hands" or uniquenesses in how they approach the design work. The limits for the various designs vary, based on the available contents, the available information, the technological enablements and constraints, and the visions of the subject matter experts and team members. How effective and relevant the respective learning designs and deliverables are may vary over time and with certain audiences, but all sunset and are retired after some period of time. Building open-source learning objects contain other challenges, such as the lack of funding, except for out-of-pocket investments, challenging definitions of learners, and other challenges (Hai-Jew, 2018).

My work in instructional design began decades ago, first as a college instructor and then later as a full-time instructional designer. I have worked in higher education

Preface

for many years, but I have also worked for publicly traded companies and nonprofit organizations, at which I have built various learning resources since the mid-1990s.

DEFINING TERMS FROM THE TITLE

One truism in teaching and learning is that terms should be defined early and as precisely as possible. It may help to define the respective terms of the title, *Form, Function, and Style in Instructional Design: Emerging Research and Opportunities*. It so happens that every part of the title is somewhat vague and open to broad interpretation

Let's start with the easier term. The "instructional design" here is conceptualized broadly, without assuming any basic approach except the following:

- Some educational theories are more applicable than others in the different environments and contexts in which the teaching and learning will occur.
- In general, the ADDIE process is relevant, involving the following steps: Analyze, Design, Develop, Implement, and Evaluate. (Learning designs are not just created and launched into the world untested, and learning designs are not about one iteration but often many based on the empirical observations about their efficacy.)
- The "form, function, and style" refer to both internal- and external-facing contents. In the "design, development, and deployment," design and development are internal (private, in-house), and deployment is external (public, for teachers and learners). All the created contents have relevance, even those which are not publicly facing.
- The research into multimedia design for learning, based on human perception, cognition, and learning, is considered highly relevant. This is so for learning that is online, face-to-face (F2F), and blended.
- Learning should be designed to human capabilities and needs.

Then, in terms of form, function, and style:

"Form" here means the inherent structure (and even sequence) of the design, the development, and the deployment of the learning resource. The informational content is part of the object's form and has its own structure and its own typical conventions. The technological form also suggests certain affordances and constraints, based on the software, learning systems, and hardware. The form of the object may be single-modal or multi-modal.

- What is the document/learning object/item format and contents?

- What order are the respective sub-elements organized in? What is the experiential sequence (or experiential sequences)?
- What do the technological affordances and constraints enable?
- What sort of digital structure is the learning object configured in? How does the object manifest?
- Is the content part of a sequence, and if so, how does it link to the respective external pieces? What does it contribute?

"Function" here refers to the what the learning resource does and how it may be used, in the design, the development, and the deployment phases.

- What does the design achieve? What strategies and tactics does it use?
- What does the digital learning object enable the user to do? What are the ranges of actions that may be taken?
- What learning and other needs are met with designed resource? What learning and other needs are not met?

"Style" indicates the "look-and-feel" and "atmospherics" applied to the learning resources. Style may also refer to the points of view in the work, the voices, the tones, the affectations, the language, and how the learners are addressed. The way learning is structured may also be a feature of the style. In digitally authored contents, these may be created from built-in templates and color palettes and other designs. Style may be organic to the design and created with an original eye and artful hand.

- What technologies are used, and how much leeway do these offer to enable the expression of style (in all the various manifestations)? What platforms are used?
- What set pieces are used in the learning sequence, and why? How are these attention-getting? How do they help learners make meaning?
- What do the respective contents and objects communicate to their users? What aesthetics are in play? Are the aesthetics pleasing?
- Is the learning resource recognizability unique, in terms of aesthetics?
- Or it is evocative of a known style?
- Do the respective styles work together with other elements of the learning to create a cohesive sense of the designed learning resource?
- How may the style be objectively described? Is it ornate or pared down? Are there obvious cultural influences? Technological ones?
- What are the instrumental or functional aspects of the style?
- What does the graphical user interface (GUI) or user interface (UI) look like? How functional is it? How is it styled?

Preface

These are some initial concepts explaining the meanings of instructional design, form, function, and style.

An extended Table of Contents (TOC) follows.

SECTION 1: ABOUT BUILDING LEARNING TO LEARNERS

Chapter 1: Cognitive Load Theory, Spacing Effect, and Working Memory Resources Depletion – Implications for Instructional Design

Ouhao Chen and Slava KalyugaIn classroom, students' learning is affected by multiple factors that influence information processing. Working memory with its limited capacity and duration plays a key role in learner ability to process information and therefore, is critical for students' performance. Cognitive load theory, based on human cognitive architecture, focuses on the instructional implications of relations between working memory and learner knowledge base in long-term memory. The ultimate goal of this theory is to generate effective instructional methods that allow managing students' working memory load to optimize their learning, indicating the relations between the Form of instructional design and the Function of instructional design. This chapter considers recent additions to the theory based on working memory resources depletion that occurs after exerting significant cognitive effort and reverses after a rest period. The discussed implications for instructional design include optimal sequencing of learning and assessment tasks using spaced and massed practice tasks, immediate and delayed tests.

Chapter 2: Applying Uses and Gratifications to Promote Cognitive and Affective Learning via Online Instructional Content

Rebecca M.L. Curnalia and Amber L. Ferris

Instructional design benefits from integration and application of communication theory to help guide practice. Uses and gratifications (U&G) is a useful approach for developing, evaluating, and selecting fully integrated, interactive course materials. U&G has assumptions related to individuals, uses, and effects that apply to a myriad of communication channels, including instructional materials. There are four considerations derived from U&G that we address in this chapter: user motives, platform affordances, user activity, and user outcomes.

Chapter 3: Intergenerational Learning Styles, Instructional Design Strategy, and Learning Efficacy

Michael G. Strawser, Marjorie M. Meier, Renee Kaufman

Instructional designers must appeal to a variety of audience members both in terms of competency and preferred learning style. Though many factors may influence learning style, generational preferences may provide instructional designers a broad base of understanding undergirding strategic educational design choices. While it would be naive, and even inaccurate, to assume that Millennials constitute the only unique generational challenge for instructional designers, their sheer presence in organizations and their education expectations have changed the game-so to speak. Thus, in an attempt to clarify generational uniqueness, this chapter will explore general generational instructional trends while positioning instructional design as a necessary answer to 21st century learning efficacy challenges.

SECTION 2: FORM, FUNCTION, AND STYLE

Chapter 4: Some Basics to the Initial Setup and Maintenance of Serialized Online Learning

Shalin Hai-Jew

Optimally, the learning sequence experienced by learners is addressed in the instructional design plan. So too is the sequencing of learning objects in the modules, related modules in the course, related courses in a degree program, and so on, from granular objects to larger ones. A variety of learning contents may be conceptualized, at a zoomed-out level, as "serialized" or a part of a series. Serialized online learning refers to any number of types of large-scale sequenced learning, such as endeavors that continue over extended time (such as a number of years), that involve a number of interrelated learning objects (like podcast series), and that serve both new learners and continuing learners. The instructional design for serialized online learning requires front-loaded design considerations and approaches that consider the continuing nature of such learning.

Chapter 5: Designing Integrated Learning Paths for Individual Lifelong Learners or Small Groups – Backwards Curriculum Design From Target Complex-Skill Capabilities for Nonformal and Informal Learning

Shalin Hai-Jew

Preface

Curriculum design is often applied to creating formal learning sequences to ensure that learners pursuing accredited coursework experience the proper learning contents, activities, life-building, and fair assessments in the proper order. In a lifelong learning context, learners will engage in a combination of formal (accredited), nonformal (byproduct learning from structured unaccredited learning contexts), and informal (unintentional) learning. For the latter two contexts, and for individual and groups of learners, there may be benefits in constructing a backwards curriculum design to enable target complex-skill capabilities (even those that require years of effort). This work explores how to create a backwards curriculum design from target complex-skill capabilities, using manually created data tables and related mind maps as early design tools. These enable advancing targeted learning by skill branches or by sequential approaches towards the target skill set.

Chapter 6: Recognizing Curricular Infusions in Extant Online Learning Contents by Types and at Varying Scales

Shalin Hai-Jew

Online learning exists in a dynamic environment, with changing research, applicable laws and policies, pedagogical approaches, and technologies. The changing external environment necessarily informs the curriculum given the need for learning relevance. Curricular infusions (CIs) occur as a practical method of integrating new elements into extant learning: values, ethics, thinking, knowledge, worldviews, practices, tools and technologies, and other elements. These infusions may occur at the most granular level of the learning object all the way to learning disciplines and domains. The method of curricular infusion enables adaptivity to occur with online learning without having to rebuild learning from scratch, so infusions could be additive to particular learning sequences or integrated with the learning objects, and other aspects of designed online learning. This work explores some of the prior research into curricular infusions and introduces some basic ways to reverse engineer curricular infusions in extant online learning.

Chapter 7: Optimizing Static and Dynamic Visual Expressions of Time-Based Events, Processes, Procedures, and Future Projections for Instructional Design

Shalin Hai-Jew

Time-based visuals are used to depict time-based events, processes, procedures, and future projections, among others. These come in 2D, 3D, and 4D types, and they may be static or dynamic, non-interactive or interactive. A simple process or procedure may be expressed visually as a timeline, a flowchart, a stacked diagram, a node-link game tree, a workflow diagram, dedicated-type sequence diagrams, or some other sequence-based visual. With the proliferation of more complex time-based sequences—with multiple paths, multiple actors, decision junctures, conditionals, and other forms of dimensionality, and with multimodal expressions and interactive digital interfaces, with processes as descriptions, theorized steps, directional procedures, projections, and other types—the visual depictions of processes and procedures have become much more complex and layered. This work describes some efforts to optimize these visual expressions through proper design, development, testing, and revision.

Chapter 8: Defining Salient Features of "Boutique" Instructional Designs and Implications for Design, Development, and Deployment

Shalin Hai-Jew

"Boutique" instructional design (ID) projects are fairly common across verticals, especially in higher education, open shared learning, government, and some commercial enterprises. In general, boutique-designed learning is small-scale, with narrowly targeted learners, *limited* development funding/access to information/development and deployment technology/human resources, and other aspects. The strategies and tactics for successful boutique projects differ in some ways than those used for mid-scale and full-scale / general ID projects. This work explores some of the dimensions of boutique ID projects and the implications of those dimensions on design, development, and deployment strategies and tactics. This work is informed by decades in the profession, a review of the literature, and analyses of related open-source and closed-source online learning objects.

SECTION 3: DATA FOR DESIGN

Chapter 9: The Respective Roles of Broad and Deep Research in Instructional Design and Development Work

Shalin Hai-Jew

The work of instructional design (ID) requires new content learning, which often requires various types of published or secondary research as well as direct elicitations from the cooperating subject matter experts (SMEs) about the topic. For instructional design projects, both design and development, a range of information is required:

- Who the target learners are

Preface

- What content knowledge is required (as knowledge, skills, and abilities)
- What pedagogical designs may be most effective
- What technologies will be required for the build
- What learning sequences, objects, assignments, and assessments are needed
- What legal and technological standards need to be abided by

This work describes research strategies for instructional design, research documentation, research citations, and applying the many acquired research insights to the instructional design and development work.

CONCLUSION

It is hoped that this collection may be of use to others who design, develop, and deploy learning resources in various contexts.

Shalin Hai-Jew
Kansas State University, USA
August 2019

REFERENCES

Hai-Jew, S. (2018). *Designing Instruction for Open Sharing*. New York: Springer Publishing.

Acknowledgment

Thanks to the respective researchers and authors, including Ouhao Chen, Slava Kalyuga, Rebecca M.L. Curnalia, Amber L. Ferris, Michael Strawser, Marjorie Meier, and Renee Kaufman. Thanks also to the excellent development team at IGI Global. I appreciate the opportunity to explore this issue.

Foremost, I am grateful to the subject matter experts and grant principal investigators (PIs) who have included me on their projects and the design and development colleagues with whom I've collaborated. Each challenge informs both the current work and future work. Thank you for the collegiality and support.

Section 1
About Building Learning to Learners

Chapter 1
Cognitive Load Theory, Spacing Effect, and Working Memory Resources Depletion:
Implications for Instructional Design

Ouhao Chen
Nanyang Technological University, Singapore

Slava Kalyuga
University of New South Wales, Australia

ABSTRACT

In classroom, student learning is affected by multiple factors that influence information processing. Working memory with its limited capacity and duration plays a key role in learner ability to process information and, therefore, is critical for student performance. Cognitive load theory, based on human cognitive architecture, focuses on the instructional implications of relations between working memory and learner knowledge base in long-term memory. The ultimate goal of this theory is to generate effective instructional methods that allow managing students' working memory load to optimize their learning, indicating the relations between the form of instructional design and the function of instructional design. This chapter considers recent additions to the theory based on working memory resources depletion that occurs after exerting significant cognitive effort and reverses after a rest period. The discussed implications for instructional design include optimal sequencing of learning and assessment tasks using spaced and massed practice tasks, immediate and delayed tests.

DOI: 10.4018/978-1-5225-9833-6.ch001

INTRODUCTION

Cognitive Load Theory (CLT) is an instructional theory that explains the effects of information processing load imposed by learning tasks on learners' cognitive system (Sweller, Merriënboer & Paas, 2019). The general goal of cognitive load theory is to generate innovative and effective instructional procedures to reduce learners' working memory load and optimize their information processing ability.

Working memory resources are limited due to its limited capacity, and this characteristic of working memory is central to the main topic of this chapter - the depletion effect. The next section provides a brief review of human cognitive architecture, its characteristics, and operation principles. Working memory and long-term memory are two major components of this architecture. In accordance with human cognitive architecture, the following section introduces the function of instructional design from the perspective of element interactivity and types of cognitive load. As the function of instructional design within the framework of cognitive load theory is to manage cognitive load, some load-reduction instructional methods are presented to address the form of instructional design and its relation with its function. Then, the working memory resources depletion effect is introduced, followed by the spaced practice design and the immediate vs. delayed tests as forms of evidence for the depletion effect. The chapter concludes with educational implications of working memory resources depletion effect for instructional design principles, including optimal sequencing of learning and assessment tasks using spaced and massed practice tasks, immediate and delayed tests.

HUMAN COGNITIVE ARCHITECTURE

Human cognitive architecture is considered as a natural information-processing system that operates based on a set of principles that determine the interaction between the external environment, working memory and long-term memory. These principles might be common to all natural information-processing systems such as human cognition or biological evolution by natural selection (Sweller & Sweller, 2006). The aspects of human cognitive architecture that are relevant to instructional issues can be summarized by five principles.

- **Information Store Principle:** All the natural information-processing systems have large stores of information that govern their behavior within the environment. For example, for biological systems, the information store is their genome (generic code store); for human cognitive architecture - it is the long-term memory's knowledge base. To perform well in a complex environment, human cognition must rely on a large amount of domain-specific knowledge (Chi, Glaser, Rees, & Steinberg, 1982) stored in long-term memory in the form of schemas (Tricot & Sweller, 2014). The goal of instruction is to increase the amount of domain-specific knowledge held in long-term memory.

- **Borrowing and Reorganizing Principle:** Most of the information in the store is borrowed from other sources and reorganized rather than just copied. The efficient way to acquire a large amount of domain-specific knowledge is to borrow information from others, such as imitating them (Bandura, 1986), listening to what they say and reading what they write. Before storing borrowed information, it usually is actively restructured, reorganized, and integrated with already available knowledge in long-term memory.
- **Randomness as Genesis Principle:** Although most information is borrowed from others, information can be initially constructed by a random generation and testing process during search-based problem solving. When the solution of a problem is not available for borrowing, possible moves are generated by random search for information or solution moves and tested for their effectiveness, with successful ones retained and unsuccessful ones discarded. This mechanism usually involves general problem-solving methods such as trial-and-error or means-ends analysis - the methods humans use in unfamiliar situations. In biological systems, this principle is realized in random mutations that could be adopted by the test of survival.
- **Narrow Limits of Change Principle:** When a natural information-processing system operates in a new environment (i.e., in the absence of information in the store that could guide its behavior in this environment), it requires a mechanism that could prevent significant random changes in its information store that might potentially damage the system. For example, in the biological evolution system, random mutations usually cause only small changes in the genome at a time. In human cognitive architecture, to prevent rapid, significant and therefore damaging changes to the knowledge base in long-term memory, the information system has to ensure that only a small amount of novel information is processed at a given time. Working memory, which has a limited processing capacity when dealing with novel information (Miller, 1956) and limited duration time (Peterson & Peterson, 1959), provides that assurance.
- Too many elements of information that are processed in working memory at the same time may exceed its capacity and cause cognitive overload. According to classical study by Miller (1956), humans cannot temporary store more than approximately seven elements of information simultaneously in short-term memory. This processing limitation of our cognitive system is a

major factor that influences the effectiveness of instruction from a cognitive load perspective. This potential working memory (or cognitive) overload happens when consciously processing a cognitive task at a specific (current) moment. It is not identical to the information overload in general, when we need to handle huge amounts of information over long periods of time. Cognitive load phenomena are associated only with conscious information processing on a scale of working memory operation, i.e., from around several to tens of seconds.

- **Environmental Organizing and Linking Principle:** When a natural information-processing system operates in a familiar environment (i.e., in the presence of information in the store that could guide its behavior), the narrow limits of change are lifted. In human cognition this means that the limited capacity of working memory only applies to processing novel information. For well-organized information held in long-term memory, there are no known limits for working memory capacity (Ericsson & Kintsch, 1995). Following appropriate stimuli from the external environment, working memory can process a huge amount of information retrieved from long-term memory to give a proper response to the external environment. If available knowledge structures (schemas) in long-term memory are used to encapsulate many information elements into larger chunks, these information-rich chunks are processed in working memory as single units, thus effectively increasing its actual capacity.

In human cognition, working memory is critical for constructing mental representations, however, it is limited in capacity and duration when dealing with unfamiliar information (Baddeley, 1986; Cowan, 2001; Miller, 1956). Accordingly, presenting a large amount of novel information to students may impose a heavy working memory load. In this situation, if the instructional design is suboptimal and imposes an additional cognitive load, working memory will be overloaded by breaking the Narrow Limits of Change Principle. Therefore, when learning materials consist of large amounts of novel information, carefully selecting instructional procedures to reduce cognitive load is critical. Still, working memory limitations do not apply to any well-organized information that has been learnt previously.

ELEMENT INTERACTIVITY AND TYPES OF COGNITIVE LOAD

Cognitive load generally refers to the load that performing a specific task imposes on our cognitive system (Sweller, Van Merrienboer, & Paas, 1998, 2019). Two dimensions have been used to consider the load: mental load (task-based dimension) and mental effort (learner-based dimension). The mental load relates to the load that is imposed by the demands from tasks, while the mental effort indicates the load that learners actually use to accommodate the demands of the task (Paas, Van Merriënboer, & Adam, 1994).

There are three types of cognitive load that have been traditionally discussed within the framework of cognitive load theory: intrinsic load, extraneous load and germane load (Paas, Renkl, & Sweller, 2003, 2004; Sweller et al., 1998, 2019; Van Merrienboer & Sweller, 2005). In this section, the three types of cognitive load will be described by using the concept of element interactivity which is the central concept in cognitive load theory.

Element Interactivity

Element interactivity is an index used to evaluate the difficulty of learning material (Chen, Kalyuga, & Sweller, 2015). An element can be a concept, a mathematical symbol or anything that can be learned. For example, to solve $x + 5 = 6$, for x, the five elements ($x, +, 5, =, 6$) that are interconnected and have to be processed simultaneously rather than individually in working memory to successfully understand the equation. These five interconnected elements, processed simultaneously in working memory, may indicate a high level of element interactivity. If instead, a non-English speaking student is asked to memorize English letters, such as A, B, C, then the level of element interactivity is low. As the student could memorize the letters one by one, individually, there is only one element (A or B or C) that needs to be processed in working memory at one time, and that element can be processed without referring to the other elements. For example, student could memorize A without referring to B and C. Therefore, this task indicates a low level of element interactivity.

Intrinsic Cognitive Load and Element Interactivity

Intrinsic cognitive load is imposed by learning material that needs to be processed in order to achieve the learning goal. This type of load depends on the nature of learning materials. As element interactivity is an index to show how difficult learning materials are, intrinsic load and element interactivity are interconnected. Let's use the same examples for element interactivity as those used above to explain the concept of intrinsic cognitive load. In order to solve $x + 5 = 6$ for x, the five elements ($x, +, 5, =, 6$) that are interconnected must be processed simultaneously in working memory for understanding the equation, which indicates high levels of element interactivity and accordingly, high levels of intrinsic cognitive load are required to achieve the learning goal. If a non-English speaking student is asked to memorize English letters, then the intrinsic load is low as this type of material is low in element interactivity.

As students' levels of prior knowledge (or levels of learner expertise) may influence the level of element interactivity (Chen, Kalyuga, & Sweller, 2016a, 2016b, 2017), learners' expertise should also be considered to determine the level of intrinsic load. While the above equation may consist of five interconnected elements for novices, it may contain only one element for experts, as their previously acquired schema for solving this type of equations can be processed as a single entity in working memory, which reduces the level of element interactivity, and so the level of intrinsic load. Therefore, working memory resources (limited by capacity of working memory) used to deal with intrinsic cognitive load that is determined by the learning goals of specific tasks directly contribute to students' learning, making this type of load productive and necessary for learning.

Extraneous Cognitive Load and Element Interactivity

Extraneous cognitive load happens when the instructional design is suboptimal. Namely, this type of load is imposed because, due to an ineffective instructional design, learners are involved in activities that are irrelevant to achieving learning goals. Therefore, the extraneous load can be altered by modifying instructional procedures and techniques.

Element interactivity also can be used for explaining extraneous cognitive load. Interconnected elements that are only derived from a task (defined by the corresponding instructional goal) cause intrinsic load, whereas elements that interact solely due to the way the instruction is designed (corresponding learning activities are selected or presented to learners) determine extraneous cognitive load (Sweller, 2010). For example, consider selecting problem solving activities to achieve the goal of learning a solution procedure (schema) for a specific type of problems, and asking learners to generate solutions by themselves (Cooper & Sweller, 1987). In the absence of relevant knowledge of solution procedures, the learners would inevitably use search-based problem-solving strategies, such as means-ends analysis. The means-ends analysis requires simultaneous handling of many element of information – initial problem state, its final state (goal), the chain of sub-goals that reduce the distance between the initial and final states, the operations that would allow transitioning between the intermediate states. Such a large number of interactive elements generated during search-based problem solving may cause a high level of cognitive load. This type of cognitive load is an extraneous cognitive load, as it is caused by instructional design, in this case, by selecting problem-solving tasks for achieving the instructional goals.

As the extraneous cognitive load is imposed by the way learning materials are selected and presented, using limited working memory resources to deal with this type of cognitive load does not contribute to students' learning. Therefore, reducing or eliminating extraneous cognitive load to free more working memory resources for dealing with intrinsic load is necessary.

Germane Cognitive Load

Even though germane cognitive load has been often considered as a separate type of productive cognitive load that directly contributes to schema acquisition and automation, in more recent versions of cognitive load theory, it is closely associated with the intrinsic cognitive load (Sweller, 2010). The three-component model of cognitive load has been recently challenged as intrinsic load and germane load are very close and difficult to clearly differentiate. Therefore, a dual model of cognitive load has been suggested that includes only intrinsic and extraneous types of cognitive load (Kalyuga, 2011). With this approach, germane cognitive load (or germane resources) is regarded as the amount of working memory resources that are actually allocated to dealing with the element interactivity associated with intrinsic cognitive load (Sweller et al., 2011). Thus, it represents a dimension of actually allocated working memory resources which is different from the dimension of cognitive load as the amount of working memory resources required by a task. The actually allocated working memory resources are influenced by factors beyond those related to purely instructional design decisions, such as learner motivation, engagement, and affect. This dimension is essential for making connection between cognitive load theory and motivational theories of learning, which represents one of the important issues to deal in future research in this field.

Total Amount of Cognitive Load

Based on the dual model of cognitive load in recent descriptions of cognitive load theory (Kalyuga, 2011; Sweller, 2010; Sweller et al., 2011), the two independent types of cognitive load - intrinsic and extraneous - are additive, and the total load formed by intrinsic and extraneous loads indicates the required working memory resources. If the total required load exceeds the available capacity of working memory, learning will be inhibited. As the capacity of working memory is traditionally regarded as constant for a given learner (relevant to her/his domain specific knowledge structures), if most of this capacity is used for dealing with extraneous, irrelevant load, fewer resources will be available for dealing with essential, intrinsic load.

Accordingly, instructional design should eliminate (ideally) or reduce extraneous load, as this kind of load has nothing to do with achieving specific learning goals.

As for intrinsic load, it should be managed by selecting appropriate learning tasks (Kalyuga, 2011). The learning task should not be too complex in order not to impose an extremely high intrinsic load and make working memory break down, however, it should not be too simple in order to be sufficiently cognitively challenging and motivating (Schnotz & Kürschner, 2007). The resources of working memory that are actually allocated to dealing with intrinsic load which is relevant to learning and schema acquisition (germane resources) need to be maximized, while resources allocated to dealing with extraneous load should be reduced.

LOAD-REDUCTION INSTRUCTIONAL DESIGNS

As extraneous load is irrelevant to learning, the main function of generating innovative and effective instructions, within the framework of cognitive load theory, is to reduce extraneous load imposed on working memory. There are different types of load-reduction instructional design methods. In this section, some classic load-reduction instructional designs (*Form*) are introduced to give readers specific illustrations of how cognitive load is managed (*Function*).

Worked Example Effect

Using worked examples could be traced back to the mid-1950s. The paradigm used in those studies was learning by examples. The example-based learning had initially aimed at the acquisition of simple concepts, then it was used to investigate learning of more complex forms of knowledge (Atkinson, Derry, Renkl, & Wortham, 2000).

A worked example includes the problem statement with associate procedures (Atkinson et al., 2000). The first example-based research conducted within the framework of cognitive load theory applied the idea of worked example-problem solving pairs (Sweller & Cooper, 1985; Cooper & Sweller, 1987), namely, students were presented with a worked example to study first, followed by solving a similar problem. This paradigm has been proved to be superior to engaging students in solving problems only, indicating the worked example effect.

The worked example effect could be directly explained by human cognitive architecture. When students are presented worked examples, the relevant knowledge structures could be borrowed (borrowing and re-organizing principle) compared to solving problems which requires random generation of solutions (producing more interactive elements which may break the narrow limit of change principle). Many research studies have found the effectiveness of using worked examples in algebra (Sweller & Cooper, 1985), statistics (Paas, 1992), geometry (Paas & Van Merriënboer, 1994; Schwonke, Renkl, Krieg, Wittwer, Aleven & Salden, 2009), physics (Reisslein, Atkinson, Seeling & Reisslein, 2006; Van Gog, Kester & Paas, 2011; Van Gog, Paas & Van Merriënboer, 2006) and other domains.

Although using worked example-problem solving pairs is superior to engaging problem solving only, the design of worked examples is critical (Catrambone, 1994; Catrambone & Holyoak, 1990; Mwangi & Sweller, 1998; Ward & Sweller, 1990; Zhu & Simon, 1987). If the internal structure of worked examples is not properly designed, the effectiveness of using worked examples may disappear due to imposing higher levels of extraneous load. The following sections describe some of such situations and appropriate designs to prevent them.

Split Attention Effect

Split attention effect stipulates that separated related sources of information must be physically integrated for students to mentally integrate them without causing high levels of extraneous load. There are two types of split sources of information: spatially and temporally separated (Sweller et al., 2011).

Spatially Separated Sources of Information

Learning geometry may frequently involve dealing with spatially separated sources of information. When students are presented a geometry example, the geometric shape and associated procedures are usually separated. In order to fully understand the material, students have to hold information from the geometric shape in working memory while searching for the relevant procedures. On the other hand, students may need to hold much of information about procedures in their working memory while searching back in the geometric shape for relevant visual components. In both cases, a heavy extraneous cognitive load could be imposed on working memory and interfere with learning. Therefore, if the two separated sources of information, a geometric shape and procedures, are physically integrated beforehand, then students do not need to search between them, which reduces levels of extraneous load. The cases of spatially separated sources of information causing split attention have been found in many research studies (e.g., Chandler & Sweller, 1992; Ayres & Youssef, 2008; Rose & Wolfe, 2000; Lee & Kalyuga, 2011).

Temporally Separated Sources of Information

This type of split-source design formats includes related sources of information that are separated in time rather than by the location. Baggett (1984) and Mayer and Anderson (1991, 1992) investigated this issue by comparing two versions of instructional design: visual and auditory sources of information were presented simultaneously or auditory information was presented before or after the relevant visual information. The results favored presenting the visual and auditory information in concurrent form rather than in the temporally separated form.

Split attention situations occur when they involve multiple sources of information that are mutually dependent and not just re-describe each other. If the multiple sources of information re-describe each other in different formats, their integration for learning may cause another structural design issue for worked examples.

The Redundancy Effect

Similar to the split attention effect, the redundancy effect also deals with multiple sources of information. However, in this case, the multiple sources of information re-describe each other, namely, a single source of information could be fully understood without referring to other sources of information. Within the framework of Cognitive Load Theory, any information that is not necessary and is irrelevant to learning should be regarded as redundant (Sweller et al., 2011).

Chandler and Sweller (1991) conducted the first study within the framework of cognitive load theory showing a redundancy effect. One group was presented with integrated text and a diagram that essentially re-described the textual information, while another group studies from the separated text and the diagram. Results favored the second group in which learners were able to ignore the redundant source of information, indicating a redundancy effect. Following this experiment, other research studies have also found the redundancy effect in other domains (Sweller & Chandler, 1994; Chandler & Sweller, 1996; Mayer, Heiser & Lonn, 2001; Kalyuga, Chandler & Sweller, 2004).

The redundancy effect may be counterintuitive (Sweller et al., 1998), as many people feel that learning the same information repeatedly in different formats should be beneficial for learning. However, the available empirical evidence tells us another story: presenting redundant information together with essential information may impose a heavy extraneous load on working memory. The learners may not be able to ignore the redundant information, especially in the integrated format, and processing redundant information may unnecessarily require allocating extra working memory resources.

Variability Effect

Unlike the above effects, the variability effect aims to maximize the level of intrinsic load in order to enhance the transfer of learning. Within the framework of cognitive load theory, variability effect is implemented by using examples that vary their context (Clark, Nguyen & Sweller, 2006). Learners who are presented with varied-context examples are assumed to be better able to distinguish the relevant and irrelevant features of worked examples (Van Merriënboer & Sweller, 2005), thus forming conditionalized schemas (Clark et al., 2006).

Paas and Van Merriënboer (1994) conducted the first experiment investigating the variability effect within the framework of Cognitive Load Theory by applying Pythagoras' theorem to calculate the distance between two points. The experiment compared low-varied worked examples which only changed the values of the problem variables with high-varied worked examples which changed both the values and the structure of the problem. The post-test transfer performance favored the group using high-varied worked examples, supporting the hypothesis of variability effect.

Variability effect was also found with examples that varied the levels of contextual interference. Low levels of contextual interference relate to a series of problems that could be solved by using the same set of skills, whereas, high levels of contextual interference relate to a series of problems that requires different sets of skills but are placed next to each other (Sweller et al., 2011). Assuming A, B, C are three different skills, then the sequence of A-A-A, B-B-B or C-C-C targets a low level of contextual interference, compared to the sequence of C-B-A, B-A-C, B-C-A for a high level of contextual interference (Van Merriënboer, Schuurman, De Croock & Paas, 2002). De Croock, van Merriënboer, and Paas (1998) found that using task sequences with high levels of context interference caused higher levels of mental effort and increased learning time, but resulted in fewer errors on the posttest transfer test, compared to the ask sequences with low levels of contextual interference.

The above instructional designs aim to reduce the extraneous load which is irrelevant to learning but to maximize the intrinsic load which is relevant to learning. However, the idea of managing cognitive load is based on the assumption that working memory resources of a learner available for dealing with a specific task are relatively constant, which has been challenged recently (Chen, Castro-Alonso, Paas, & Sweller, 2018).

WOKING MEMORY RESOURCE DEPLETION

Depletion Phenomena

Depletion phenomena happen when two tasks must be processed in immediate sequence, leading to worse performance on the second task because of working memory capacity reduction following the first task. For example, Persson, Welsh, Jonides, and Reuter-Lorenz (2007) indicated that when dealing with higher cognitive processes, resources might be temporarily depleted. Persson et al. (2007) applied a within-subject experimental design to investigate the depletion effect. In their experiment, participants were required to do verbal generation task based on the presented nouns. Participants were placed in low and high interference conditions. For the low interference condition, possible associate responses to the nouns were limited (e.g., SCISSORS—CUT), while for the high interference condition, the nouns allowed several obvious suitable response options (e.g., BALL—THROW, KICK, BOUNCE). Participants were fatigued with three distinct interference resolution processes for 18 minutes, followed by a test including tasks that required different interference resolution mechanisms. The results indicated that the test performance was affected only when test items required the same resources that were initially depleted, with no performance depression on test items using different cognitive resources.

Anguera et al., (2012) followed the depletion approach of Persson et al. (2007). They had designed visuomotor tasks to selectively fatigue spatial working memory, then evaluated the participants' performance on tasks that were related or unrelated to the corresponding cognitive processes. Results indicated that the depletion of working memory resources negatively influenced the rate of early visuomotor adaptation. Also, intentionally training working memory capacity could not improve the rate of visuomotor adaptation.

The depletion effect has also been discussed in connection with self-control which happens when a person tries to change the way he or she would think, feel or behave (Muraven & Baumeister, 2000). Muraven, Tice and Baumeister (1998) found that when performing two consecutive acts of self-control, the performance on the second act could be depressed. The impaired performance happened even when two different acts of self-control were involved. The provided explanation suggested that varied types of self-control consumed the same resource (or self-control strength) which is very limited and therefore could be depleted quickly. This self-regulatory depletion mode has been tested with different types of tasks (Baumeister, Bratslavsky, Muraven, & Tice, 1998; DeWall, Baumeister, Stillman, & Gailliot, 2007; Muraven et al., 1998; Schmeichel, Vohs, & Baumeister, 2003).

Schmeichel et al. (2003) assigned participants into self-regulation and non-regulation groups. In the self-regulation group, participants were required to regulate emotion or attention initially, while participants in the non-regulation group were not required to do those exercises. The results showed that depletion was found with the tasks requiring complex thinking, such as logical and reasoning tasks (Study 1), cognitive extrapolation tasks (Study 2), and a test of thoughtful reading comprehension (Study 3), but no evidence of depletion was found for memory and recall tests. In their Experiment 1, Muraven, Shmueli and Burkley (2006) used two tasks that required solving moderately difficult multiplication problems (math problem condition) and suppressing the thought of a white bear (thought suppression condition). In the thought suppression condition, learners were required to write down their thoughts but without thinking about the white bear (Wegner, Schneider, Carter, & White, 1987). It was assumed that only thought suppression condition would deplete the resources compared to working on arithmetic problems that was automatic. In Experiment 2, participants were required to type a paragraph either with letter e or without it. The condition involving typing without e required high levels of self-control. The tasks were then changed to trying cookies and celery in Experiment 3. All experiments indicated that participants using self-regulation depleted resources and performed worse in an intervening test of self-control compared to participants without resource depletion.

Constant Working Memory Resource Assumption

Based on a dual model of cognitive load (Kalyuga, 2011), two independent types of cognitive load, intrinsic and extraneous cognitive load, are additive. The Narrow Limits of Change Principle assumes that the working memory resource of a specific individual available for dealing with a specific task is relatively constant (Chen et al., 2018). Therefore, this assumption may provide a baseline for discussing relations between intrinsic and extraneous types of cognitive load. Specifically, if the total amount of intrinsic and extraneous cognitive load exceeds the assumed constant working memory capacity, learning will be restricted. To optimize students' learning, instructions should be designed to minimize extraneous cognitive load which is irrelevant to achieving specific learning goals, to accordingly increase the relative amount of working memory resources left to deal with the intrinsic cognitive load.

However, the assumption of a constant working memory resource in cognitive load theory may have been challenged recently (Chen et al., 2018). In cognitive load theory, the traditional and only factor influencing working memory capacity is the content of long-term memory - the organized knowledge structures (schemas) related to the task at hand. Based on human cognitive architecture, working memory has limited capacity when processing novel information for which there is no related knowledge in learner long-term memory, with no known limits for well-organized information held in long-term memory via Environmental Organizing and Linking Principle. Namely, the more schemas that are relevant to the task are stored in long-term memory, the fewer working memory resource may be consumed. Therefore, the working memory resource is assumed to be alterable by the content of long-term memory only. However, it has been indicated that intensive cognitive effort may deplete working memory resources due to a working memory capacity reduction after heavy cognitive processing (Chen et al., 2018), suggesting that long-term memory may not be the only factor affecting the characteristics of working memory.

Working Memory Resources Depletion Effect and Cognitive Load Theory

The working memory resources depletion could be discussed within the framework of cognitive load theory. Particularly, working memory resources deplete when the two sequential tasks have similar cognitive elements, and the reduced working memory capacity depresses the performance on the second task due to increased cognitive load. However, research indicates that after some rest, the resources available for the second task could be restored (Tyler & Burns, 2008), resulting in reduced cognitive load.

There is little empirical research investigating the effect of cognitive effort on resource depletion directly. Experiments conducted by Schmeichel (2007) provide some empirical evidence. In the first experiment, participants who were required to ignore irrelevant words of a person speaking with no copy of the narrated text on the screen, depleted their working memory resources, compared to others without this requirement. Similarly, students who were asked to write a story without using the letters *a* or *n* performed worse on a working memory capacity test than the students without this restriction in the second experiment. In the last experiment, a group of participants was required to exaggerate their emotions when watching a movie compared to another cohort who watched movie normally. The cohort watching the movie normally depleted fewer working memory resources than those who had to put much effort in exaggerating their emotions.

Schmeichel et al. (2003) found similar results to those obtained by Schmeichel (2007). Even though the working memory capacity was not measured in their study, they used reasoning, problem solving, or reading comprehension tasks as measures of the resulting performance. The results indicated again that with resource depletion, the learner performance on reasoning, problem solving or reading tasks became depressed.

Compared to Schmeichel's et al. (2003) results on general depletion effects, Healey, Hasher, and Danilova (2011) provided empirical evidence of some specific working memory depletion effects. They varied stimuli that were to be ignored in the first task, but had to be remembered afterwards. The multiple experiments showed that ignoring words in the initial task depressed the performance on the following working memory test that was words-based (Experiment 1), but not on the test that was arrows-based (Experiment 2). Similarly, the performance on arrow-based working memory test was impaired if ignoring arrows was required in the first task (Experiment 3), but no depression on working memory test that was words-based was observed (Experiment 4). Therefore, the working memory resource depletion may happen when there are similarities between to-be-ignored stimuli in the beginning and to-be-remembered stimuli on the following working memory test. However, none of those experiments used educationally-relevant materials. Schmeichel et al. (2003) also observed general depletion effects by using self-control tasks and found that depletion might not be applicable to simple tasks. For example, the resource depletion effect was not found with nonsense syllable memorization task (Schmeichel et al., 2003).

Overall, the previous research has not studied the resource depletion effect with realistic learning tasks but rather, investigated general cognitive processing with typical experimental psychology tasks. However, the spacing effect discussed in the next section may be used as a means for investigating resource depletion in learning-relevant environments.

RESOURCE DEPLETION: EVIDENCE FROM SPACED PRACTICE DESIGN

The spacing effect demonstrates that studying learning materials presented with time spaces between learning tasks is superior to studying all the content presented under massed conditions. This effect, which is also called the massed vs. spaced effect, has been well-documented in learning research (Gluckman, Vlach, & Sandhofer, 2014; Kapler, Weston, & Wiseheart, 2015).

To test the working memory resource depletion effect, a spaced practice design was used by Chen et al. (2018). Two experiments tested two hypotheses about possible explanations of the spacing effect: 1) the spacing effect is caused by working memory resource depletion following a massed practice; 2) a lower content test score and more working memory resource depletion would be found after the massed practice. The first experiment used a quasi-experimental design. Participants in one class were allocated to the massed practice condition with another class allocated to the spaced condition. Three pairs of worked example-problem solving tasks were designed to teach Year 4 students how to calculate fraction addition, where two fractions had different denominators. In the massed condition, students received the three pairs at one time, whereas in the spaced condition, each of the three pairs was taught on three separate consecutive days. All the three pairs were presented via a projection on the screen. Each slide was set a fixed time for presentation, with the total learning time equal for both conditions. The massed condition involved a working memory capacity test directly after learning the last pair, while in the spaced condition, the same test was conducted on the fourth day. The working memory test was also presented on the screen with the same projector, but students were required to give answers on the provided answer sheet.

The test items for the working memory test were a set of equations, such as $5 + 6 + 2 = 13$. Students were required to judge whether the equation was correct. If the equation was correct, they chose smiling face, if not, they chose sad face on the answer sheet. Also, students were instructed to remember the first digits of the equations, such as 5 for $5 + 6 + 2 = 13$, and then recall them in the same order on the answer sheet. However, they were not allowed to record the to-be-remembered first digits and to choose the smiling or sad faces anywhere on the answer sheet during the presentation of the whole set of equations. They could only record their answers when they were instructed to do so. Therefore, during the presentation of the whole set of equations, participants had to process and store information in their working memory. There were multiple levels of test items designed for the working memory capacity test to increase the difficulty of the test. For different levels, there were different numbers of test items: the higher the level, the more test items it involved. For example, for Level 2, there were two items (namely, only judging two equations and memorizing two digits), while for Level 3, there were three test items etc. Participants in both conditions also completed a content-based test after the working memory capacity test. The results confirmed the hypotheses: the spaced condition was superior to the massed condition on the content test and indicated a higher working memory capacity compared to the massed condition.

The second experiment used the same procedures and materials, but a counterbalanced design was applied. In Week 1, one class was assigned to the massed condition, and another class was allocated to the spaced condition. In Week 2, while using different learning materials, the class of the massed condition in Week 1 was allocated to the spaced condition with the class of the spaced condition in Week 1 was allocated to the massed condition. The results of Experiment 1 were replicated in Experiment 2 – again, the spaced condition was superior to the massed condition on the content test and indicated a higher working memory capacity.

The results of these two experiments may have some important theoretical and practical implications. Concerning the theoretical implications, the two experiments may have set up a new perspective of cognitive load theory with working memory resources depletion phenomena following the significant cognitive effort. Also, the two experiments demonstrated the spacing effect, and may have provided another explanation for this effect. Namely, the spacing effect may be caused by working memory resource depletion after massed practice rather than distributed study-phase retrieval only (Delaney, Verkoeijen, & Spirgel, 2010). Regarding practical implications, working memory resources depletion and potentially increased cognitive load need to be taken into consideration when sequencing tasks that may require significant cognitive effort. For example, using the spaced design may be more suitable for students compared to the massed presentation, as more working memory resource can be used for learning using the spaced design.

RESOURCE DEPLETION: EVIDENCE FROM IMMEDIATE VS. DELAYED TESTING DESIGNS

In the conceptual design of spaced practice, time is used as a factor that influences working memory resources depletion and restoration. Spreading the tests across different time periods, such as using immediate vs. delayed tests, might also have the same effect.

Previously published evidence has demonstrated that students can show higher scores on delayed testing as compared to immediate assessments (e.g., Roediger & Karpicke, 2006; Rohrer & Taylor, 2007; Soderstrom & Bjork, 2015). A potential explanation for these findings, consistent with cognitive load theory, is that working memory resources can be depleted and later replenished (see Chen et al., 2018). The working memory resources depletion effect implies that a delayed test can be superior to an immediate test because delayed assessments allow time for working memory resources to replenish from previous processing, while immediate testing adds cognitive load to working memory that has already been depleted by the preceding learning activities (Chen, Yeo, & Kalyuga, submitted). In Chen et al.'s (submitted) experiment, 23 Year 2 primary school students were presented with four worked examples for learning about the subtraction of two unlike fractions. After a learning phase, a working memory resources test was conducted to all students. The test was the same as the one used for testing spaced practice design described in the previous section. An immediate test for subtraction of two unlike fractions was administered on the first day of experiment. On the second day, all students came back to do a delayed post-test with the same testing content (there was no feedback given after the immediate test). Results showed higher scores on the delayed test due to more working memory resources depleted for the immediate test. This phenomenon has clear implications for the design of learning materials involving learner assessment, especially diagnostic (summative) testing: when dealing with cognitively effortful materials, the assessment tasks should better be delayed rather than administered immediately after the learning tasks.

FUTURE RESEARCH DIRECTIONS

The working memory resources depletion effect within the framework of cognitive load theory has opened a new direction for future research. Based on the results of Chen et al. (2018), working memory resources tests may be used in investigating other cognitive load effects, such as the worked example effect. One of the factors contributing to the superiority of using worked examples compared to problem solving tasks might be causing less working memory resources depleted. Also, all cognitive load effects have been investigated from the perspective of working memory load only, however, learner motivation and emotional states may also affect the allocation of working memory resources (Chen, Castro-Alonso, Paas & Sweller, 2018). Therefore, in future research, these factors need to be integrated into conceptual framework of cognitive load theory.

Similar to spacing effect, the working memory resources depletion may be used to explain the interleaving effect by comparing a blocked design with an interleaved design. Once the empirical evidence is obtained using measures of learner working memory capacity, specific instructional recommendations could be provided for school teachers on sequencing learning tasks and practice exercises.

CONCLUSION

Cognitive load theory, based on contemporary knowledge of human cognitive architecture, aims to generate innovative and effective instructional techniques (*Form*) to optimize students' learning by managing learner working memory load (*Function*). Traditionally, cognitive load theory assumes a constant amount working memory resources for a given learner and the task. However, the results from spaced practice experiments may have challenged this assumption, indicating that working memory resources may be depleted after heavy cognitive effort and be restored after a rest period. Therefore, the constant working memory resource assumption may need to be revised to extend cognitive load theory by incorporating the working memory resource depletion phenomenon. The obvious instructional implication of this phenomenon is the suggestion to manage the sequences of effortful tasks of a similar nature in a way that they do not follow each other immediately, but rather intermixed with other tasks and some breaks or rest time in-between. In particular, the spaced design of a series of tasks may be superior to their massed presentation for students' learning, as there could be more working memory resources depleted after massed practice compared to spaced design.

REFERENCES

Anguera, J. A., Bernard, J. A., Jaeggi, S. M., Buschkuehl, M., Benson, B. L., Jennett, S., ... Seidler, R. D. (2012). The effects of working memory resource depletion and training on sensorimotor adaptation. *Behavioural Brain Research*, *228*(1), 107–115. doi:10.1016/j.bbr.2011.11.040 PMID:22155489

Atkinson, D., Derry, S. J., Renkl, A., & Wortham, D. (2000). Learning from examples: Instructional principles from the worked examples research. *Review of Educational Research*, *70*(2), 181–214. doi:10.3102/00346543070002181

Ayres, P., & Youssef, A. (2008). Investigating the influence of transitory information and motivation during instructional animations. *Proceedings of the 8th international conference on International conference for the learning sciences*, 1.

Baddeley, A. (1986). *Working Memory*. Oxford, UK: Clarendon Press.

Baggett, P. (1984). Role of temporal overlap of visual and auditory material in forming dual media associations. *Journal of Educational Psychology*, *76*(3), 408–417. doi:10.1037/0022-0663.76.3.408

Bandura, A. (1986). *Social foundations of thought and action: A social cognitive theory*. Englewood Cliffs, NJ: Prentice-Hall.

Baumeister, R. F., Bratslavsky, E., Muraven, M., & Tice, D. M. (1998). Ego depletion: Is the active self a limited resource? *Journal of Personality and Social Psychology*, *74*(5), 1252–1265. doi:10.1037/0022-3514.74.5.1252 PMID:9599441

Catrambone, R. (1994). Improving examples to improve transfer to novel problems. *Memory & Cognition*, *22*(5), 606–615. doi:10.3758/BF03198399 PMID:7968556

Catrambone, R., & Holyoak, K. J. (1990). Learning subgoals and methods for solving probability problems. *Memory & Cognition*, *18*(6), 593–603. doi:10.3758/BF03197102 PMID:2266861

Chandler, P., & Sweller, J. (1991). Cognitive load theory and the format of instruction. *Cognition and Instruction*, *8*(4), 293–332. doi:10.12071532690xci0804_2

Chandler, P., & Sweller, J. (1992). The split-attention effect as a factor in the design of instruction. *The British Journal of Educational Psychology*, *62*(2), 233–246. doi:10.1111/j.2044-8279.1992.tb01017.x

Chandler, P., & Sweller, J. (1996). Cognitive load while learning to use a computer program. *Applied Cognitive Psychology*, *10*(2), 151–170. doi:10.1002/(SICI)1099-0720(199604)10:2<151::AID-ACP380>3.0.CO;2-U

Chen, O., Castro-Alonso, J. C., Paas, F., & Sweller, J. (2018). Extending Cognitive Load Theory to Incorporate Working Memory Resource Depletion: Evidence from the Spacing Effect. *Educational Psychology Review*, *30*(2), 483–501. doi:10.100710648-017-9426-2

Chen, O., Castro-Alonso, J. C., Paas, F., & Sweller, J. (2018). Undesirable difficulty effects in the learning of high-element interactivity materials. *Frontiers in Psychology*, 9, 1483. doi:10.3389/fpsyg.2018.01483 PMID:30150964

Chen, O., Kalyuga, S., & Sweller, J. (2015). The worked example effect, the generation effect, and element interactivity. *Journal of Educational Psychology*, 107(3), 689–704. doi:10.1037/edu0000018

Chen, O., Kalyuga, S., & Sweller, J. (2016a). When instruction is needed. *The Educational and Developmental Psychologist*, 33(2), 149–162. doi:10.1017/edp.2016.16

Chen, O., Kalyuga, S., & Sweller, J. (2016b). The relations between the worked example and generation effects on immediate and delayed tests. *Learning and Instruction*, 45, 20–30. doi:10.1016/j.learninstruc.2016.06.007

Chen, O., Kalyuga, S., & Sweller, J. (2017). The expertise reversal effect is a variant of the more general element interactivity effect. *Educational Psychology Review*, 29(2), 393–405. doi:10.100710648-016-9359-1

Chen, O., Yeo, S., & Kalyuga, S. (Manuscript submitted for publication). Working memory resources depletion can explain why delayed testing is superior to immediate testing. *The Educational and Developmental Psychologist*.

Chi, M., Glaser, R., Rees, E., & Steinberg, R. (1982). Expertise in problem solving. In R. Sternberg (Ed.), Advances in the psychology of human intelligence (pp. 7–75). Hillsdale, NJ: Lawrence Erlbaum Associates.

Clark, R. C., Nguyen, F., & Sweller, J. (2006). *Efficiency in Learning: Evidence-Based Guidelines to Manage Cognitive Load*. San Francisco: Pfeiffer.

Cooper, G., & Sweller, J. (1987). Effects of schema acquisition and rule automation on mathematical problem-solving transfer. *Journal of Educational Psychology*, 79(4), 347–362. doi:10.1037/0022-0663.79.4.347

Cowan, N. (2001). Metatheory of storage capacity limits. *Behavioral and Brain Sciences*, 24(1), 154–176. doi:10.1017/S0140525X0161392X

De Croock, M. B., Van Merriënboer, J. J., & Paas, F. G. (1998). High versus low contextual interference in simulation-based training of troubleshooting skills: Effects on transfer performance and invested mental effort. *Computers in Human Behavior*, 14(2), 249–267. doi:10.1016/S0747-5632(98)00005-3

Delaney, P. F., Verkoeijen, P. P., & Spirgel, A. (2010). Spacing and testing effects: A deeply critical, lengthy, and at times discursive review of the literature. *Psychology of Learning and Motivation*, *53*, 63–147. doi:10.1016/S0079-7421(10)53003-2

DeWall, C. N., Baumeister, R. F., Stillman, T. F., & Gailliot, M. T. (2007). Violence restrained: Effects of self-regulation and its depletion on aggression. *Journal of Experimental Social Psychology*, *43*(1), 62–76. doi:10.1016/j.jesp.2005.12.005

Ericsson, K. A., & Kintsch, W. (1995). Long-term working memory. *Psychological Review*, *102*(2), 211–245. doi:10.1037/0033-295X.102.2.211 PMID:7740089

Geary, D. C. (2007). An evolutionary perspective on learning disability in mathematics. *Developmental Neuropsychology*, *32*(1), 471–519. doi:10.1080/87565640701360924 PMID:17650991

Geary, D. C. (2008). An evolutionarily informed education science. *Educational Psychologist*, *43*(4), 179–195. doi:10.1080/00461520802392133

Gluckman, M., Vlach, H. A., & Sandhofer, C. M. (2014). Spacing simultaneously promotes multiple forms of learning in children's science curriculum. *Applied Cognitive Psychology*, *28*(2), 266–273. doi:10.1002/acp.2997

Healey, M. K., Hasher, L., & Danilova, E. (2011). The stability of working memory: Do previous tasks influence complex span? *Journal of Experimental Psychology. General*, *140*(4), 573–585. doi:10.1037/a0024587 PMID:21767041

Kalyuga, S. (2011). Cognitive load theory: How many types of load does it really need? *Educational Psychology Review*, *23*(1), 1–19. doi:10.100710648-010-9150-7

Kalyuga, S., Chandler, P., & Sweller, J. (2004). When redundant on-screen text in multimedia technical instruction can interfere with learning. *Human Factors: The Journal of the Human Factors and Ergonomics Society*, *46*(3), 567–581. doi:10.1518/hfes.46.3.567.50405 PMID:15573552

Kapler, I. V., Weston, T., & Wiseheart, M. (2015). Spacing in a simulated undergraduate classroom: Long-term benefits for factual and higher-level learning. *Learning and Instruction*, *36*, 38–45. doi:10.1016/j.learninstruc.2014.11.001

Lee, C. H., & Kalyuga, S. (2011). Effectiveness of different pinyin presentation formats in learning Chinese characters: A cognitive load perspective. *Language Learning*, *61*(4), 1099–1118. doi:10.1111/j.1467-9922.2011.00666.x

Mayer, R. E., & Anderson, R. B. (1991). Animations need narrations: An experimental test of a dual-coding hypothesis. *Journal of Educational Psychology*, *83*(4), 484–490. doi:10.1037/0022-0663.83.4.484

Mayer, R. E., & Anderson, R. B. (1992). The instructive animation: Helping students build connections between words and pictures in multimedia learning. *Journal of Educational Psychology, 84*(4), 444–452. doi:10.1037/0022-0663.84.4.444

Mayer, R. E., Heiser, J., & Lonn, S. (2001). Cognitive constraints on multimedia learning: When presenting more material results in less understanding. *Journal of Educational Psychology, 93*(1), 187–198. doi:10.1037/0022-0663.93.1.187

Miller, G. A. (1956). The magical number seven, plus or minus two: Some limits on our capacity for processing information. *Psychological Review, 63*(2), 81–97. doi:10.1037/h0043158 PMID:13310704

Muraven, M., & Baumeister, R. F. (2000). Self-regulation and depletion of limited resources: Does self-control resemble a muscle? *Psychological Bulletin, 126*(2), 247–259. doi:10.1037/0033-2909.126.2.247 PMID:10748642

Muraven, M., Shmueli, D., & Burkley, E. (2006). Conserving self-control strength. *Journal of Personality and Social Psychology, 91*(3), 524–537. doi:10.1037/0022-3514.91.3.524 PMID:16938035

Muraven, M., Tice, D. M., & Baumeister, R. F. (1998). Self-control as a limited resource: Regulatory depletion patterns. *Journal of Personality and Social Psychology, 74*(3), 774–789. doi:10.1037/0022-3514.74.3.774 PMID:9523419

Mwangi, W., & Sweller, J. (1998). Learning to solve compare word problems: The effect of example format and generating self-explanations. *Cognition and Instruction, 16*(2), 173–199. doi:10.12071532690xci1602_2

Paas, F. (1992). Training strategies for attaining transfer of problem-solving skill in statistics: A cognitive-load approach. *Journal of Educational Psychology, 84*(4), 429–434. doi:10.1037/0022-0663.84.4.429

Paas, F., Renkl, A., & Sweller, J. (2003). Cognitive load theory and instructional design: Recent developments. *Educational Psychologist, 38*(1), 1–4. doi:10.1207/S15326985EP3801_1

Paas, F., Renkl, A., & Sweller, J. (2004). Cognitive load theory: Instructional implications of the interaction between information structures and cognitive architecture. *Instructional Science, 32*(1/2), 1–8. doi:10.1023/B:TRUC.0000021806.17516.d0

Paas, F., & Van Merriënboer, J. J. (1994). Variability of worked examples and transfer of geometrical problem-solving skills: A cognitive-load approach. *Journal of Educational Psychology, 86*(1), 122–133. doi:10.1037/0022-0663.86.1.122

Paas, F. G., Van Merriënboer, J. J., & Adam, J. J. (1994). Measurement of cognitive load in instructional research. *Perceptual and Motor Skills*, *79*(1), 419–430. doi:10.2466/pms.1994.79.1.419 PMID:7808878

Persson, J., Welsh, K. M., Jonides, J., & Reuter-Lorenz, P. A. (2007). Cognitive fatigue of executive processes: Interaction between interference resolution tasks. *Neuropsychologia*, *45*(7), 1571–1579. doi:10.1016/j.neuropsychologia.2006.12.007 PMID:17227678

Peterson, L., & Peterson, M. J. (1959). Short-term retention of individual verbal items. *Journal of Experimental Psychology*, *58*(3), 193–198. doi:10.1037/h0049234 PMID:14432252

Reisslein, J., Atkinson, R. K., Seeling, P., & Reisslein, M. (2006). Encountering the expertise reversal effect with a computer-based environment on electrical circuit analysis. *Learning and Instruction*, *16*(2), 92–103. doi:10.1016/j.learninstruc.2006.02.008

Roediger, H. L. III, & Karpicke, J. D. (2006). Test-enhanced learning: Taking memory tests improves long-term retention. *Psychological Science*, *17*(3), 249–255. doi:10.1111/j.1467-9280.2006.01693.x PMID:16507066

Rohrer, D., & Taylor, K. (2007). The shuffling of mathematics problems improves learning. *Instructional Science*, *35*(6), 481–498. doi:10.100711251-007-9015-8

Rose, J. M., & Wolfe, C. J. (2000). The effects of system design alternatives on the acquisition of tax knowledge from a computerized tax decision aid. *Accounting, Organizations and Society*, *25*(3), 285–306. doi:10.1016/S0361-3682(99)00048-3

Schmeichel, B. J. (2007). Attention control, memory updating, and emotion regulation temporarily reduce the capacity for executive control. *Journal of Experimental Psychology. General*, *136*(2), 241–255. doi:10.1037/0096-3445.136.2.241 PMID:17500649

Schmeichel, B. J., Vohs, K. D., & Baumeister, R. F. (2003). Intellectual performance and ego depletion: Role of the self in logical reasoning and other information processing. *Journal of Personality and Social Psychology*, *85*(1), 33–46. doi:10.1037/0022-3514.85.1.33 PMID:12872883

Schnotz, W., & Kürschner, C. (2007). A reconsideration of cognitive load theory. *Educational Psychology Review*, *19*(4), 469–508. doi:10.100710648-007-9053-4

Schwonke, R., Renkl, A., Krieg, C., Wittwer, J., Aleven, V., & Salden, R. (2009). The worked-example effect: Not an artefact of lousy control conditions. *Computers in Human Behavior, 25*(2), 258–266. doi:10.1016/j.chb.2008.12.011

Soderstrom, N. C., & Bjork, R. A. (2015). Learning versus performance: An integrative review. *Perspectives on Psychological Science, 10*(2), 176–199. doi:10.1177/1745691615569000 PMID:25910388

Sweller, J. (2010). Element interactivity and intrinsic, extraneous, and germane cognitive load. *Educational Psychology Review, 22*(2), 123–138. doi:10.100710648-010-9128-5

Sweller, J., Ayres, P., & Kalyuga, S. (2011). *Cognitive load theory*. New York: Springer. doi:10.1007/978-1-4419-8126-4

Sweller, J., & Chandler, P. (1994). Why some material is difficult to learn. *Cognition and Instruction, 12*(3), 185–233. doi:10.12071532690xci1203_1

Sweller, J., & Cooper, G. A. (1985). The use of worked examples as a substitute for problem solving in learning algebra. *Cognition and Instruction, 2*(1), 59–89. doi:10.12071532690xci0201_3

Sweller, J., & Sweller, S. (2006). Natural information processing systems. *Evolutionary Psychology, 4*(1), 434–458. doi:10.1177/147470490600400135

Sweller, J., Van Merrienboer, J. J., & Paas, F. G. (1998). Cognitive architecture and instructional design. *Educational Psychology Review, 10*(3), 251–296. doi:10.1023/A:1022193728205

Sweller, J., Van Merriënboer, J. J. G., & Paas, F. (2019). Cognitive architecture and instructional design: 20 years later. *Educational Psychology Review, 31*(2), 261–292; Advanced Online Publication. doi:10.100710648-019-09465-5

Tricot, A., & Sweller, J. (2014). Domain-specific knowledge and why teaching generic skills does not work. *Educational Psychology Review, 26*(2), 265–283. doi:10.100710648-013-9243-1

Tyler, J. M., & Burns, K. C. (2008). After depletion: The replenishment of the self's regulatory resources. *Self and Identity, 7*(3), 305–321. doi:10.1080/15298860701799997

Van Gog, T., Kester, L., & Paas, F. (2011). Effects of worked examples, example-problem, and problem-example pairs on novices' learning. *Contemporary Educational Psychology, 36*(3), 212–218. doi:10.1016/j.cedpsych.2010.10.004

Van Gog, T., Paas, F., & van Merriënboer, J. J. (2006). Effects of process-oriented worked examples on troubleshooting transfer performance. *Learning and Instruction, 16*(2), 154–164. doi:10.1016/j.learninstruc.2006.02.003

Van Merriënboer, J. J., Schuurman, J., De Croock, M., & Paas, F. (2002). Redirecting learners' attention during training: Effects on cognitive load, transfer test performance and training efficiency. *Learning and Instruction, 12*(1), 11–37. doi:10.1016/S0959-4752(01)00020-2

Van Merrienboer, J. J., & Sweller, J. (2005). Cognitive load theory and complex learning: Recent developments and future directions. *Educational Psychology Review, 17*(2), 147–177. doi:10.100710648-005-3951-0

Ward, M., & Sweller, J. (1990). Structuring effective worked examples. *Cognition and Instruction, 7*(1), 1–39. doi:10.12071532690xci0701_1

Wegner, D. M., Schneider, D. J., Carter, S. R., & White, T. L. (1987). Paradoxical effects of thought suppression. *Journal of Personality and Social Psychology, 53*(1), 5–13. doi:10.1037/0022-3514.53.1.5 PMID:3612492

Zhu, X., & Simon, H. A. (1987). Learning mathematics from examples and by doing. *Cognition and Instruction, 4*(3), 137–166. doi:10.12071532690xci0403_1

KEY TERMS AND DEFINITIONS

Cognitive Load Theory: An instructional theory for generating effective instructional methods based on knowledge of human cognitive architecture.

Human Cognitive Architecture: The base of cognitive load theory, revealing the relations between working memory and long-term memory.

Long-Term Memory: Permanent storage of learned knowledge structures.

Redundancy Effect: An instructional effect indicating that for more efficient learning, any unnecessary information should be eliminated rather than included.

Spaced Practice Design (Spacing Effect): An effect indicating the superiority of studying learning materials presented with time spaces between learning tasks compared to studying learning materials presented without time spaces.

Split-Attention Effect: An instructional effect indicating that for more efficient learning, multiple separated sources of interdependent information must be physically integrated.

Worked Example Effect: An instructional effect indicating the superiority of using worked examples rather than problem solving tasks.

Working Memory: A cognitive system with a limited capacity that is responsible for temporarily holding and processing information.

Working Memory Resources Depletion: A depletion of working memory resources that happens after heavy cognitive processing.

Chapter 2
Applying Uses and Gratifications to Promote Cognitive and Affective Learning via Online Instructional Content

Rebecca M. L. Curnalia
Youngstown State University, USA

Amber L. Ferris
University of Akron, USA

ABSTRACT

Instructional design benefits from integration and application of communication theory to help guide practice. Uses and gratifications (U&G) is a useful approach for developing, evaluating, and selecting fully integrated, interactive course materials. U&G has assumptions related to individuals, uses, and effects that apply to a myriad of communication channels, including instructional materials. There are four considerations derived from U&G that the authors address in this chapter: user motives, platform affordances, user activity, and user outcomes.

INTRODUCTION

Uses and gratifications (U&G) is a useful approach for developing, evaluating, and selecting fully integrated, interactive course materials. U&G offers suggestions for

DOI: 10.4018/978-1-5225-9833-6.ch002

how the characteristics of users (students or other learners) relate to their use of the features in online instructional content and, as a result, the learning outcomes in courses that use online instructional content.

Instructional design would benefit from integration and application of communication theory to help guide practice. Sprague (1993) argued that research in communication education did not use the breadth of communication theory to explore instructional practices and outcomes, and later pointed out that the lack of theory led to conceptual muddiness and an over-simplification of the complexities of instructional communication (Sprague, 2002). For example, there has been an understandable but narrow focus in the instructional literature on teachers' prosocial behaviors, such as immediacy, relationship-building, and affect.

Sprague (2002) rightly challenged teacher-scholars in communication to apply new theories, work across disciplinary boundaries, and ask bigger questions about strategies for student learning: It comes down to the question of our ultimate goal as teacher educators. If we want to know how to help teachers achieve the perception that they have supported student learning, we can rely on the current models, but if we want to help teachers engage in behaviors that have high probability of leading to significant cognitive learning, there is still much to investigate (p. 352). To that end, U&G has assumptions related to individuals, uses, and effects that apply to a myriad of communication channels, including instructional technologies like interactive textbooks.

Converged Online Instructional Materials

Converged, online instructional materials are used in traditional courses, distance education courses, and flipped courses. They are a shift from flat e-textbooks to interactive resources that encourage self-paced and more self-directed learning that is then supplemented by the course instructor.

E-textbooks have been offered since 2001 and their features have evolved to incorporate multimedia, interactive discussions, activities, quizzes, and adaptation to students' learning. Textbooks have converged with learning management system (LMS) functionalities so that fully online course packages, such as text content with embedded videos, engagement opportunities, and assessments are available for adoption and for instructor development. Moreover, with the growth of open educational resources, instructors can design fully converged online courses in their own university's LMS.

Media convergence, or the merging of different media formats into a new form of media, offers unique opportunities for expanding access and engagement. Convergence also changes audiences, giving users more options and more control over what they use, when they use it, and how they use it (Jenkins, 2004). User control is one of the key tenets of U&G: individuals have a choice when using media and they choose if, when, and how to use media to fulfill their needs (Rubin, 2009).

The challenge for designers lies in choosing the layout, features, and functions that will engage students and encourage their active use of instructional resources. At present, people are still more likely to prefer print over fully integrated online material (Baron, Calixte, & Havewala, 2017) and satisfaction with previous online learning materials predicts future selection of that modality as well as the outcomes of the course material (Liaw & Huang, 2016). U&G offers a framework for considering instructional options and designing fully integrated online instructional content that may motivate more active, involved users. There are four considerations derived from U&G that we address in this chapter: user motives, platform affordances, user activity, and user outcomes.

USES AND GRATIFICATIONS OF ONLINE INSTRUCTIONAL RESOURCES

U&G was one of the first theories to be applied to new communication media (Rubin, 2009). Interactive e-textbooks are hosted online and have elements of traditional textbooks, such as text and images, but they also take advantage of the features of new communication media. For example, interactive course materials may incorporate embedded questions, tests, instructional resources like hyperlinks to examples and videos, and engagement features that require student participation such as discussions and activities. Early research on these instructional features suggest that students learn more when instructional resources incorporate these features, but that many students do not always choose to use the features. U&G clarifies who is likely to use this technology (users' motives), why they would use it (needs, traits, circumstances), how they would use it (audience activity, interaction, attention), and the effects associated with that use (cognitive, affective, and behavioral) (Papacharissi, 2008).

U&G has also been cited as a useful approach for exploring computer-assisted instruction, particularly given the theory's focus on interactivity (Khuen, 1994). U&G has also been recommended as an approach for understanding instructors' adoption of learning management systems (Park, Lee, & Cheong, 2013). Thus, U&G is a useful lens for considering instructional technologies such as interactive textbooks and the features that may be most useful to and used by students.

U&G researchers view media consumers as selective and active: People's needs motivate them; people choose which communication to consume to fulfill those needs and choose among available options; people's external and internal motives, as well as structural access, affect how actively or passively they engage with content; people's activeness affects their emotional and cognitive involvement before, during, and after interactions; and activeness, in the form of involvement, attention, and cognitive processing, influences cognitive, emotional, and behavioral message effects (Rubin, 1984; Rubin, 1990; Levy, 1983; Levy & Windhal, 1984).

Thinking about the assertions of U&G in the context of teaching and learning, U&G offers useful insight into instructional technology:

- Students have different needs, traits and circumstances, and they will choose to use course materials that they expect will fulfill their needs.
- Students' use of course materials will exist on a spectrum from active to passive, which will affect their cognitive involvement in the material before, during, and after use.
- Students' involvement in course material will affect the long-term emotional, cognitive, and behavioral effects of the material.

Thus, the features (or affordances) and content of media need to align with the needs that users are seeking to fulfill in order for gratifications to be obtained and people to continue to use that type of content (Palmgreen & Rayburn, 1982).

Affordances

Affordances are the features of platforms that "enable or constrain behavior" (Rathnayake & Winter, 2018, p. 373). Sundar and Limperos (2013) linked motives for using new media with the affordances of Web 2.0 technology using Sundar's (2008) MAIN model of platform affordances: modality, agency, interactivity, and navigability. In short, the MAIN model suggests that affordances such as multimedia, user control, ability to interact, and ease of navigation fulfill more motivations for users and increase repeated use and engagement.

The integration of multiple affordances on teaching platforms improves student learning. For example, Limperos, Buckner, Kaufman, and Frisby (2015) studied online learning and found that media-rich lectures, which included both text and video, resulted in increased perceived and real learning compared to less media-rich lectures. Features such as forums, discussions, and feedback also are used to create immediacy and promote student learning via online instructional content (Dixson, Greenwell, Rogers-Stacy, Weister, & Lauer, 2017). Affordances and use of those affordances promote interactivity, attention, ability to modify and manage content, and help students process the information, connect, and engage. Rathnayake and Winter (2018) identified a series of affordances that linked to motives for using different platforms:

- **Realism**: Similarity to real life, being like face-to-face interactions, and being a way of experiencing the world.
- **Coolness**: Being distinctive, new, innovative features, and interfaces that are different.
- **Social Presence**: Sense of being immersed, experience of being present, and experiencing things via the platform.
- **Agency**: Have real interactions, allow opinion expression, identity expression, and having a say.
- **Community**: Part of a community, build a network, contribute to community / society.
- **Bandwagon**: Learning about others, reading comments to avoid conflicts, adjust one's responses.
- **Filter / Control**: Limit visibility of one's own posts, review information before posting, using media one's own way.
- **Interaction**: Interacting via a platform, specifying needs and preferences.
- **Activity**: Complete necessary tasks, feel active, not being passive, being able to do many things.
- **Responsiveness**: Platform is responsive, feel in charge, give control to users, and able to control interactions.
- **Browsing**: Get a variety of information, get many types of information, enable browsing, enable linking of information, incorporate visuals.
- **Play**: Escape reality, get entertaining information, entertaining features.

Motives

Though there are many possible affordances, not all users will engage with or benefit from all features used in online instructional content. According to U&G, users engage with content and features differently as a result of their motives. Motives are the reasons people have for their choice to use particular media content. Motives for media use stem from users' needs, traits, and circumstances (Rubin, 2002). For example, some students may not be motivated in a particular course because it is outside of their major (a circumstance) or they may not enjoy learning (a trait), but they may be required to complete the class (need). These students will approach and use online course material more passively, but might be engaged through use of features such as short skimmable modules, brief videos, and quick (single-item) assessments.

Various typologies of motives have been developed to explore why people select media channels and content to fulfill their needs. Generally, motives range from intentional and active to incidental and passive (Rubin, 2002). In the example of the disinterested students above, they are likely to have more passive motives, which include using media to pass time, as a distraction, and when there is nothing better to do. If students are likely to be passive, then design and features should be developed to address their disposition: content that is portable and offers rich multimedia. Further, for active students, content interactivity and diverse usability features would be necessary for them to be satisfied with their user experience: ability to highlight, take notes, find more information on a topic, and so on. Satisfying students' diverse needs should, in turn, increase repeated use and promote activity.

Generally speaking, research suggests that motivation is both internal, or related to one's states and traits, *and* external, or related to the situation or circumstances. For example, internal motivation is an explanation of students' reading behavior from an early age, and includes individual beliefs about the value of reading and one's sense of self efficacy (Gambrell, Palmer, Codling, & Mazzoni, 1996). In terms of external motivation to read, teachers' uses of textbook content in the course affects students' motivations and behavior in different ways. For example, having reading quizzes gets students to come to class, but students appear to learn more when they complete activities and receive extensive feedback on the activity that applies reading material (Ryan, 2006). Thus, reliance on features in instructional material needs to be balanced with the types of assessments that promote deep learning.

Internal Motivations to Consider When Designing Instructional Content

According to Park (2013), there are three basic needs related to student motivations to engage in content: autonomy, competence, and relatedness. Park asserts that when students are allowed to have control over content or make choices in their readings, when they feel challenged or can receive positive reinforcement, and can feel connected to and respected by significant others, they are more likely to engage in self-determined motivation to read. These needs can also be related to the integration of technology into the classroom to support learning.

Individual student needs and personality traits may also be a key factor in the use of mediated course content. In their study on the use of Web 2.0 technologies in the classroom, del Barrio-Garcia, Arquero, and Romero-Frias (2015) found that the need for cognition was a key factor related to e-learning. Students with a high need for cognition were more likely to have a favorable view of e-learning technologies if they felt they enhanced their learning experience and if they were perceived as being useful. However, the key factor for low need for cognition students in e-learning perceptions was most strongly related to the ease-of-use.

In their study on open source textbooks, Jhangiani and Jhangiani (2017) found that the most important feature of the open source book was having immediate access to content. Other important factors included cost savings, convenience and portability, the abilities to print pages and keep the book forever, and the ability to share content. However, the downfalls of e-books for students included the increased distractions and difficulties with reading online, the inability to highlight or make notes in the text, and needing to have internet access to read the book.

External Motivations to Consider When Designing Instructional Content

Designers can also incorporate elements that encourage motivated use of instructional materials. In a study on predictors related to students' textbook reading, Gurung and Martin (2011) found that students were more likely to read their psychology textbooks based on the quality of visual content, the study aids, and the examples/tables. Additionally, when instructors explicitly stated the need to read or designed course assignments around the reading (i.e., homework or quizzes) students were more likely to complete assigned readings. Indeed, surveys of students have lead to a list of desired features including being able to bookmark content, highlight content, use supplemental multimedia content like hyperlinks and videos, and link to definitions (Sheen & Luximon, 2015).

When assessing the usefulness of Web 2.0 technologies to create learning environments (such as Twitter, Facebook, blogging, wikis), del Barrio-Garcia et al. (2015) found that new technologies were viewed as having a positive value to their learning experience, particularly when there were collaborative learning opportunities. Additionally, students who believed that these technologies were useful and who had a positive attitude toward using technology were more likely to feel satisfied in the e-learning experience.

Usability and Efficacy

Ease-of-use and students' technological abilities are key with respect to e-book use. In their study on student perceptions related to e-books, Wiese and du Plessis (2014) found that usefulness and ease-of-use were related to preferences between print books and e-books. Interestingly, when asked about the important features of e-books, interactivity functions were ranked near the bottom of the list, whereas convenience, access, reliability, and the ability to highlight ranked highest. It is interesting to note that integrating Web 2.0 features was viewed positively by students, however in a learning context, these features were less important. Additionally, having a table of contents on the left side of the screen when reading was viewed as being helpful for navigation of content (Kim, 2009).

One key barrier to adoption of fully online instructional material is also a lack of instructor development (Denoyelles & Seilhamer, 2013). Though features like interactive quizzes, collaborative activities, and discussions can encourage students to actively engage with materials, developing these features may seem time-consuming to instructors. Indeed, institutional support is necessary to encourage and help faculty develop the content for interactive e-textbook materials in their classes.

Fulfilling Motives by Strategically Using Affordances Encourages Active Use

When people's needs are fulfilled by new media options they tend to be more active and involved during use (Ruggerio, 2000). In U&G, activity refers to attention, feelings of involvement, cognitive effort, and interaction with the content (Rubin, 2009). When there is utility *and* intentional use, people tend to be more active in their use. More active, instrumental uses lead to different activity during media use and, as a result, different outcomes. More to the point, Rubin (2009) pointed out that a motivated and involved user should learn more from content and that learning should be more long-term.

Clearly, instructors and designers want students to be active users of instructional content: using features and functions, engaging with the material, thinking about it, discussing it, and so on. Active reading involves scanning the content to get oriented, thinking about the content, linking content to other knowledge, and checking understanding of the content (McNamara, Levinstein, & Boonthum, 2004). These are the key aspects of active reading that lead to retention and integration of knowledge in memory.

Course materials should enable and encourage active reading strategies to encourage active use of course content. To promote active use, developers should ensure the clarity of layout, modularity of the materials, thoughtful integration of aligned assessments and activities, and ease for faculty to personalize and taylor content to their students. Moreover, the online course materials should mimic the features of traditional books that active readers make use of: note taking, clear indexes, and highlighting, as these aspects of active reading appear to be lacking in online course content use (Schugar, Schugar, & Penny, 2011).

One of the great benefits of digital texts is the ability to enhance user activity. When digital readings are more engaging and interactive, students have been shown to reap the benefits of this active learning environment. Chen and Chen (2014) conducted a study on fifth grade students' use of a collaborative reading annotation system compared to traditional print texts. Results showed that when students were able to interact with the text by highlighting and taking notes in the system, as well as collaborate with peers to discuss readings via discussion boards, they exhibited stronger improvements in reading comprehension and the use of different reading strategies than the paper-based reading students.

CREATING INTERACTIVE COURSE MATERIALS THAT ALIGN WITH STUDENTS' NEEDS, MOTIVES, AND CMC USES

The U&G perspective links motives to use of features and user activity, which includes attention, information processing, engagement, satisfaction, feelings of connection, and retention (Rubin, 2009). Active use, in turn, influences the persistence of informational effects. Users who are actively engaged with the content report more involvement, more satisfaction, and more liking or connection with media (Rubin, 2009). In instructional contexts, recognizing the motives of content users them integrating elements and course designs that fit users' motives and encourage active use, should lead to more cognitive and affective learning. Cognitive learning is retention of information and affective learning is an attitude toward the course and the subject matter of the course (Russo & Benson, 2005). Both are important components of learning.

In short, U&G is a lens to consider the features of interactive course materials that will fulfill students' motives. Adjusting content to accommodate students' motives should lead to more satisfying user experiences, or more affective outcomes from the course. Integrating instructional elements to encourage students to actively use interactive instructional materials to promote cognitive engagement should lead to more cognitive learning.

The preceding discussion outlines what features have emerged through the evolution of e-textbooks that bring us to the completed converged interactive e-textbooks options available today. We have reviewed some of the features that seem to engage students the most, and some of the shortcomings of previous and current e-textbook offerings. Interactive e-textbooks have the options available to integrate the elements of traditional learning management systems such as online grading and online quizzes, with rich multimedia and Web 2.0 features present in online courses, and imbed these elements in meaningful, high-quality content that are typical of traditional print academic textbooks. There are some suggestions, taken from U&G, about how to build an interactive textbook that should appeal to students, even if they do not use all of the features of the text to its fullest (see Table 1).

CONCLUDING THOUGHTS

Taking a media theory approach to new instructional technologies in general, and interactive textbook options in particular, will likely be a fruitful avenue for instructional communication research moving forward. Indeed, new instructional technologies, like all new media options, create the opportunity to explore new'

Table 1. Summary of the features linked to learners' motives and needs

Technology Features	User Needs
Usability: product easy to access and use	• Navigation (ToC) that is clear • Readability features: changeable text size, spacing, headings, full-page viewing option • Bookmarking • Note taking • Highlighting • Search • Clear layout, formatting • Affordable • Shown the features of the text (video or in class)
Portability: product works in the lives of students	• Works across devices • Works offline • Printable
Interactivity: Text incorporates opportunities to try out and apply knowledge throughout	• Collaborative activities • Discussion sections • Interactive assessments throughout • Opportunity to practice (e.g., flashcards, practice test questions, etc.)
Multimedia: product offers a rich media experience, having features similar to a webpage	• Embedded video: lectures, examples, as part of activities • Hyperlinks to examples, definitions, additional resources • Images, GIFs

Customizability: content can be edited, rearranged, and assessments or examples added that link directly to course being taught	• Faculty can tailor the content to students, course level, and course outcomes:
	    o Add, reorder, or remove content
	    o Add or remove assessments and activities

motives, types of involvement and user activity, and new media features that may help students engage course material and learn more deeply.

A more thorough application of U&G, particularly the expectancy approach to U&G that emphasizes what people expect to get out of new communication media, may also help clarify faculty adoption and development of interactive digital course materials. In the current environment, where there are many features available that may promote students' access, engagement, activity, and attention, it is important to consider the needs and motives of faculty who develop textbook content and make adoption decisions. At present, there are many digital instructional options available, but their development was slow, the learning curve was steep, and we appear to be clinging to the old standby of print materials in the absence of meaningful insight into ways that we might build and use more effective course materials.

REFERENCES

Baron, N. S., Calixte, R. M., & Havewala, M. (2017). The persistence of print among university students: An exploratory study. *Telematics and Informatics*, *34*(5), 590–604. doi:10.1016/j.tele.2016.11.008

del Barrio-Garcia, S., Arquero, J. L., & Romero-Frais, E. (2015). Personal learning environments acceptance model: The role of need for cognition, e-learning satisfaction and students' perceptions. *Journal of Educational Technology & Society*, *18*, 129–141.

Dixson, M. D., Greenwell, M. R., Rogers-Stacy, C., Weister, T., & Lauer, S. (2017). Nonverbal immediacy behaviors and online student engagement: Bringing past instructional research into the present virtual classroom. *Communication Education*, *66*(1), 37–53. doi:10.1080/03634523.2016.1209222

Gambrell, L., Palmer, B., Codling, R., & Mazzoni, S. (1996). Assessing motivation to read. *The Reading Teacher*, *49*(7), 518–533. doi:10.1598/RT.49.7.2

Gurung, R. A. R., & Martin, R. C. (2011). Predicting textbook reading: The textbook assessment and usage scale. *Teaching of Psychology*, *38*(1), 22–28. doi:10.1177/0098628310390913

Jenkins, H. (2004). The cultural logic of media convergence. *International Journal of Cultural Studies*, *7*(1), 33–43. doi:10.1177/1367877904040603

Jhangiani, R., & Jhangiani, S. (2017). Investigating the perceptions, use, and impact of open textbooks: A survey of post-secondary students in British Columbia. *International Review of Research in Open and Distributed Learning, 18*. Retrieved from http://www.irrodl.org/index.php/irrodl/article/view/3012/4214

Kim, M. H. (2009). Analysis of user preferences on the structure of digital textbook contents. *The Journal of the Korea Contents Association*, *9*(12), 900–911. doi:10.5392/JKCA.2009.9.12.900

Kuehn, S. A. (1994). Computer-mediated communication in instructional settings: A research agenda. *Communication Education*, *43*(2), 171–183. doi:10.1080/03634529409378974

Levy, M. R. (1983). Conceptualizing and measuring aspects of audience "activity.". *The Journalism Quarterly*, *60*(1), 109–115. doi:10.1177/107769908306000118

Levy, M. R., & Windhal, S. (1984). Audience activity and gratifications. *Communication Research*, *11*(1), 51–78. doi:10.1177/009365084011001003

Liaw, S. S., & Huang, H. M. (2016). Investigating learner attitudes toward e-books as learning tools based on the activity theory approach. *Interactive Learning Environments, 24*(3), 625–643. doi:10.1080/10494820.2014.915416

Limperos, A. M., Buckner, M. M., Kaufmann, R., & Frisby, B. N. (2015). Online teaching and technological affordances: An experimental investigation into the impact of modality and clarity on perceived and actual learning. *Computers & Education, 83*, 1–9. doi:10.1016/j.compedu.2014.12.015

McNamara, D. S., Levinstein, I. B., & Boonthum, C. (2004). iSTART: Interactive strategy training for active reading and thinking. *Behavior Research Methods, Instruments, & Computers, 36*(2), 222–233. doi:10.3758/BF03195567 PMID:15354687

Palmgreen, P., & Rayburn, J. D. II. (1982). Gratifications sought and media exposure an expectancy value model. *Communication Research, 9*(4), 561–580. doi:10.1177/009365082009004004

Papacharissi, Z. (2008). Uses and gratifications. In M. Salwen & C. Stacks (Eds.), *An integrated approach to communication theory and research* (pp. 137–152). New York: Lawrence Erlbaum.

Park, N., Lee, K. M., & Cheong, P. H. (2007). University instructors' acceptance of electronic courseware: An application of the technology acceptance model. *Journal of Computer-Mediated Communication, 13*(1), 163–186. doi:10.1111/j.1083-6101.2007.00391.x

Rathnayake, C., & Winter, J. S. (2018). Carrying forward the uses and grats 2.0 agenda: An affordance-driven measure of social media uses and gratifications. *Journal of Broadcasting & Electronic Media, 62*(3), 371–389. doi:10.1080/08838151.2018.1451861

Rubin, A. M. (1984). Ritualized and instrumental television viewing. *Journal of Communication, 34*(3), 67–78. doi:10.1111/j.1460-2466.1984.tb02174.x

Rubin, A. M. (2002). The uses and gratifications perspective of media effects. In J. Bryant & D. Zillman (Eds.), *Media effects: Advances in theory and research* (pp. 525–548). Mahwah, NJ: Lawrence Erlbaum.

Rubin, A. M. (2009). Uses and gratifications. In R. L. Nabi & M. B. Oliver (Eds.), *The SAGE handbook of media processes and effects* (pp. 147–159). Los Angeles, CA: Sage.

Ruggiero, T. E. (2000). Uses and gratifications theory in the 21st century. *Mass Communication & Society*, *3*(1), 3–37. doi:10.1207/S15327825MCS0301_02

Russo, T., & Benson, S. (2005). Learning with invisible others: Perceptions of online presence and their relationship to cognitive and affective learning. *International Forum of Educational Technology and Society, 8*, 54-62.

Ryan, T. E. (2006). Motivating novice students to read their textbooks. *Journal of Instructional Psychology*, *33*, 135–140.

Schugar, J. T., Schugar, H., & Penny, C. (2011). A Nook or a book? Comparing college students' reading comprehension levels, critical reading, and study skills. *International Journal of Technology in Teaching and Learning*, *7*(2), 174–192.

Sheen, K. A., & Luximon, Y. (2015, August). The Future of Electronic Textbooks from a User Perspective. In Lecture Notes in Computer Science (pp. 704-713). Springer. doi:10.1007/978-3-319-20609-7_66

Sprague, J. (1993). Retrieving the research agenda for communication education: Asking the pedagogical questions that are "embarrassments to theory". *Communication Education*, *42*(2), 106–122. doi:10.1080/03634529309378919

Sprague, J. (2002). Communication education: The spiral continues. *Communication Education*, *51*(4), 337–354. doi:10.1080/03634520216532

Sundar, S. S. (2008). The MAIN model: A heuristic approach to understanding technology effects on credibility. In M. J. Metzger & A. J. Flanagin (Eds.), *Digital media, youth, and credibility* (pp. 73–100). Cambridge, MA: MIT Press.

Sundar, S. S., & Limperos, A. M. (2013). Uses and grats 2.0: New gratifications for new media. *Journal of Broadcasting & Electronic Media*, *57*(4), 504–525. doi:10.1080/08838151.2013.845827

Chapter 3
Intergenerational Learning Styles, Instructional Design Strategy, and Learning Efficacy

Michael G. Strawser
Bellarmine University, USA

Renee Kaufmann
University of Kentucky, USA

ABSTRACT

Instructional designers must appeal to a variety of audience members both in terms of competency and preferred learning style. Though many factors may influence learning style, generational preferences may provide instructional designers a broad base of understanding undergirding strategic educational design choices. While it would be naive, and even inaccurate, to assume that Millennials constitute the only unique generational challenge for instructional designers, their sheer presence in organizations and their education expectations have changed the game—so to speak. Thus, in an attempt to clarify generational uniqueness, this chapter will explore general generational instructional trends while positioning instructional design as a necessary answer to 21st century learning efficacy challenges.

A GENERATIONAL NARRATIVE

The instructional design landscape, specifically instructional audiences, are becoming more diverse. While diversity may present itself in a variety of forms in an institution (e.g., ethnicity, gender, socioeconomic, etc.), one particularly fascinating trend is the generational diversity many institutions are experiencing (Schullery, 2013). While it would be naive, and even inaccurate, to assume that Millennials constitute the only unique generational challenge for instructional designers, their sheer presence in organizations and their education expectations have changed the game-so to speak. Thus, in an attempt to clarify generational uniqueness, this chapter will explore general generational instructional trends while positioning instructional design as a necessary answer to 21st century learning efficacy challenges.

First, it is important for instructional designers to know that Millennials, one oft-discussed generation, now represent a significant portion of the workforce. In 2013, Millennials constituted roughly ⅓ of the U.S. workforce and by 2030 Millennials will comprise up to 75% of the total U.S. workforce (Pew Research Center, 2010). Millennials, those born between 1982-2004, have a reputation for being seen as lazy, entitled, and high maintenance (Morreale & Staley, 2016), yet, they are also are highly networked, appreciate experiences, and are tech-savvy. In a recent *Time* article, Joel Stein (2013) said this about Millennials:

They are the most threatening and exciting generation since the baby boomers brought about social revolution, not because they're trying to take over the Establishment but because they're growing up without one. The Industrial Revolution made individuals far more powerful–they could move to a city, start a business, read and form organizations. The information revolution has further empowered individuals by handing them the technology to compete against huge organizations: hackers vs. corporations, bloggers vs. newspapers, terrorists vs. nation-states, YouTube directors vs. studios, app-makers vs. entire industries. Millennials don't need us. That's why we're scared of them. (para. 4)

In terms of education and training, Millennials desire flexibility, promotion opportunities, and an environment that highlights professional coaching and instruction. It is important to remember that before developing 21st century training initiatives, trainers must have a generational awareness, especially in relation to Millennial workers.

Instructional designers must appeal to a variety of audience members both in terms of competency and preferred learning style. Though many factors may influence learning style, generational preferences may provide instructional designers a broad base of understanding undergirding strategic educational design choices. For example, Millennials, compared to previous generations, prefer active and engaged learning (Nimon, 2007). This preference should inform choices regarding which opportunities are included for educational participation and involvement. The evolving "learning landscape mandates that we engage students as co-consumers/owners of ideas and approaches in the classroom [and we know] that millennials fare better when teachers provide flexible structure that allows for guided creativity" (Hosek & Titsworth, 2016, p. 359).

The same truths that resound in higher education classrooms create similar questions for instructional designers who are experiencing a new and generationally diverse workforce.

How should we respond to these changing demands?

How should we engage Millennials inside the classroom and the workplace?

How should we harness the digital connectedness of Millennials as a positive educational environment characteristic?

These questions cannot be ignored in the midst of a changing professional demographic. Thus, considering this reality in conjunction with traditional design best practices informs a new set of expectations and strategies for instructional designers to incorporate into design preferences. This chapter highlights diverse learning styles specifically from a generational perspective and discusses appropriate best practices for engaging a variety of generations, especially Millennials, in educational opportunities.

DEMONSTRATE EFFECTIVE AND APPROPRIATE INSTRUCTIONAL DESIGN

As designers navigate best practices, it is important to remember that every audience member is unique and even as we try to create generational distinctions in audiences, individual members of each generation respond differently to content and delivery. Yet, generational characteristics can help developers design more targeted and more salient content, activities, and examples, thereby enhancing the effectiveness of the training offered. While instructional design is, obviously, still necessary in K-12 and post-secondary environments, it has become even more important in corporate contexts. To contextualize, Singh (2016) defines corporate training programs as those designed by organizations to impart skills and competencies for the workplace. Additionally, training is a hallmark of good management and is vital for organizational success and sustainability (Singh, 2016). Given the importance of training in the workplace and to an organization's success, considering factors such as generational characteristics that equip trainers with greater insight of those being trained elevates the quality of training that trainers can offer. This section, unlike the previous generational overview, establishes a direct connection between generational characteristics and instructional design as an essential component of 21st century training.

Demonstrating effective and appropriate instructional design is a necessity for the modern trainer because of varying audiences and the incredible range of learning preferences represented in organizations. To combat, or address, audience differences and learning preferences, trainers must implement true models of instructional design and reach different learning styles through corresponding instructional strategies and methodologies.

In any training endeavor, instructional design is primary. Hemingway (2008) reminds designers that knowing your audience is a crucial component of any training module or initiative. New and improved training techniques are needed to help retain younger Generation Y employees. This new generation will not sit still for traditional training, and they want interactive and multimedia technology. Millennials would do well with life and career-enhancement training that resonates with their cultural upbringing: the information revolution, multi-tasking, etc. It is important to remember that the development of a learner-centered course cannot start with the development of the learning materials and learning activities. In fact,

Instructional designers must first meet with the business unit manager, ask analysis questions, document the analysis data, craft the course design, create a design document, and get approval from the manager. Only then is the designer ready to begin the development phase of instructional systems design. (Lopker, para 2).

Instructional design, then, becomes not just a means to an end, but a vital process in the corporate training machine.

There have been several training and development frameworks that help establish clarity for how and why a training initiative should be developed. For instance, in 1980, Knowles identified four assumptions to make about maturing learners: (1) they gain self-direction; (2) they gather experience, a useful resource to which to build learning; (3) their focus on getting a job and succeeding in their careers tends to dominate motivation for learning; (4) they expect what they learn to have immediate application. Kirkpatrick, in 1979, developed an evaluative training method that included four levels: (1) Reactions (i.e., Satisfaction); (2) Learning (i.e., Acquisition of knowledge or skills); (3) Behaviors (i.e., Application of knowledge in the workplace); and (4) Results (i.e., Broader indicators like increased sales, improved quality and higher productivity, or reduced costs). These decades old foundations clarify the process of evaluating and creating courses that reach the adult learner and provide a roadmap for success.

Training and development programs require diligence and purpose on the part of the designer. While training programs can consist of five steps which are "analysis, instructional design, validation, implementation and evaluation" (Singh, 2016, p. 311), these traditional duties, like assessing needs, designing training programs, facilitating programs, supporting the transfer of training, and evaluating training, are all necessary components of an instructional design mentality - no matter the audience.

With that said, the technology needs of the younger workforce has gradually shifted content expectations, thus reinforcing the need for applied and intentional instructional design. O'Brien (2009) notes that technology is a great way to bridge the generational divide in training initiatives, but we must remain mindful of mixed generational audiences and plan training modules accordingly (i.e., instructional design). She goes on to say that images, metaphors, and technology must meet the needs of individual audiences (O'Brien, 2009). Further, Jha (2017) asserts that "while employees in older age brackets prefer traditional, classroom methods of training, younger individuals seek interactive, technology-based learning experiences" (p. 201).

Intergenerational workplaces require training and development design that meets training and organizational needs and appeals to multiple generational and individual preferences. To say it another way, learning contexts still require learning goals and lesson objectives (O'Brien, 2009), even when the instructional design and strategies used attempt to cater to or accommodate multiple penchants for learning. Therefore, instructional design becomes even more important in light of intergenerational workplaces. According to Jha (2017)

A stream of young, bright workers is in the making as Gen Y gears up to take on fresh workplace roles. These tech-centric, socially-adept individuals are swiftly chalking out the trends of the future. From communication modes to training and learning methods, entire company strategies are being built around the expectations of this young league of talent who view technology as vital to their professional live. (p. 201)

Different generations and different types of learners may require more or less guidance (O'Brien, 2009). In order to adapt to an intergenerational workplace and provide organizations with initiatives that attend to the various and sometimes disparate needs or preferences associated with each generation, trainers must incorporate known generational preferences into the instructional design of trainings offered. Only by demonstrating the ability to flexibly address the training audience, one that is undoubtedly complicated by multiple generations with distinct values and biases, can trainers provide organizations with effective training.

RATIONALE: A BRAVE NEW TRAINING WORLD

With the impending tidal wave of Millennials in the professional workforce, designers must step back and analyze current instructional strategies and modalities related to 21st century initiatives. Thus, this section provides a brief overview of the brave new training world and establishes the need for diverse training initiatives built on a solid instructional design foundation.

Each generation has a mix of workplace culture preferences that directly impact training and development instructional design. For instance, Traditionalists (born between 1900-1945) value directions and guidance while Gen Xers (born between 1965-1981) want to work independently. Boomers (born between 1946-1964) enjoy working in and leading teams while Millennials (born between 1982-2004) enjoy the collaborative nature of teams but will tend to more actively avoid leadership positions. These differences highlight some immense challenges. It is important, then, to establish a generational awareness to enhance and encourage employee engagement.

Millennials, also called Generation Y, garner significant attention in the media and from organizations. Recruiting Millennial talent is important but retaining Millennial talent, and preparing Generation Y for corporate engagement, is necessary as well. Singh (2016) says this about modern day training initiatives and the response to intergenerational needs:

With the new generation of talent entering the workplace, with high levels of education and with new technology in their DNA, the corporate learning also has to be designed in a way that would bring out the best from this new generation workforce who shun the nine to five lifestyle and bring with them new expectations, norms and values in the workplace. Corporate learning must respond by fulfilling five criteria namely: online on-demand (wherein knowledge should be available at fingertips whenever possible); personalized (wherein information should be tailor made for the individual's specific needs); contextual (wherein learning should be embedded to business processes); collaborative (wherein employees should be able to use the creativity of all their colleagues worldwide both inside and outside their company); and trusted source (wherein the information should be qualitative and should be from a reliable source). (p. 313)

Designers can actively engage in this brave new training world and design curricula that responds to generational needs for organizational relevance, meaningful work, and effective professional development.

The Generation Y desire for active and engaging professional development directly connects to their rapid and ever-evolving technology proficiency. Unfortunately, Traditionalists and Boomers may not be as tech-savvy as Millennials or even members of Generation X, thus creating an even broader spectrum for training and instructional modality that is crucial for the 21st century instructional designer.

Ultimately, we are participants in a brave new training world. Tried and true strategies, without reinforcement from principles like the best practices within this volume, may no longer be sufficient for the modern training context. As such, trainers need to think strategically about engaging a variety of learning preferences and designing training initiatives with a foundation of appropriate and effective instructional design principles. The following sections will preview learning styles and provide relevant strategies for instructional design that engages multiple generations and learning preferences.

LEARNING STYLE OVERVIEW

Learning styles have received considerable attention, warranting the development of several learning styles models. Since the initial introduction of learning styles, research supports the effectiveness of incorporating strategies that specifically address various learning styles into instruction (Felder & Brent, 2005). Felder and Brent (2005) warn that "if completely individualized instruction is impractical and one-size-fits-all is ineffective for most students, a more balanced approach that attempts to accommodate the diverse needs of the students in a class at least some of the time is the best an instructor can do" (p. 57). Designers, too, benefit from appealing to the learning styles of their diverse audiences (Beebe, Mottet, & Roach, 2013). Hence, understanding what learning styles are and a popular learning styles model, Kolb's (1956) experiential learning styles model can help 21st century designers tailor instruction to the diverse learners.

Kolb's model designates four different broad categories of learners - divergers, assimilators, convergers, and accommodators. Each of the categories draw on "how [learners] take in information" and "how [learners] process information" (Felder & Brent, 2005, p. 59-60). Divergers rely on experience and reflection. They prefer observation to active participation or experiences, and they seek to find connections between the information gathered and previous experiences. Reflecting on the new information and connections help them learn. Beebe, Mottet, and Roach (2013) point out that divergers "tend to be innovative, imaginative, and concerned with personal relevance" (p. 47). Assimilators utilize abstract thinking and reflection. Assimilators prefer to rely on experts' insights as opposed to experiencing something for themselves. They also value straightforward and organized information. Convergers also utilize abstract thinking, like assimilators, but prefer active experimentation to reflection. This means that convergent learners prefer experiencing things rather than reflecting or observing. Convergers favor problem-solving approaches that allow them to test ideas and generate solutions. Accommodators make sense of information via experience and active learning. Even more so than convergers, accommodators enjoy a "getting your hands dirty" or trial-by-error opportunity to understand information. Accommodators tackle learning by discovery. Though each person may have a preferred learning style, though, everyone can learn when taught from any of these four perspectives. Importantly, rounding the learning cycle by designing instructional content and materials that appeal to all learning styles and encourage learners to expand their information acquisition and processing abilities is critical to appropriately and effectively experiential learning theory. All four learning styles (or preferences) are likely to be represented among training participants in the workforce, and developers need to consider the various learning styles when engaging in instructional design.

Along with the generational differences, learning styles provides an additional insight into designing training that appeals to diverse, intergenerational audiences. Based on characteristics of the different generations, we understand that previous generations may be more accustomed to recognizing a teacher or trainer as an authority figure, following directions without question, and work autonomously (Lovely, 2012; Worley, 2011). Millennials tend to prefer team-based, collaborative approaches; using technology; expect immediate results; and privilege the outcome to the process (Stewart, 2009; Worley, 2011). In light of learning styles, older generations may be reticent to acknowledge their own learning styles and instead believe the that learning only occurs when an instructor lectures about the information. Without explanations for why new teaching strategies are used and how the strategies best facilitate the learning process, traditionalists, baby boomers, and Generation Xers may not embrace a training design that requires active participation. Further, millennials may expect the integration of technology for both reflective and active learning. For example, typing a blog entry or participating in an online discussion rather than handwriting a journal may be more salient to Millennial learners who process information via reflection. For active Millennial learners, using a video game to simulate communication skills or conducting Internet research to inform a new creation or experiment are ways to integrate technology into trainings. To address how learners take in information, intergenerational contexts present unique opportunities. By pairing trainees with individuals from different generations, trainees can benefit from listening to and connecting with experiences of others, thereby broadening the breadth of experience and knowledge of all trainees. Additionally, commonalities through more abstract ideas can be discussed and shared, further generating well-developed and clear, organized ideas to be tested and used.

EFFECTIVE INSTRUCTIONAL DESIGN FOR INTERGENERATIONAL LEARNING STYLES

Coupling intergenerational differences with Kolb's (1956) learning model, developers can best adapt their instructional design to most effectively tailor instruction to workplace participants. Felder and Best (2005) specify instructional roles per learning style - the motivator, the expert, the coach, and the facilitator. Generational differences present an instructional role continuum ranging from the authority figure to the facilitator. Importantly, each of these roles can be embodied by a trainer in order to best meet the learning needs of trainees. How, then, should developers effectively design training for intergenerational learning styles?

A 21st century designer, attempting to round the learning cycle and engage in the brave new training world, should establish generational awareness, develop technology-friendly initiatives, and encourage mentoring as part of training programs. Establishing generational awareness includes educating others about varying approaches to learning informed by the values ascribed to each generation. However, Beebe et al. (2013) and Lovely (2012) caution against using stereotypes to every person. Instead, apply generational characteristics (and learning styles or preferences) as a starting point that should be challenged and reconsidered in light of the unique person encountered. Especially for developers or designers who may not have the luxury of meeting with each individual participant though, knowing the disparate generational values and the generational makeup of your audience can help you design initiatives that align with the various values that may be represented. Further, incorporating information about generational characteristics in design initiatives may help others embrace multiple instructional strategies.

Developing technology-friendly initiatives is particularly important to be relevant in the 21st century. Yet, recognize that some generations have less familiarity and perhaps confidence with technology than other generations (Beebe et al., 2013). Whereas Traditionalists, Baby Boomers, and Generation Xers may remember a time before color television, smartphones, and laptops with Wi-Fi, Millennials depend on multiple technologies for daily life (Lovely, 2012). Thus, integrating technology into instruction may be critical to achieving the desired training objectives but needs to be done so with mindful consideration of individuals comfort levels with using technology as well as acceptance of technology and belief in its dependability. Further, individuals may have different preferences for technology use. For example, a Millennial may be familiar and comfortable with a given technology and believe in its dependability but still prefer not to use a particular technology regularly (Lovely, 2012). When integrating technology, it is critical that the technology chosen appropriately fits at least one of the learning styles. Articulating your rationale for using a particular technology to trainees is important for successful integration.

Perhaps the best technique for cultivating a positive and productive intergenerational educational environment is to promote peer-to-peer interactions through mentoring and peer training. Beebe and colleagues (2013) put forth several instructional strategies for each learning style including "mentor/mentee relationships" for divergers, "individual research projects" for assimilators, "'problem-based' training methods" for convergers, and "[placing] trainees in the field or on job sites" as well as "internship programs" for accommodators (p. 47-49). Each of these strategies can benefit from structuring and fostering intergenerational interactions that enhance learning and satisfaction with the experience. For example, pairing individuals from different generations offers divergers the ability to converse and reflect on information with another person who may be able to contribute different experiences and perspectives to the conversation. Appealing to the assimilator learning style by posing a research project or the converger learning style by introducing a problem to solve may be coupled with peer-to-peer interactions and working with intergenerational partners or groups. Accommodators, who appreciate hands-on, action-based experiences, may be most likely to benefit from an internship or shadow experiences where older and younger generations may practice communication skills. Jha (2017), speaking particularly about technology skills, encourages corporations to consider peer-to-peer training so that younger generations can train older counterparts. The benefit of learning with and from individuals from multiple generations is not limited to technology. Contrarily, other communication skills such as expressing disagreement, listening, and decision-making may be informed by generational values and rounding the learning cycle in a way that brings to light these values so that they can be reconciled for an intergenerational workplace is an advantageous instructional design for trainers to employ.

Establishing generational awareness, developing technology-friendly initiatives, and encouraging mentoring and intergenerational peer interactions are critical instructional strategies for the 21st designer. Considering generational differences and learning styles together as essential factors informing instructional design prompts us to address the diverse values and learning preferences present in a corporate audience. In order for a 21st century designer to be most effective, we must appeal to a diverse audience and create productive learning content and materials that catalyze learning.

CONCLUSION

Generational difference is one component of a learner's background, and as evidenced by the research cited in this chapter, an important and salient component for trainers to consider when designing instruction, particularly for an intergenerational audience. As Baird and Fisher remind us, "In andragogy, the learner's background is an essential component" (p. 7). It is important for trainers to establish a generational awareness and design training initiatives that reach unique learners. The information presented in this chapter reinforces the necessity for trainers to demonstrate effective and appropriate instructional design.

REFERENCES

Beebe, S. A., Mottet, T. P., & Roach, K. D. (2013). *Training and development: Communicating for success* (2nd ed.). Upper Saddle River, NJ: Pearson Education.

Felder, R. M., & Brent, R. (2005). Understanding student differences. *Journal of Engineering Education, 94*(1), 57–72. doi:10.1002/j.2168-9830.2005.tb00829.x

Hosek, A., & Titsworth, S. (2016). Scripting knowledge and experience for Millennial students. *Communication Education, 65*(3), 357–359. doi:10.1080/03634523.2016.1177844

Jha, P. (2017, January 15). The future of learning. *Business Today (Norwich)*, 200–202.

Kirkpatrick, D. (1979). Techniques for evaluating training programs. *Training & Development* Journal, 33, 78-92.

Knowles, M. (1980). *The modern practice of adult education: From pedagogy to andragogy* (2nd ed.). New York, NY: Association Press.

Lopker, G. (2016, May 3). 10 training and development tips for instructional designers and trainers [Blog post]. Retrieved from https://www.td.org/Publications/Blogs/L-and-D-Blog/2016/05/10-Training-Development-Tips-for-Instructional-Designers-and-Trainers

Lovely, S. (2012). Boomers and millennials: Vive la difference. *Journal of Staff Development, 33*, 56–59.

Morreale, S. P., & Staley, C. M. (2016). Millennials, teaching and learning, and the elephant in the classroom. *Communication Education, 65*(3), 370–373.

Nimon, S. (2007). Generation Y and higher education: The other Y2K. *Journal of Institutional Research, 13*, 24–41.

O'Brien, M. (2009, August). The e-learning industry: Facing the challenges of Web 2.0. *Forum* New Media, New Relations, 6, 57-61.

Pew Research Center. (2010). Millennials: A portrait of generation next. Retrieved from http://www.pewsocialtrends.org/files/2010/10/millennials-confident-connected-open-to-change.pdf

Schullery, N. M. (2013). Workplace engagement and generational differences in values. *Business Communication Quarterly, 76*, 252–265.

Singh, S. (2016). Impact and effectiveness of corporate training programs through industry-academia tie-ups. *Journal of Commerce & Management Thought, 7*, 309-319. Doi:10.5958/0976-478X.2016.00021.5

Stein, J. (2016, May). Millennials: The me me me generation. *Time.* Retrieved from http://time.com/247/millennials-the-me-me-me-generation/

Stewart, K. (2009). Lessons from teaching millennials. *College Teaching, 57*(2), 111–118. doi:10.3200/CTCH.57.2.111-118

Worley, K. (2011). Educating college students of the net generation. *Adult Learning, 22*(3), 31–39. doi:10.1177/104515951102200305

Section 2
Form, Function, and Style

Chapter 4

Some Basics to the Initial Setup and Maintenance of Serialized Online Learning

Shalin Hai-Jew
https://orcid.org/0000-0002-8863-0175
Kansas State University, USA

ABSTRACT

Optimally, the learning sequence experienced by learners is addressed in the instructional design plan. So too is the sequencing of learning objects in the modules, related modules in the course, related courses in a degree program, and so on, from granular objects to larger ones. A variety of learning contents may be conceptualized, at a zoomed-out level, as "serialized" or a part of a series. Serialized online learning refers to any number of types of large-scale sequenced learning, such as endeavors that continue over extended time (such as a number of years), that involve a number of interrelated learning objects (like podcast series), and that serve both new learners and continuing learners. The instructional design for serialized online learning requires front-loaded design considerations and approaches that consider the continuing nature of such learning.

INTRODUCTION

In applied instructional design, sequences have virtually always been part of the consideration. What are the assumed pre-requisites for the learning? What order should the experienced learning occur in (Simple to complex? Developmental to more advanced?)? What about the sequence of learning activities? (For example,

DOI: 10.4018/978-1-5225-9833-6.ch004

before a field trip or a group simulation, what should the lead-up learning consist of?) What is a reasonable sequence of learning outcomes? In an analytical case study, what information should learners have access to first and then in what sequence thereafter, to highlight different available insights? How should learners transition from one level of knowledge to another? If a process or procedure is taught, what base knowledge should be available to learners, and then how should the sequences be represented for optimal performance? In learning where social interactions are required, what should be the order of interactivity—and to what depth and to what learning ends?

At a zoomed-out level would be large-scale serialized online learning, including projects that continue over years, the creation of a number of interrelated learning objects (in large sets or large series, like podcast series or online encyclopedias), and that serve both new learners and continuing learners. What has not generally been addressed is how to plan, design, and develop such serialized online learning in a way that supports the learners, whether they are new or continuing ones. For example, such serialized online learning may include the following:

- A large set of similar or related learning objects
- A podcast series
- A video series
- An electronic book series
- A public wiki based on a particular topic or domain, and others

This work provides some initial design considerations for large-scale serialized online learning, with some basic assumptions:

- Large-scale serialized learning generally deals with complex learning in particular domains and related fields. The complexity in the learning may be understood cumulatively.
- Large-scale serialized learning will attract a range of learners with evolving needs over time. Some learners will be new ones, and others will be continuing ones.
  ○ Learners tend to prefer consistency and recognizable patterning.
- The teams that contribute to long-running serialized learning projects will experience turnover and so will need to integrate new contributors (including new leadership) over time. The work standards need to be transferable, and the work practices need to be robust over time.
- The content domain space will evolve and change over time.

Some Basics to the Initial Setup and Maintenance of Serialized Online Learning

- The technological underpinnings for the online learning will evolve over time, so some digital preservation efforts will be important, along with endeavors for future-proofing.
- Large-scale serialized learning may be closed-source or open-source or some combination.

This work explores some of the considerations for building large-scale serialized online learning, with a focus on initial setups of such projects and some maintenance. While most instructional designs are for discrete-sized objects (learning objects, modules, courses, etc.), this challenge involves open-endedness in terms of the series of learning contents and longitudinal time in terms of learning object / learning resource production. The underlying research informing this work stems from decades in the area of online learning design and development.

REVIEW OF THE LITERATURE

At some level, all learning has some intersection with the world, for authentic learning. Some offers focuses on "real-life learning tasks" as the base motive for the learning (van Merriënboer & Stoyanov, 2008, p. 84). One of the main survival demands of modern life is to handle complexity, with the requisite perspective(s), knowledge, decision making capabilities, and resources.

One researcher proposed a descriptive rendition of problem types as the following: "logical problems, algorithmic problems, story problems, rule-using problems, decision making problems, trouble-shooting problems, diagnosis-solution problems, strategic performance problems, case analysis problems, design problems, (and) dilemmas" each requiring different learning activities to acquire (Jonassen, 2000, pp. 74 - 75). How the "problem space" is conceptualized is relevant "because rich problem representations most clearly distinguish experts from novices and scaffold working memory (an essential cognitive component in problem solving)" (Jonassen, 2000, p. 82). Finally, this typology, while informative in an academic space, may be even a little textbook and non-inclusive of real-world hard problems writ large. Teaching and learning has been undergoing a "movement towards ill-structured problem-solving, domain-general competencies, expert learning, metacognitive skills, and broad reference situations" (van Merriënboer & Stoyanov, 2008, p. 84).

There are well-structured problems, which are defined and identifiable, with known required thinking and actions to solve. Worked problems can enhance learners' capabilities of acquiring the necessary schemas to understand and solve the challenges. The intuition is that "instruction-based learning took fewer trials than trial-and-error learning to reach a similar performance level"…and "repeated instructions" were even better than single instruction (Ruge, Karcz, Mark, Martin, Zwosta, & Wolfensteller, 2018, p. 4).

Then, too, there are ill-structured problems, hard problems, complex ones, which do not have worked solutions. These require awareness, wisdom, accurate information, complex collaborations, mixed skillsets, and various resources. These problems do not have pre-defined paths for their solution, if indeed, they are solvable. Hard problems in various fields can remain open ones for hundreds of years, and in some cases, they may remain extant (with various proofs of impossibility). In some cases, ill-structured problems pose different design problems along the way, with many parts unsurfaced and elusively undefined:

Ill-definition means that the design problem being solved itself develops as design progresses. Further, criteria in design may remain tacit throughout (Woodbury, Mohiuddin, Cichy, & Mueller, 2017, p. 40)

To function effectively, learners need the proper knowledge, skills and abilities (KSAs) (van Merrienboer, Kirschner, & Kester, 2003), and they need the ability to coordinate and cooperate. To effectively address ill-structured problems (which lack tested prior worked solutions), people need both domain-specific and domain-general competencies:

Recent research points out that different intellectual skills are needed for solving well-structured problems, which rely on applicative or recurrent skills that are highly domain-specific, and ill-structured problems, which rely not only on applicative but also on interpretive or non-recurrent skills that are less domain-specific (Cho & Jonassen, 2002; Hong, Jonassen, & McGee, 2003; Van Merriënboer, 1997). In this respect, the meaning of domain-specific and domain-general competencies is also changing because the combination of both is needed to solve ill-structured problems. (van Merriënboer & Stoyanov, 2008, p. 71)

Ill-structured problems are conceptualized as being "more situated" (context-dependent) with well-structured problems relying "more on general problem-solving skills, such as means-ends analysis" (Jonassen, 2000, p. 68) although the opposite can also be true where "ill-structured problems, in the form of dilemmas, can be fairly abstract" (Jonassen, 2000, p. 68). To solve ill-structured problems, knowledge alone is insufficient and inert. They need to think creatively and divergently (not in ways that everyone else has thought about the challenge before), from a place of deep knowledge of particular areas of expertise but also from outside that domain. They need to be able to apply analogical solutions. They need to be able to apply knowledge, skills and abilities from one area to another, through transfer. Said another way, the intrinsic cognitive load--"a basic component of the material" (Sweller, 1994, p. 295)—is by definition higher for ill-structured hard problems. The difficulty level is intrinsic. To solve these, they must apply simultaneous learning with schemas that interact (Sweller, 1994, p. 295). Learning relevant pieces in isolation, without application to the constraints in the challenge, will not be sufficient. Problem solving requires "cognitive operations" that are properly sequenced and goal-directed (Anderson, 1980, p. 257, as cited in Jonassen, 2000, p. 65).

To make complex tasks more understandable, most break the challenge down into respective parts and solve the individual parts. Perhaps they may reorganize the tasks into meaningful sequences. Perhaps the orders of the sequences may result in solving more critical parts of a complex challenge with fewer unintended outcomes, less negative second- and third-order effects. Others may start at the macro level and reframe the challenge there, and work the issue from the outside in. With complex problems, there may be desirable end states and "equifinality" in some cases (different solution approaches resulting in the same end-state solution) or not (different solution approaches resulting in different end-state solutions).

In terms of large-scale serialized online learning, both novices and experts will be accessing the contents. Providing the same instruction to both novices and experts can be problematic. For the novices, advanced directions may be impossible to comprehend, at one extreme. At the other, experts may experience the "expertise reversal effect" in which instructional methods decline as "levels of learner knowledge in a domain change" (Kalyuga, 2007, p. 510). There has to be an artful approach in the presentation of learning tasks so as not to "unbalance" the executive function: "…if external guidance is provided to learners who have sufficient knowledge base for dealing with the same units of information, learners would have to relate and reconcile the related components of available long-term memory base and externally provided guidance. Such integration processes may impose an additional working memory load and reduce resources available for learning new knowledge" (Kalyuga, 2007, pp. 512 - 513). Said another way: "If learners already have acquired information, requiring them to process that information again via the borrowing and reorganising (sic) principle may result in an extraneous cognitive load due to the narrow limits of change principle. Learners who already have acquired information will be unnecessarily processing excess interacting elements" (Sweller, Ayres, & Kalyuga, 2011, pp. 155 – 156).

For novices, by definition, they aspire to ultimate expertise, even if this requires years of effort.

High-level professional expertise requires years of extensive learning and practice in a specific domain (Ericsson et al. 1993) and involves many essential attributes in addition to the relevant knowledge base. However, one of the most important characteristics of expertise in any domain is the availability of a large number of domain-specific organized knowledge structures (schemas). High-level professional experts are in most cases also experts in solving specific routine tasks in their domains. Task-specific expertise is the ability to perform fluently in a specific class of tasks. A typical indicator of such expertise is performing rapidly advanced stages of solution by skipping some (or all) intermediate steps. Developing task-specific expertise is an important and necessary prerequisite for becoming a higher-level expert in a broader domain. (Kalyuga, 2007, p. 511)

In general, experts can call on prior experiences and can recognize emergent patterns for their analysis. They can engage complexity without being overwhelmed. They may have a sense of what steps to take to arrive at accurate outcomes. They may assess situations and focus on the proper "signals" or "indicators," without being overwhelmed by the "noise" in the context. They may have evolved heuristics or rules-of-thumb to apply to the situation. They may have expectations of outcomes that are more accurate to the world than may be achieved by non-experts. They can troubleshoot with improved efficacy. They have some over-learned behaviors that enable automaticity in appropriate contexts. They may bring into play the different measures of different intelligences needed, such as visual intelligence, logico-mathematical intelligence, symbolic intelligence, and psychomotor skills. To be relevant, all experts have to have the ability to learn. Dealing with complexity requires the ability to engage "with materials incorporating an enormous number of interacting elements" (van Merriënboer & Sweller, June 2005, p. 156). Experts have conceptual models of reality that can inform their work (while non-experts in the domain often have mental models, which are incomplete or inaccurate or only partially formed). Long-term memory in people is important in dealing with complexity:

Working memory has no known limitations when dealing with information retrieved from long-term memory (Ericsson and Kintsch, 1995; Sweller, 2003, 2004). In effect, long-term memory alters the characteristics of working memory. Long-term memory holds cognitive schemata that vary in their degree of complexity and automation... In this sense, schemata can act as a central executive, organizing information or knowledge that needs to be processed in working memory (van Merriënboer & Sweller, June 2005, pp. 148 - 149)

Acquiring this complex knowledge requires attentional resources and investments of time. One authoring team observes:

Some Basics to the Initial Setup and Maintenance of Serialized Online Learning

Structures with all items repeated in different orders in different parts of the structure… require attention for learning. Such structures may require hierarchic representation, the construction of which takes attention (Cohen, Ivry, & Keele, 1990, p. 17).

Sequencing theory suggests the importance of purposeful setup of the learning. Some suggest the decomposing of complex tasks into part-tasks, teaching those parts, and then having learners practice the parts as a sequenced whole. Some overlearning may be needed to make parts of the sequence automatic. In general, sequences progress from the simple to the complex ["van Merriënboer recommends that case types within whole-task practice be sequenced from simple to more complex cases" (Wiley, June 2000, p. 71)]. There are other sequencing regimes based on other logics and learner needs.

INITIAL SETUP AND MAINTENANCE OF LARGE-SCALE SERIALIZED ONLINE LEARNING

One way to think about serialized online learning design is to place two important dimensions on a 2x2 table. The two elements are the target learners and time. Serialization is about the creation of a series of learning contents that are somewhat interrelated and that meet the needs of the learners, with a high level of quality. The four quadrants in Figure 01 include meeting the needs of new learners in the present, new learners in the future, returning or continuing learners in the present, and returning or continuing learners in the future. (This is a reading of the quadrants from the top-left cell, across to the right, then down to the left, and across to the right.) Ideally, the learning resources would be designed and developed once, tested for efficacy, and revised, and then versioned for all learners. Notice that over time, new learners become returning ones (per the down-pointing arrow), and continuing learners may become future learners, if they maintain the interest, and if the evolving learning resource continues to provide learner value. If the cognitive scaffolding is designed appropriately, novice learners and expert learners are each supported in their respective needs based on differentiated instruction.

There are multiple ways to approach serialized online learning.

- One approach is to write out a plan, design the elements of the related learning, and develop the learning contents and test from there. This approach may be informed by learning theories and other sources. This is a classic top-down approach.
- Another approach is to go right to development, evolve the learning resources for a time, and then evaluating what was created to see what elements should

Figure 1. Large-scale serialized online learning: considering target learners and brief-to-extended time (in a 2x2 table)

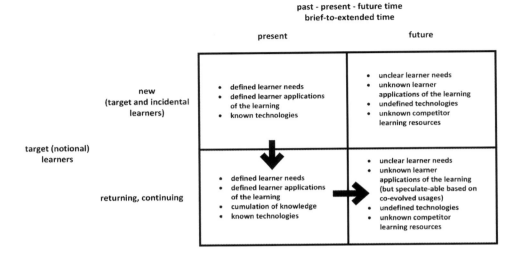

be kept for the serialized online learning designs. Those may be documented in a project stylebook, and the stylebook may be used for the project. This is a classic bottom-up approach.

A core concept is that in the learning, there are constants which provide a sense of familiarity and safety and confidence. Then there are also variations, such as the learning contents, that add value to the learning and that update the knowledge, skills, and abilities (KSAs) of the learners. The combination should offer ways for learners to apply their cognition to the new learning and not waste attention and focus on extraneous cognitive loads (stemming from poor design, attentional distractors, and others). (Table 1)

Table 1. Combining constants and variations in large-scale serialized online learning

Constants	Variations
• Overall purposes • General target learners • Domain of learning (including periphery) • Learning sequences • Look-and-feel • Interactivity • Sense of welcome to all learners	• Informational contents • Spokespersons • Pedagogical designs • Technologies • Opt-in learning experiences

Some Basics to the Initial Setup and Maintenance of Serialized Online Learning

Essentially, considering serialized online learning is an add-on consideration to a typical instructional design sequence (Figure 2 and Table 2), which tends to be recursive (with designer/developers completing the work in a semi-linear way but moving backwards as needed as new information is captured and new observations are made) and cyclical in the serial context, with repetitions of the cycle to enable the creation of the learning resources. A lot of work is front-loaded, so that "throughlines" may be created for the learning, to maintain coherence, while enabling designer/developer improvisation. The openness of the considerations enable individuals and teams to meet needs as they arise, so even though there is initial planning, the idea is that the plans are living documents that evolve over time. The point is to avoid being overly scripted or overly regimented.

Discussion

As noted earlier, the serialized online learning may be film series, podcast series, wikis, blogs, simulation series, and others. At core, designing and developing serialized online learning involves some combination of the following:

- building learning without a clear end point

Figure 2. The instructional design and development cycle

Table 2. Planning for the serialized online learning (step 2) as part of the instructional design and development cycle

Steps of the Design and Development Sequence	Related Work Questions
1. Light Pre-Assessment of the Instructional Design Project	• What are the learning objectives? What are ways to achieve those learning objectives? • What domain topics will be addressed, and why? • Who are the target learners? Who are the novices, and who are the experts? What are their respective needs? • What technologies are available for the project? • What are the available resources? • What is the timeline for this work? • What are the legal requirements for this work? Policy requirements? Technical requirements? • Which are the funding entities, and what are their requirements?

continued on following page

Some Basics to the Initial Setup and Maintenance of Serialized Online Learning

Table 2. Continued

Steps of the Design and Development Sequence	Related Work Questions
2. Planning for Serialized Online Learning*	**Content Authenticity** • What are ways to ensure that the learning contents are authentic to the world? What are ways to ensure that the learner experience is authentic to the world? **Learner Needs** • What are ways to address the needs of novice learners? The needs of the in-between state learners? The needs of expert learners? • What are resources that may be made available to the novice learners? The in-between state learners? The expert ones? • What are ways to align the learning to the motives of the novice learners? The in-between state learners? The expert learners? • How can opt-in cognitive scaffolding be offered for less knowledgeable learners? How can more apt examples be provided for the novice learners? How can the expertise of the experts be drawn out in ways that are helpful to their learning? • How can new learners be accommodated in the serial learning? How can expert learners' be accommodated in the serial learning (based on their prior experiences, their expectations, their patterning, and others)? • How can feedback loops be created to understand the respective learners' usage of the learning resources and what they are getting out of it? • If a new direction is desired, how can these considerations of learner needs inform the changes? How can there be a balance of a sense of continuance while new objectives and contents and pedagogical methods are in play? **Important Core Elements** • What are the animating values and principles and objectives which guide the instructional design? How far reaching are these? Will these serve the project well into the near-term, mid-term, and far-term future? **Throughlines** • What sorts of "throughlines" should be designed and developed for a sense of continuity? A character or number of characters? A consistent narrator? An origin story? Designed sequences of learning? Templating of learning contents? Recurring symbols? Atmospherics? **Work Documentation (for Onboarding, for Continuance)** • What sorts of work documentation is required for easier handoffs to the designers/developers and the teams that collaborate around this work? (Reverse-engineering design standards from the completed learning resources is an imprecise process. It can be difficult to infer intentionality from the finished objects. Undocumented work can leave users guessing as to original intentions and guidelines. Usually, what is left to institutional memory goes unremembered and is lost.) Should there be project stylebooks? Defined project color themes and palettes? Logos and symbols? Other elements? **Competitiveness** • How can the learning resources maintain competitiveness in contest with the other extant learning resources? How can the serialized learning resources maintain competitiveness into the future? **Future Proofing** • Over time, how can the information or contents be protected for versioning and future-proofing? What are ways to transcode digital contents with the least lossiness (lost information)? How can designer/developers benefit from the ability to separate informational contents and how those contents are delivered (with on-the-fly re-packaging)? **Project Management** • What are ways to ensure that the project is resourced into the future?
3. Learning Content Development	• How should the learning contents be presented? • What are the most important interactive and other features necessary in the learning? • What technologies are most important? • What should the look and feel be?
4. Alpha and Beta Testing	• What sorts of in-house testing should be done to ensure functionality of the learning objects? Legality? Alignment with branding? (alpha testing) • What sorts of testing of the draft learning contents be done with focus groups of learners? What sort of feedback would be useful from these participants? (beta testing)

continued on following page

Some Basics to the Initial Setup and Maintenance of Serialized Online Learning

Table 2. Continued

Steps of the Design and Development Sequence	Related Work Questions
5. Revision	• What needs to be revised, redesigned, re-developed, after the alpha and beta testing?
6. Deployment	• How should the learning be set up on the online learning platform? How will the learning contents be delivered to the target audience(s)?
7. Learner and Learning Monitoring	• What aspects of learner monitoring are most important to track, and why? How will this information be used for revision of the learning resources? (How can learner privacy and learner identities be protected? How can personally identifiable information or "PII" be avoided in the data collection?) • What aspects of the learning monitoring are most important to track, and why? How will this information be used for revision of the learning resources?
8. Learning Content Updating	• When should the learning resources be updated, and how? What aspects of the learning are most time-sensitive for updating, and why? (If a work is "defunct," should be it retired? Archived? Left alone?)
9. Repetition of Entire Cycle for Follow-on Contents	• Once a part of the serialized online learning has been designed and launched, the cycle repeats. In many cases, simultaneous efforts are used to design and develop and launch contents, with the necessary levels of testing and revision.

- building learning to acquire complex skill sets
- building learning to enable the solving of ill-structured hard problems
- building learning to an audience of both novices and experts (over time)
- building online learning to a dynamic technological understructure

The resulting learning objects may be aggregated into designed learning sequences. They may be disaggregated and used by others as parts of other learning sequences. (This means that every disaggregate-able piece has to be able to stand alone and provide informational and learning value individually, for learners taking on different tracks.) The learning contents may be used in unprincipled and even naïve applied ways. The usage may be in open-entry open-exit trainings. They may be parts of online courses. They may be harnessed by informal learning-based online communities.

For those who inherit a set of trainings or course contents, they need to review the learning contents, the work documentation, and other aspects—and design to the relevant aspects of the materials. They have to ask, What are the critical elements of the learning that should be borne forward? What learning objectives are relevant to this time and to future learners? What learning activities will be relevant for learners today and into the future? Why? What style elements may be updated? What technologies need to be updated for relevance into the future? In other words, these designer/developers who inherit the work have to understand what to cherish from history, how to update the instructional designs into the future and what to make wholly new and what changes to bring about. The "emulation" may be relevant only to a point, and then there should be innovations and improvisations, riffing off a theme.

The original online learning series may continue for a time, and then there may be spinoffs, semi-derivative byproducts from the original. Those who design spinoffs have important considerations as well. They have more leeway to introduce innovations and different contents, but they have to have some overlap with the original, whether this is about content (the same learning albeit for a different age group of learners, for example), parallel learning or follow-on learning, style or other features. Spinoffs are usually done to capitalize on the name recognition of the original contents and to benefit from the learner base of the original (to move them to new contents), and other practical reasons. Designers of spinoffs often have more freedom to innovate than those who merely inherit an assignment and have to "ghost" the work in the same vein as the originals.

The work handoff, whether for continuing design and development or for spinoffs, will require professional knowledge and skills.

This work examines large-scale serialized online learning as a separate class of online learning resources that requires more pre-planning and forethought to enable effective learning over time, for both new learners and continuing ones.

FUTURE RESEARCH DIRECTIONS

To extend this initial work, researchers may explore their own large-scale serial learning projects and record instructional design and development strategies and test what works and what doesn't, in case-based research. This would require either pilot-testing the learning contents and going live with them and collecting data from live learners (once initial alpha and beta testing have been completed). Based on their collected data, they may be able to observe types of instruction which are efficacious for some types of learning over others. They may be able to identify gaps in their design and development work. They may be able to explain methods for expanding their applied imagination in constructive ways to expand serialized online learning for optimal accurate knowledge retention, decision making, skill creation and development, ability creation and maintenance, and related knowledge, skills and abilities ("KSA")-transfer.

It would help also to know if there is optimal macro-scale sequencing for particular types of learning and practice.

Another approach may involve ad hoc serialized learning, such as in non-formal (non-credit-based learning sequences) and informal (learning as a byproduct of experiences) in lifelong learning contexts. Are there some *ad hoc* sequences that make more sense than others? Are there longitudinal patterns that make sense for such learning? Are there times when particular learning resources are optimal?

As yet, this approach of analyzing serialized designed learning and instruction is highly under-explored.

CONCLUSION

One of the leading thinkers in the design of learning objects wrote, "We can only create what we can imagine" (Hodgins, 2002, p. 282). The ability to deploy the human imagination to solve problems in the real is critical, and understanding serialized online learning may enhance what instructional designers and developers see and imagine, and how they may strive to meet the needs of learners in all their diversities in this particular "use case." This "serialized" framing provides an anticipatory depth, whether or not the learning is directed and closed-sourced or open-sourced, and whether or not the learning is formal academic learning (theory-heavy, designed for complexity and transfer) or applied trainings (practice and process-oriented, designed for application in work places).

With how much goes into digital content creation, IDs should not approach the work as "day trading" or as "one-offs" but consider the creation of long-term learning value and to actualize these plans where possible.

REFERENCES

Cohen, A., Ivry, R. I., & Keele, S. W. (1990). Attention and structure in sequence learning. *Journal of Experimental Psychology*, *16*(1), 17–30.

Hodgins, H. W. (2002). The future of learning objects. In *The Instructional Use of Learning Objects* (pp. 281–298). Bloomington, IN: Agency for Instructional Technology, and Association for Educational Communications & Technology.

Jonassen, D.H. (2000). Toward a design theory of problem solving. *Educational Technology Research and Development (ETR&D)*, *48*(4), 63 – 85.

Kalyuga, S. (2007). Expertise reversal effect and its implications for learner-tailored instruction. *Educational Psychology Review*, *19*(4), 509–539. doi:10.100710648-007-9054-3

Ruge, H., Karcz, T., Mark, T., Martin, V., Zwosta, K., & Wolfensteller, U. (2018). On the efficiency of instruction-based rule encoding. *Acta Psychologica*, *184*, 4–19. doi:10.1016/j.actpsy.2017.04.005 PMID:28427713

Sweller, J. (1994). Cognitive load theory, learning difficulty, and instructional design. *Learning and Instruction*, *4*(4), 295–312. doi:10.1016/0959-4752(94)90003-5

Sweller, J., Ayres, P., & Kalyuga, S. (2011). The expertise reversal effect. In J. Sweller, P. Ayres, & S. Kalyuga's (Eds.), Cognitive Load Theory. Explorations in the Learning Sciences, Instructional Systems and Performance Technologies. New York: Springer Science + Business Media, LLC. doi:10.1007/978-1-4419-8126-4_12

van Merriënboer, J. J. G., Kirschner, P. A., & Kester, L. (2003). Taking the load off a learner's mind: Instructional design for complex learning. *Educational Psychologist*, *38*(1), 5–13. doi:10.1207/S15326985EP3801_2

van Merriënboer, J. J. G., & Stoyanov, S. (2008). Learners in a changing learning landscape: Reflections from an instructional design perspective. In J. Visser & M. Visser-Valfrey (Eds.), Learners in a Changing Learning Landscape (pp. 69 – 90). Academic Press. doi:10.1007/978-1-4020-8299-3_4

van Merriënboer, J. J. G., & Sweller, J. (2005, June). Cognitive Load Theory and complex learning: Recent developments and future directions. *Educational Psychology Review*, *17*(2), 147–177. doi:10.100710648-005-3951-0

Wiley, D. A., II. (2000). *Learning object design and sequencing theory* (Doctoral dissertation). Brigham Young University.

Woodbury, R., Mohiuddin, A., Cichy, M., & Mueller, V. (2017). Interactive design galleries: A general approach to interacting with design alternatives. *Design Studies*, *52*, 40–72. doi:10.1016/j.destud.2017.05.001

ADDITIONAL READING

Clark, R. C., & Mayer, R. E. (2016). e-Learning and the Science of Instruction: Proven Guidelines for Consumers and Designers of Multimedia Learning (4th ed.). Hoboken, NJ: John Wiley & Sons, Inc.

KEY TERMS AND DEFINITIONS

Atmospherics: Mood (such as from designed elements).
Continuance: In existence over time, continuing, enduring.
Lossiness: The irrecoverable giving up or forfeiture of information (often in a process).

Some Basics to the Initial Setup and Maintenance of Serialized Online Learning

Serialized: Part of a series; regular installments (often in sequence).
Style: Distinctive instantiation (of learning).

Chapter 5
Designing Integrated Learning Paths for Individual Lifelong Learners and/or Small Groups:
Backwards Curriculum Design From Target Complex-Skill Capabilities (for Nonformal Informal Learning)

Shalin Hai-Jew
https://orcid.org/0000-0002-8863-0175
Kansas State University, USA

ABSTRACT

Curriculum design is often applied to creating formal learning sequences to ensure that learners pursuing accredited coursework experience the proper learning contents, activities, life-building, and fair assessments in the proper order. In a lifelong learning context, learners will engage in a combination of formal (accredited), nonformal (byproduct learning from structured unaccredited learning contexts), and informal (unintentional) learning. For the latter two contexts, and for individual and groups of learners, there may be benefits in constructing a backwards curriculum design to enable target complex-skill capabilities (even those that require years of effort). This work explores how to create a backwards curriculum design from target complex-skill capabilities, using manually created data tables and related mind maps as early design tools. These enable advancing targeted learning by skill branches or by sequential approaches towards the target skillset.

DOI: 10.4018/978-1-5225-9833-6.ch005

Designing Integrated Learning Paths for Individual Lifelong Learners and/or Small Groups

INTRODUCTION

A "curriculum" represents "the expression of educational ideas in practice" and is based on "the Latin word for track" (Prideaux, 2003, p. 268), so it refers to a learning path, a course of study in accredited schools and universities. Another definition suggests that a curriculum "is an ideological, social and aspirational document that must reflect local circumstances and needs" and "is made up of all the experiences learners will have that enable them to reach their intended achievements from the course" (Grant, 2010, p. 1). "Curriculum design" is an outgrowth of efforts to create formal accredited coursework, in pre-K12 through doctoral studies programs. As a matter of practice, curriculum design involves reasoned, data-based, and systematized building of blocks and sequences of learning to ensure that the target learning objectives are achieved effectively. In political framing, there are stated curriculums, hidden or sub-textual ones, and omitted ones (what is left out), in any curriculum design (CD). Ideally, such designs should consider the whole learner and their overall well-being as well as the necessary "knowledge, skills, and abilities / attitudes" ("KSAs"), from a term originated by staff at the U.S. Office of Personnel Management:

Knowledge, Skills, and Abilities *(KSAs): The attributes required to perform a job and are generally demonstrated through qualifying service, education, or training.*

Knowledge*: A body of information applied directly to the performance of a function.* **Skill***: An observable competence to perform a learned psychomotor act.* **Ability***: Is competence to perform an observable behavior or a behavior that results in an observable product. ("Knowledge, skills, and abilities," Nov. 17, 2018)*

The advent of the Social Web has meant that a wide variety of learning resources have become available to the broad public. The Web 2.0 technologies have broadened the sharing methods for curriculum resources (Xie, Bai, Li, & Yin, 2014). Some of these are open-source, others open-access, and others behind paywalls. Regardless, there are numerous available resources for learning: social videos, games, published research articles, datasets, simulations, image sets, immersive virtual worlds, and others. Many resources are hosted online, on repositories, in digital libraries, on learning management systems, image-sharing platforms, video sharing platforms, and others. Massive open online courses (MOOCs) enable a defined-path to various skillsets. And beyond MOOCs, in this contemporaneous space, lifelong learners may pursue professional / personal / hobbyist learning interests outside of formal channels. They may pursue nonformal learning from non-credit learning contexts and informal learning through the experiences of everyday life and without learning goal orientation. In these pursuits, curriculum design may be applied more broadly, in less formal contexts but with more ambitious "hard problem" sorts of learning goals as the end point. [This approach assumes that critical learning developmental windows were met in childhood, so learners can bring their full capabilities to the lifelong (and mastery) learning space. Complex learning requires serious study skills and discipline. Cobbling handpicked and machine-picked resources to develop knowledge, skills and attitudes / abilities or "KSAs" outside organizational structures means that learners have to self-provision in many aspects. The DIY aspect may seem simple, but much effort is required behind the scenes.]

Some researchers have offered a model of "guiding principles for learning in the 21st century," and they suggest that there should be a mix of learning support and assessment (Hughes & Acedo, 2014, as cited in Acedo & Hughes, 2014, p. 515). They suggest foundational skills including academic honesty, critical thinking, creativity, information literacy, and other requisites. They write: "Creativity and critical thinking intersect at the levels of problem solving, argument analysis and decision-making: they are the habits of mind that students need to address high levels of complexity, challenge and unfamiliarity" as 21st-century citizens (Acedo & Hughes, 2014, p. 518). These researchers observe that the human mind "thrives on highly complex polyvalent environments" (Acedo & Hughes, 2014, p. 504).

With open-source learning contents, unique CDs may be designed at the micro (individual) and meso (group) levels with blocks cobbled from open-shared learning resources and sequencing based on the individual and group learning needs. Beginning with the end for curriculum design for complex learning in non-formal and informal learning contexts can be advantageous in enabling goal-focused learning using open-shared learning resources that enables thinking through long-term time investments to achieve ambitious outcomes. There are also learning competitions, conferences, and other events. This lifelong-and-mastery learning curriculum design (CD) approach may be less formal than for a full program design, degree design, interdisciplinary program design, or other sequence in an academic context. This approach adds a planning component that is not particularly common in nonformal and informal types of lifelong learning.

As conceptualized, this approach...

- requires less focus on subject disciplinary limitations
- lowers the need for the purity of applied theories and models (in formal curriculum design)
- enables usage of open-shared learning resources on the Web and Internet
- may involve the cobbling of a mix of open-available and copyrighted contents (with legal usages)

Designing Integrated Learning Paths for Individual Lifelong Learners and/or Small Groups

- may involve the creation of on-the-fly learning resources which may be wholly new

- enables the holistic focus on the acquisition of complex skill sets with plenty of dependencies
- enables the focus on acquiring skills requiring years of effort (over longitudinal time)
- may accommodate particular learner preferences and unique needs (in participatory learning design)

- may accommodate unexpected "found" discovery paths along the way
- enables learner decision-making about paths forward and inquiry-based explorations (learner agency and independence)
- enables adaptivity to learner needs, with controlled complexity (and an experiential learning approach)
- is time-flexible around learners' lives (when applied at the micro level)
- enables on-the-fly adjustments to the curriculum design to meet learner's felt needs

- focuses on experimentation in learning sequences

- enables social learning among groups of learners
- enables social learning (when applied to small groups at the meso level)
- enables on-the-fly adjustments to the curriculum design to meet learners felt needs (in a social group)

- enables some feedback from the learning blocks, learning sequences, and the world writ large (whether reinforcement or otherwise)

- enables learner engagement in the real world for learning

Ultimately, this approach may open up a broader range of learning opportunities, particularly for complex and long-term learning. Backwards design is mission-oriented with defined measurable outcomes for goal-based learning.

REVIEW OF THE LITERATURE

"Curriculum development" has been in existence since the mid-1800s (Tyack, 1974, as cited in Kelting-Gibson, 2005, p. 27), according to one source, and it may have been around even longer based on a search through the Google Books Ngram Viewer (Figure 1).

Over the years, a number of approaches have been used to design curriculums, including understandings of the natures of humans; various considerations of idealized learners; competing value systems (including political ones), and others.

Various learning theories, based on hundreds of years of research, are considered important to inform the learning designs. One design model explicitly maps learning theories, which include the following: behaviorism, pre-conscious learning, reflective learning, experiential learning, learning in HE (higher education), conversational framework, and communities of practice (Conole, Dyke, Oliver, & Seale, 2004, pp. 25 - 26), with contributions by many of the foremost thinkers in the education space.

The three-stage backward curriculum design process includes defining the "desired results,...multiple sources of data...and appropriate action plans" to achieve those particular aims (McTighe & Thomas, Feb. 2003, p. 1). The second step requires the "acceptable evidence" of the efficacy or inefficacy of the learning and informs the planned "learning experiences and instruction" (Wiggins & McTighe, 1998, as cited in Kelting-Gibson, 2005, p. 28). Assessment of the learning is a critical aspect in backwards design (Wiggins & McTighe, 1998, as cited in Hendrickson, Jan. 2006, p. 31), and as such, in backward design, assessments should be clarified first to inform the design of "the most appropriate learning activities and instruction" (Wiggins, Feb. 2012, Slide 56).

Some research suggests that "curriculum design using the backward design model" outperformed curriculum designs "using a traditional model on all six

Figure 1. "Curriculum development" and "instructional design" on Google Books Ngram Viewer

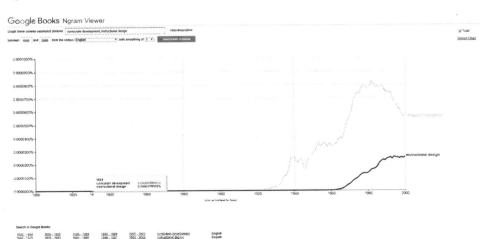

components" (of Danielson's Framework for Professional Practice ("demonstrating knowledge of content and pedagogy, demonstrating knowledge of students, selecting suitable instructional goals, demonstrating knowledge of resources, designing coherent instruction, and assessing student learning") (Kelting-Gibson, 2005, p. 26), aligning with the idea that some of the best curricular designs are designed in a backward way (Wiggins & McTighe, 1998). After all, the approach is built around outcomes, defined as "successful performance" (Wiggins, Feb. 2012, Slide 60), with the requisite knowledge, skills, and attitudes/abilities (KSAs). The effort in this for learners involves "engaging work and competent understanding" (Wiggins, Feb. 2012). The originators of this approach suggest the importance of systems approaches to understand the dynamics around the curriculum (McTighe & Thomas, Feb. 2003, p. 4).

"High quality curriculum development" is thought to include the following sequences: analysis, design, construction, evaluation, and implementation (Gustafson & Branch, 1997; Visscher-Voerman, Gustafson & Branch, 1997; Visscher-Voerman, Gustafson, & Plomp, 1999, as cited in McKenney, Nieveen, & van den Akker, 2002, p. 25). More specifically, analysis involves "performing problem analysis, task analysis, context analysis, content analysis"; design involves "deciding on substantive parts or components of the curriculum, such as: aims and objectives, subject matter, learning and instructional strategies, learner tests, timing, location"; construction involves "creating and revising prototypes of the curriculum"; evaluation involves "testing the quality of the prototypes or final deliverable," and implementation involves "applying the curriculum in practice" (McKenney, Nieveen, & van den Akker, 2002, p. 25). This formal sequence often involves cross-functional team work, and the work requires complex adherences to higher education policies, professional standards (including ethics), and domain practices. Graves "model of curriculum design" (2000) includes "assessing needs, formulating goals and objectives, developing materials, designing an assessment plan, organising (sic) the course, conceptualising (sic) content," to inform the course designing…and also "defining the context" and "articulating beliefs" to better address the context in which the learning is occurring (Graves, 2000, as cited in Nation & Macalister, 2010, p. 136).

Also, curriculum design rationales are informed by practical considerations like learning objectives and learning outcomes; in many cases, there is so-called "teaching to the test" based on in-domain professional assessments for various types of certifications. Intended learning outcomes may lead directly to the development of particular learning paths (Tangworakitthaworn, Gilbert, & Wills, 2013). In highly dynamic fields, curriculums have to be created to differentiate between "fads" vs. "fundamentals" (Lightfoot, Sept./Oct. 1999). Various stakeholder groups have to be considered in the designs. Individual students' concerns are relevant, but curriculum design capabilities generally focus on the "public interest" when considering program graduates, company stockholders and "all of public" (Lightfoot, Sept./Oct. 1999, p. 45), with the concerns of business entities, legislative bodies, and educators more often focused on the long-term (p. 47).

In terms of practices, the curricular organization may be understood in four approaches: "a strict disciplinary curriculum, an integrated curriculum, a problem-based curriculum, (and) an apprenticeship model" described in order as "organized around disciplines, with no explicit introductions or skills" for disciplinary focuses, "organized around disciplines, with skills and projects interwoven" for integrated curriculums, "organized around problems, with disciplines interwoven" for problem-based curriculums, and "based on projects, with no organized introductions of disciplines" for apprenticeship curriculums (Edström, Gunnarsson, & Gustafsson, 2007, p. 88). [For this backwards design for lifelong and mastery learning in nonformal and informal learning, the designs most align with "integrated curriculum" and "problem-based curriculum" and "apprenticeship models".] The authors describe various integrations of learning by interspersing target learning, running target learning in a parallel way with other learning, or integrating target learning into an extant curriculum (Edström, Gunnarsson, & Gustafsson, 2007, p. 89), and in the approach here, any of these interwoven approaches may apply.

Researchers have created designs of curricula for complementary school-work contexts or what they call a "hybrid" curricular approach or "vocational education and training" (VET) (Zitter, Hoeve, & de Bruijn, 2016). The curriculum may be conceptualized along two overlapping axes: connected to realistic on the horizontal (left-right), and acquisition to participation on the vertical (top-down). The resulting quadrants describe different aspects of the work-school curriculums (Zitter, Hoeve, & de Bruijn, 2016, p. 115). [For this work, the backwards design of lifelong and mastery learning for nonformal and informal learning would best fit at the bottom right "realistic-participation" quadrant with "high-fidelity" to the world. In their model, the "realistic-participation quadrant" involves on-the-job training, apprenticeships, and work experiences (Zitter, Hoeve, & de Bruijn, 2016).] The empirical evidence in curriculum design does not suggest that there is any "one best choice for framing a curriculum as a whole or any of its parts" but only that the curriculum "should simply be fit for the purpose and context of its place and day" (Grant, 2010, p. 1), which suggests that there is no equifinality of design but only of learning outcomes (whether those are achieved to satisfaction or not).

How the curricular materials are harnessed depends on those who use the contents to teach and how they interpret the curricular materials in terms of the "enactment perspective" (Choppin, 2011, p. 333), described as *"orientations* toward the use of curriculum materials (Remillard and Bryans 2004), *curriculum vision* (Drake and Sherin 2009), and *pedagogical design capacity* (Brown 2009), respectively" (Choppin, 2011, p. 333). Engagement with curricular resources may enhance teachers' developing competence in the use of teaching materials and their *"curriculum vision"* (Drake & Sherin, 2009, as cited in Choppin, 2001, p. 334) and their "pedagogical design capacity" (Brown, 2009, as cited in Choppin, 2011, p. 334). The resourcing of available curricular materials requires understanding of learner needs, their state of understanding, their learning progress, different ways to harness the learning contents, and ways to support learner uses of the learning materials.

The interactions between "users and curriculum materials" has been labeled "curriculum ergonomics" (Choppin, McDuffie, Drake, & Davis, 2018, p. 75). This seems to be a new area of expertise involving focuses on five areas:

(1) teachers' relationships with and capacity to use curriculum resources; (2) alignment between design intentions and patterns of curriculum use; (3) ways in which curriculum resources influence instruction; (4) ways in which curriculum features are purposefully designed to achieve an educative purpose; and (5) the dissolution of boundaries between design and use. (Choppin, McDuffie, Drake, & Davis, 2018, p. 75)

This approach was conceptualize as a spinoff from "cognitive ergonomics" or "the interactions among humans, systems, machines (including computers), and the environment in terms of how work gets done" (Choppin, McDuffie, Drake, & Davis, 2018, p. 75).

BACKWARDS CURRICULUM DESIGN FROM COMPLEX SKILLSETS IN THE NONFORMAL AND INFORMAL LEARNING SPACES

The core assertion is this work is that it is possible to engage some semi-formal curriculum design practices in order to reverse-build curricular paths for lifelong learning (for nonformal and informal learning) using open-shared learning resources from the desired end point (defined here as "target complex-skill capabilities" and related learning outcomes). Here, the focus will be on requisite knowledge, skills, and attitudes/abilities (KSAs) as personal learner characteristics. The learning paths may be for individuals or for groups. Generally, such curriculum designs will not have the socio-political aspects, nor the policy and standards aspects, of the more formal learning design ones. At this time, the approach is a somewhat experimental one.

To see how this might work, a light proof-of-concept may be created based on a complex skill set disaggregated as knowledge, skills and attitudes/abilities (KSAs). To start, Figure 2 shows a sequence of capabilities that may be required to achieve the research and publishing skillset. Table 1 shows the breakdown in terms of the respective KSAs, and the respective steps are portrayed as mind map visuals in the 15 figures that follow. While these mind maps might be suggestive of a sequence, down the left and then down the right sides, these can actually occur out of the implied order. The specificities of a curriculum might be the second or third-degree out from the subnodes around the central node in each mind map. The mixes of trees suggest some time sequences, but they also suggest flexibility, with some parts able to be worked piecemeal and others in branches. These mind maps may be further explored as combined sequence maps, for a more holistic approach. Curriculum maps have long been designed to show "the links between the elements of the curriculum" (Prideaux, 2003, p. 272), and this is another option: "A map for students will place them at the centre and will have a different focus from a map prepared for teachers, administrators, or accrediting authorities. They all have a common purpose, however, in showing the scope, complexity, and cohesion of the curriculum" (p. 272). Or they may be perceived as a set of learning activities (Figure 18), as depicted near the end of the chapter.

The data in Table 1 might have action verbs that show both observable outcomes but also internal-state perceptions (from the learner point-of-view); that is purposeful because both are important. Another way to understand the ideas in Table 1 is to bring in the concept of thresholds. For example, what is a sufficient threshold of quality in terms of the creation of data visualizations? What is sufficient self-sufficiency? Another approach is to mix up the higher-order level of operations. The sequence in Figure 2 is a rough order of the learning based on a theorized sequence of necessary work to achieve the research and publishing, but it is highly unlikely that a learning sequence would map to this exactly. A person may acquire understanding of a software tool for data analytics. Then maybe this person might acquire knowledge of how to transcode data from an online video sharing site. And so on. Breaking apart the mental concept of sequentiality may be useful. (The numbering here in Table 1 may be just for reference.) Also, this work suggests integrated learning paths, with overlapping learning at any one time. Some of the learning may have cross-pollination and mixed influences; for example, some software tools enable the whole sequence of work from data cleaning to model setups to model analysis to data visualizations.

Figures 3 through 17 are the mind maps, and these give a sense of the combinatorial complexity of the work for the ambitious target skill set.

It would seem to make sense that curriculum designs be coherent and fairly comprehensive…but also that they are practically doable. Figure 18 suggests these respective mind maps are part of a set but has not offered the next step in terms of integrations and possible direct sequences.

Designing Integrated Learning Paths for Individual Lifelong Learners and/or Small Groups

Figure 2. A complex skillset for research work: A sequence in 15 steps

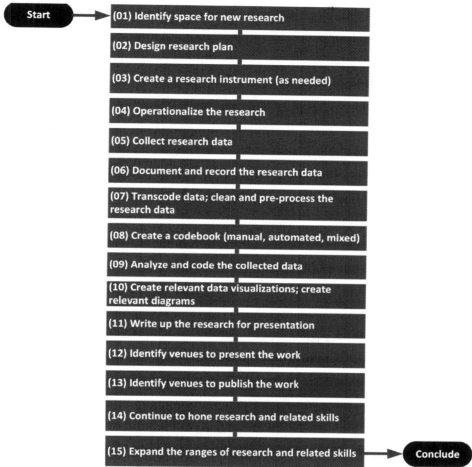

Discussion

In terms of designing curriculums for individuals and small groups, these may enable a clearer sense of planning, with defined objectives and sequences and resources. For many, acquisitions of new learning involve zoomed-in points-of-view and maybe incremental planning. Many in-world options for learning resources may be non-obvious. A micro- and meso-scale sense of backwards curriculum design applied to nonformal and informal learning may change these factors and enable a more effective approach to the acquisition of complex skill sets.

Designing Integrated Learning Paths for Individual Lifelong Learners and/or Small Groups

Table 1. Using interlinked ksas (knowledge, skills, and attitudes/abilities) to break down a complex skillset (The sections with empty bullets in the Skills column indicate the discipline- or domain-level uniquenesses.)

Performance-Level Learning Objectives	Competency / Targeted Capability	Knowledge	Skills	Attitudes ("Abilities" in some KSAs)
(1) Identify space for new research (or challenges to existing research)	Maintain precursor knowledge for the particular field	• Domain field knowledge • Domain field practices • Domain field research methods • Domain field technologies	• Reading and comprehension of the historical information, conceptual information, and prior published research • Describing of the main thinkers and contributors in the field • Summarization of the main ideas and practices in a field	• A learning approach to the field • A contributory approach to the field
	Maintain up-to-date knowledge in the field	• Contemporary domain knowledge	• Reading up on the latest published research and gray literature • Engaging in multimedia related to the field	• Open-mindedness to technologies, change, new research methods, new ideas, and others • Openness to others' participation
	Harness peripheral and interdisciplinary knowledge linked to the target domain	• Cross-domain knowledge of fields peripheral to the target domain	•	•
	Identify sources for trustworthy information in the field	• Knowledge of trustworthy sources	•	•
	Review contemporaneous research practices	• Knowledge of research practices (both central and peripheral)	•	•
	Review contemporaneous applied research ethics	• Knowledge of contemporary applied research ethics	•	•
	Identify gaps in discipline knowledge	• Gaps in discipline knowledge, absences of potential information	•	•
	Discern what has not already been done before in a discipline or field	• Gaps in research practices in the discipline or field	• Understanding the field sufficient and the potentials in the field sufficiently to identify gaps	• Considering fields to be active instead of settled • Assuming one has something to contribute to others
	Conceptualize some possible original research topics	• Application of an educated imagination to a discipline	• Formulating actionable research questions	• Assuming the space for innovation
	Define personal motivations and interests and KSAs in the particular field	• Accurate self-awareness and self-knowledge of motivations and KSAs in relation to the discipline (particularly in terms of capabilities)	• Self-assessment of motivations and KSAs in relation to the discipline	• Professional ambition • Professional hopefulness • Sense of professional possibilities
	Assess whether one has the resources and wherewithal to achieve the research	• Practical knowledge of what it takes to achieve research successfully • Sense of resources available for research	• Taking stock of a research context • Assessing or auditing available resources	• Practical approaches to research and documentation

continued on following page

Designing Integrated Learning Paths for Individual Lifelong Learners and/or Small Groups

Table 1. Continued

Performance-Level Learning Objectives	Competency / Targeted Capability	Knowledge	Skills	Attitudes ("Abilities" in some KSAs)
(2) Design research plan	Think of research objectives or goals	• Creating defined research objectives or goals	• Writing research objectives and goals that are practical	• Having confidence that one has the skills to contribute in terms of research
	Conceptualize appropriate research designs for the particular research objectives	• Formulating effective research designs based on research objectives	• Writing research designs that accurately describe the goals	• Having confidence that one has the research sensibility to set relevant research goals • Having confidence that one has the judgment to define achievable research goals
	Build "after" others' research (emulation, but done legally)	• Understanding the most salient points of others' research and designing new research to follow that	• Assess the parts of others' work that may be relevant to a particular research context • Designing research in relevant emulative ways	• Be willing to learn from others
	Design appropriate research processes	• Setting up original research that is somewhat emulative of others' research	• Designing research processes in proper ways and with the proper sequences • Writing research plans in actionable ways	• Considering the importance of accurate documentation • Understanding the importance of documentation processes to enhance the research work
	Ensure that the research design follows all legal standards	• Understanding the latest in legal requirements for research	• Conducting targeted research to understand the applicable research rules • Adhering to legal standards in research design	• Acknowledging the importance of being law abiding
	Ensure that the research design adheres to all research standards	• Listing the research standards in the field	• Abiding by the research standards in the field	• Respecting research standards in applied contexts
	Acquire proper oversight and permissions to conduct the research legally	• Understanding whom to acquire permission from and with what information and other resources	• Following through on the steps required to conduct research legally	• Respecting the oversight roles of other professional in the research space
	Ensure that the research is doable or executable (within resource and time and talent limits)	• Evaluating research for practical doability given local contexts	• Applying evaluative standards to one's own research to understand the practical doability	• Understanding the need for practical considerations in research
	If future actualization of the research design veers off of legal or ethical or appropriate, be able to recognize the danger and make proper adjustments	• Analyzing research to ensure continuing evaluation of research to ensure that it continues to adhere to legal and / or ethics standards	• Applying continuing evaluation of research to ensure that it continues to adhere to legal and / or ethics standards	• Adhering to legal and ethical standards in research
	Document the research design at a deep level of specificity	• Knowing how to maintain accurate notes • Knowing how to maintain accurate records (before-during-after research)	• Keeping accurate notes during the research • Maintaining accurate records (before- during-after research)	• Sense the importance of keeping accurate records
	Document the research design with some alternate paths and some flexibility	•	•	•

continued on following page

Table 1. Continued

Performance-Level Learning Objectives	Competency / Targeted Capability	Knowledge	Skills	Attitudes ("Abilities" in some KSAs)
(3) Create a research instrument (as needed)	Review existing possible research instruments	• Identification of the various available research instruments for the particular research • Knowledge of the respective tool features and dimensions required for the particular research effort	• Ability to vet software for proper selection and application	• Openness to using a range of software tools • Openness to acquiring new skills
	Design an original research instrument (to achieve particular objectives)	• Identifying the conventions of particular research instruments	• Applying conventions of respective research instruments to their design for a particular research context	• Understanding the strengths and limits of respective features of research instruments
	Test the research instrument for efficacy by consulting with content experts and other experts	• Knowledge of various ways to pilot-test a research instrument with experts	• Pilot-testing a research instrument with expert feedback • Pilot-testing a research instrument through statistical analyses	• Having a sense of excellence in terms of instrumentation to collect information
	Run statistical analyses for principal components analysis or factor analysis to explore apparent constructs	• Knowledge of various ways to pilot-test a research instrument with human respondent	• Process data for statistical analyses runs • Run the software programs for statistical analyses • Export the data as needed • Export data visualizations as needed	• Caring about rigorous standards in the uses of instruments for the collecting of data
	Acquire rights as needed to align with legal responsibilities	• Knowing who to acquire legal rights from for particular resources for a test instrument	• Making a professional and legally binding request of resources for a test instrument	• Taking a responsible attitude for ensuring that a test instrument is legally put together and deployed
	Revise the instrument	• Understanding how to translate research data and feedback into revisions to the test instrument	• Forming plans to revise the research instrument based on research and feedback	• Taking a rigorous approach in thinking about research instruments and their role in research
	Format the instrument for different versions to meet different needs	• Understanding the various types of formatting that may be done for different functionalities of the research instrument	• Creating different formats of the research instrument based on different needs (for versioning)	• Mental flexibility in understanding the usage of the instrument in different contexts
	Deploy the instrument	• Knowing what user needs are when responding to a research instrument	• Setting up the instrument for responses by people	• Caring about the user needs in terms of the research instrument
	Set up ways to share the instrument (if relevant)	• Considering ways to share the research instrument	• Enabling the sharing of the research instrument	• Focusing on ways to share research instruments (and related work with other researchers)
(4) Operationalize the research	Create information and methods for informed consent of research participants	• Awareness of informed consent • Awareness of elements required for an informed consent for target respondent	• Writing an effective informed consent • Writing an informed consent that is clear to research participants (and enabling access to further information, if desired)	• Caring about research participants • Caring that research participants are making decisions that are informed and optimally in line with their well being

continued on following page

Designing Integrated Learning Paths for Individual Lifelong Learners and/or Small Groups

Table 1. Continued

Performance-Level Learning Objectives	Competency / Targeted Capability	Knowledge	Skills	Attitudes ("Abilities" in some KSAs)
	Attain legal oversight for the research	• Knowledge of proper legal oversight of the research	• Acquire legal oversight of the research to ensure protections for participants, the researchers, and the institution of higher education, among others stakeholders	• Caring about adhering to legal standards while conducting research • Caring about protecting all stakeholders in research
	Acquire legal rights to necessary resources	• Being aware of what resources may be owned by others under copyright or other rights	• Ensuring that a research instrument is legally created, with all proper rights releases	• Taking a long-term view of research instruments • Protecting the interests of various stakeholders in the creation of research instruments
	Acquire necessary software and other tools	• Knowing how to acquire requisite software and other tools	• Acquiring requisite software and other tools	• Valuing the importance of acquiring software and other tools legally and fairly
	Follow research design plan and processes	• Know-how about how to actualize a research plan	• Operationalizing or actualizing the research design plan and processes in the real	• Considering the importance of follow-through based on an approved research design plan
	Identify individuals to participate in the research (while upholding the rules of sampling)	• Awareness about how to follow research guidelines for proper respondent sampling	• Acquiring proper numbers and types of respondents through adherence to approved methods	• Upholding the importance of random sampling where possible (and if using lesser standards, adapting methods or qualifying the research)
	Elicit feedback and information and data in a variety of ways	• Information about how to elicit feedback from others without introducing bias	• Neutral ways to elicit information	• Engaging with research participants as effectively as possible to elicit their points-of-view
	Document the work	• Knowledge about the types of data required for documenting the research work	• Ability to document the research work • Finding ways to use the documentation of the research work	• Valuing keeping records of the research work for later reference
	Report to grant funders and others within deadlines	• Awareness of what grant funders expect from their grant recipients	• Working to provide the requested and relevant information to grant funders in a timely fashion	• Valuing the relationship with grant funders • Respecting the role of grant funders in terms of some oversight
	Maintain a working budget	• Understand how to calculate a project burn rate	• Maintain a budget within the limits	• Understanding the need to keep projects on track by not over-taxing budgets and resources
(5) Collect research data	Engage in data collection from various research contexts	• Data collection methods (in a preservationist way) from different research contexts	• Ability to collect data from various contexts	• A sensibility that relevant data may be collected from various contexts
	Record the feedback with accuracy and comprehensiveness	• Knowledge of how to capture people's feedback thoroughly and accurately	• Capturing people's feedback thoroughly and accurately	• Consideration for the accuracy of recording others' insights in a research context
	Create research notes and / or a research journal	• Knowing what may be relevant to record in research notes and / or a research journal	• Capturing relevant or salient information in research notes and / or a research journal	• Valuing documentation of research work as having informational value
	Ensure that the data collection is done in a consistent way	• Awareness of consistency in data collection	• Maintaining consistent methods in data collection for the research	• Caring about the consistency of the data collection

continued on following page

Table 1. Continued

Performance-Level Learning Objectives	Competency / Targeted Capability	Knowledge	Skills	Attitudes ("Abilities" in some KSAs)
(6) Document and record the research data	Maintain the accuracy of the collected data	• Being aware of what actions may change the underlying data inside of and outside of technology systems	• Being sufficiently careful to protect the accuracy of the collected data	• Valuing data accuracy as of paramount importance, with implications on the research
	Create and maintain a pristine and comprehensive master set of all the data—raw, trace, and other	• Knowing how to create master datasets and keeping these in pristine condition for re-use	• Protecting pristine master datasets in order to have clean data for analysis	• Caring about protecting data integrity • Caring about maintaining flexibility in data analytics
	Create related metadata to maintain a history of the data	• Knowledge of a consistent metadata approach to labeling digital data	• Applying metadata to digital resources (published contents, gray literature, primary research, and others)	• Valuing informative metadata • Valuing the ability to access data sources (of research) using metadata
	Set up an effective archive for the research information	• Knowledge of how to set up a database (or other storage type)	• Setting up a database (or storage type) • Ensuring proper file labeling • Ensuring search functions	• Caring about ease of access to collected information for research
	Use preservationist methods to protect the data into the future	• Understandings of digital and analog preservationist methods to protect data and information	• Preserving analog data and information • Preserving digital data and information	• Valuing data and information of different forms • Valuing the access of future generations to past and contemporary knowledge
(7) Transcode data; clean and pre-process the research data	Transcode the data (analog, and other) for digital readability	• How to transcode the respective types of data into usable formats (and those that may ultimately have preservationist qualities)	• Transcoding data from analog to digital (and / or vice versa • Maintaining accuracy in the transcoding (and applying sufficient oversight to ensure accuracy)	• Valuing data of all types, no matter the format of the data • Caring about the accuracy of transcoded data
	Create clean translations of data between languages	• Understanding the complexities of languages • Respecting the nuances of respective languages • Understanding the need for accuracy in translating between languages	• Translating between languages • Using various technologies to verify the translations between languages	• Respecting various languages and their unique aspects
	Create transcripts of the video or audio or mixed-modal research interactions and elicitations	• Understandings of transcript conventions (particularly related to original data formats)	• Turning auditory files into textual ones for manual and automated analytics	• Valuing various data formats (which enable different types of data analytics)
	Pre-process or clean the quantitative datasets	• Understanding how to pre-process or clean data in effective ways for the different types of statistical analyses and machine learning and other processes (often requiring different cleaning for different processes)	• Pre-processing the master set data in different ways (for different types of analytics)	• Appreciating how different types of data pre-processing and cleaning may have nuanced effects on the data analytics outcomes

continued on following page

Designing Integrated Learning Paths for Individual Lifelong Learners and/or Small Groups

Table 1. Continued

Performance-Level Learning Objectives	Competency / Targeted Capability	Knowledge	Skills	Attitudes ("Abilities" in some KSAs)
	Combine datasets as needed for queries	• Understanding how combining various datasets and datatypes will affect the resulting datasets	• Combining various datasets to enable queries and other types of processing	• Appreciating how data can be quite nuanced
	Separate datasets as needed for queries	• Understanding how separating various datasets and data types will affect the resulting datasets	• Separating various datasets to enable queries and other types of processing	• Appreciating how data can be quite nuanced
(8) Create a codebook (manual, automated, mixed)	Define the applied theories, models, frameworks, or concepts used in top-down manual coding	• Applied theories, models, frameworks or concepts • Knowledge of how concepts apply to data • Understanding how data from research may inform theories, models, framework and / or concepts	• Selecting relevant theories, models, frameworks, and / or concepts • Applying concepts to data in accurate and creative ways	• Valuing theories in academic and research spaces • Valuing models in academic and research spaces • Valuing frameworks in academic and research spaces • Valuing concepts in academic and research spaces • Valuing top-down coding (sometimes in combination with bottom-up coding)
	Define the practices in bottom-up coding (such as those based on grounded theory) in manual coding	• Methods for bottom-up coding from the available data	• Application of bottom-up coding from the available data • Documentation of the coding (for code analysis)	• Valuing the affordances of bottom-up coding (sometimes in combination with top-down coding)
	Run some autocoding methods for some types of autocoded codebooks, including sentiment analysis, topic modeling, and others	• How to create computer-generated codebooks	• Running autocoding methods for sentiment analysis • Running autocoding methods for topic modeling • Running autocoding methods from manually-generated codebooks	• Valuing the complementarity of machine coding (and machine learning) to quantitative, qualitative, and mixed methods research)
	Run custom autocoding	• Understanding how to create a manual codebook to full saturation • Knowing how to set up a software program to emulate a human coding "fist"	• Creating a manual codebook to full saturation regarding a particular target topic (informed by concepts, data, or a combination of both) • Applying the manual codebook to data using automated means • Analyzing the results of the coded data	• Appreciating what may be coded in an automated way based on a manual codebook • Understanding that new insights may surface from this endeavor
	Create thorough README documentation for the codebook	• Conceptualizing what is important about the documentation for a codebook	• Writing documentation around the creation of a codebook	• Understanding the need for those who inherit a codebook from a researcher to understand how that codebook was created and how it should be used, among others • Valuing the ability to share a codebook with other researchers
	Maintain records of the respective autocoded codebooks as macros or scripts or programs	• Knowing how to maintain codebooks as macros, scripts, or programs	• Saving a codebook as a macro, scripts, or a program	• Understanding the value of a digital codebook as a macro or program for use into the future, and / or for sharing with other researchers • Valuing record-keeping • Valuing data preservation • Valuing sharing • Valuing publication

continued on following page

Table 1. Continued

Performance-Level Learning Objectives	Competency / Targeted Capability	Knowledge	Skills	Attitudes ("Abilities" in some KSAs)
	Maintain records of the respective codebooks in digital format (for records, for sharing, for publication, for computational analysis, and other applications)	• Keeping digital records of different codebooks in digital format for later reference	• Maintaining digital records of different codebooks in digital format for later reference	• Understanding the value of digital codebooks for documentary value • Valuing record-keeping • Valuing data preservation • Valuing sharing • Valuing publication
	Maintain records of the respective codebooks in print format (for records, for sharing, for publication, and other applications)	• How to create effective print format copies of codebooks	• Keeping effective print format copies of codebooks for records, for sharing, for publication, and other applications	• Valuing record-keeping • Valuing data preservation • Valuing sharing • Valuing publication
(9) Analyze and code the collected data	Code the data strategically and in a variety of ways	• Knowledge about coding data in incremental and insightful ways	• Coding data in incremental and insightful ways	• Valuing ways to add insights to data through coding (labeling and categorizing and otherwise mapping meaning to raw data)
	Analyze the coded data for further insights	• Knowledge about how to iterate through coding and coded data for fresh insights	• Iterating through coding and coded data for fresh insights	• Valuing working through data through multiple iterations (often over time) for new insights
	Run analytics on the codebook	• Methods for eliciting research, analysis, and other insights from codebooks	• Analyzing codebooks manually • Analyzing codebooks through autocoding	• Valuing learning about analytics applied to raw data through codebooks
	Run analytics on the coding (in parts, in whole)	• Methods for eliciting research, analysis, and other insights from coding	• Analyzing coding manually • Analyzing coding through autocoding	• Valuing learning about analytics applied to raw data through coding
	Apply statistical analysis techniques accurately	• Methods for applying statistical analysis techniques	• Applying statistical analysis techniques • Framing and describing statistical analysis techniques effectively	• Valuing the insights available from rigorous statistical analyses of various types
	Use the correct statistical analysis packages or programs for the particular analyses (and data)	• Understanding of what the respective affordances and capabilities of statistical analysis packages and programs are for various data analysis applications	• Selecting and acquiring the appropriate statistical analysis packages and / or programs for particular functions	• Valuing the various affordances and enablements of data analytics software
	Create analytics-based data visualizations from the data analytics	• Creating meaningful data visualizations from data • Knowledge of conventions of various types of data visualizations	• Creating meaningful data visualizations	• Valuing the communicating data information through visualizations and diagrams
	Draw manual models as needed	• Knowledge of convention of models and diagrams • Ways to harness technologies for the manual drawing of models and diagrams	• Drawing models manually using technologies • Drawing diagrams manually using technologies	• Valuing visual communication in sharing concepts

continued on following page

Designing Integrated Learning Paths for Individual Lifelong Learners and/or Small Groups

Table 1. Continued

Performance-Level Learning Objectives	Competency / Targeted Capability	Knowledge	Skills	Attitudes ("Abilities" in some KSAs)
	Apply relevant human analysis of the computation-based data analytics results	• Appropriate human analysis of computation-based data analytics results	• Application of relevant human analysis of the computation-based data analytics results	• Valuing human analysis of computation-based data analytics results (and not just reporting on statistical analytics but actually applying analytical approaches)
	Conduct in-depth analysis about the relevance of the data in-world	• Application of reasoning to research data to understand potential applications in the world	• Applying systems analysis to understand how research data may apply to the world	• Understanding practical and potential effects of research findings and data in the world
	Create follow-on questions that arise from the data and data analytics	• Conceptualizing follow-on research questions after initial research and related data analytics	• Thinking of potential follow-on research questions • Building on existing research and research findings to advance the work and the field	• Valuing the conceptualization of follow-on research • Valuing continuance of research in research spaces
	Explore "long tails" and outlier cases	• Considering less frequent examples of an observed phenomenon	• Exploring "long tails" and outlier cases for different types of insights	• Valuing off-cases • Going beyond population-level descriptive statistics (and measures of central tendency) • Learning from exemplars of one
(10) Create relevant data visualizations and informational diagrams	Clean and pre-process the data appropriately to create data visualizations	• How to clean and pre-process data without introducing error in resulting data analyses and data visualizations	• Cleaning and pre-processing data for data analyses and data visualizations	• Respecting the need for finesse in cleaning data for data analytics and data visualization
	Review the visual conventions for particular data (to match the underlying data with the visual elements)	• Knowledge of the types of data visualizations that align with particular underlying data • Knowledge of the most effective data visualizations for particular data • Knowledge of how data visualizations may be designed to inform on the underlying data (for accurate understandings)	• Outputting the proper data visualizations related to the underlying data	• Valuing the need for user understanding of the particular data visualization (and its underlying data)
	Apply visual conventions for the particular data visualizations and informational diagrams	• Understanding visual convention for various types of data visualizations and informational diagrams	• Applying appropriate visual convention for the various types of data visualizations and informational diagrams	• Valuing user understandings of data visualizations and informational diagrams
	Label the parts of the data visualization appropriately	• Understanding proper labeling of data visualizations (and respective parts) for clarity and precision	• Applying proper labeling of data visualizations (and respective parts) for clarity and precision	• Valuing clarity in the interpretation of data visualizations through proper labeling
	Apply informative names to the data visualizations	• Naming protocols and conventions for data visualizations	• Applying proper and informative names to data visualizations • Being consistent in the naming of data visualizations in a shared project	• Valuing clarity in the naming of data visualizations

continued on following page

85

Table 1. Continued

Performance-Level Learning Objectives	Competency / Targeted Capability	Knowledge	Skills	Attitudes ("Abilities" in some KSAs)
	Apply color in relevant ways to the data visualizations	• Understanding color theory • Understanding color palettes • Understanding color themes	• Applying color in relevant ways to data visualizations • visualizations	• Valuing the potential role of color in communicating information in data visualizations
	Ensure that visuals are accessible for those with visual acuity issues	• Understanding color contrasts • Understanding color blindness	• Applying color in accessible ways to data visualizations • Using proper data labeling with numbers and other aspects to communicate frequencies and intensities (and never color alone) • Ensuring that every part of a data visualization communicates the information in clear visual ways	• Valuing accessibility in data visualizations and informational graphics
	Maintain consistency in data visualizations and naming protocols for images in a series	• Knowing how to maintain consistency in data visualization renderings and naming protocols	• Maintaining consistency in data visualizations in a series	• Valuing consistency in data visualizations in a series
	Create diagrams / illustrations based on models and concepts (manual and digital-assisted and fully-digital-created)	• Knowing how to render diagrams and illustrations from concepts	• Rendering diagrams and illustrations from concepts and other abstractions	• Valuing the visual expression of ideas
	Ensure that visuals are understandable in stand-alone ways (in case the visual is separated from the original context or is consumed in a stand-alone way)	• Knowing how to communicate ideas through stand-alone visuals	• Communicating ideas through stand-alone visuals, without dependencies on the context for meaning	• Valuing the human practices of disaggregating parts and pieces of online presentations
	Export the visuals in the appropriate formats with the appropriate features in order for the various contexts in which the visuals will be used (presentation, print, website, and others)	• How to render visuals in a variety of digital and analog formats for different presentation contexts	• Rendering digital and analog visuals in a variety of formats for different presentation contexts	• Understanding that the visuals will be used in a variety of contexts and will require different needs and dimensions and features
	Ensure that visuals used in contexts have lead-up and lead-away information	• Understanding how to integrate a data visualization into a context with lead-up and lead-away text	• Creating lead-up and lead-away information to visuals in a presentation or other context	• Valuing integration of data visuals in particular contexts
(11) Write up the research for presentation	Select what is relevant from the research, the data, and related information	• How to describe research in academic styles and convention	• Writing up research in academic styles and conventions	• Valuing the sharing of original research to an audience of academic peers
	Explain the work and logic with clarity	• How to explain how the research was conducted and the data analyzed with clarity	• Explaining how the research was conducted and the data analyzed	• Valuing clarity in the sharing of research information

continued on following page

Designing Integrated Learning Paths for Individual Lifelong Learners and/or Small Groups

Table 1. Continued

Performance-Level Learning Objectives	Competency / Targeted Capability	Knowledge	Skills	Attitudes ("Abilities" in some KSAs)
	Create finalized visuals to communicate information	• Creating effective visuals	• Outputting visuals to communicate information with clarity	• Valuing clarity in visual communication
	Write with clarity	• Communicating effectively with text	• Writing with clarity	• Valuing clarity in textual communication
	Ensure the accuracy of the source citations through research	• Ability to cite sources to the required source citation method	• Citing sources in proper form	• Valuing giving credit where it is due
	Critique the work as thoroughly as possible	• Reviewing academic manuscript for quality	• Evaluating the academic paper for gaps in information, poor writing, and other potential standards lapses	• Caring about academic standards in academic papers
	Revise	• Ability to revise a work to quality	• Revising the academic manuscript to quality	• Caring about achieving academic standards
	Run the work through an automated grammar and spell check	• Knowing how to run a grammar and spell check effectively	• Running a grammar and spell check over the manuscript	• Valuing precision and accuracy in grammar and spelling
	Go through an editorial and / or peer review process	• Understanding expectations in editorial review processes • Understanding expectations in peer review processes	• Going through an editorial and / or peer review process constructively	• Respecting the establishing of editorial and peer review standards in academic publishing
	Revise the work to quality	• Knowing how to revise a draft work to quality through analysis and revision	• Revising the academic manuscript to quality	• Respecting the need for hard work to revise an academic manuscript to quality
	Do not engage in multiple submissions of the manuscript at the same time	• Knowledge of the social norms and policies against multiple submissions of manuscript to multiple potential publishers	• Submitting one manuscript at a time to a single publisher (until a decision is rendered)	• Respecting publisher processes by not offering a manuscript for consideration to multiple publishers at the same time
	Adhere to legal requirements for publishing (such as intellectual property rights, and others)	• Knowledge of legal requirements for publishing	• Applying legal requirements for publishing	• Respecting the legal standards for publishing
	Evaluate how the research findings may affect practices in the world (implications)	• Understanding how research findings may be suggestive of in-world practices	• Applying concepts and research and tools to in-world contexts	• Thinking beyond current practices to the potentials in other practices
(12) Identify venues to present the work	Identify reasonable venues with audiences potentially interested in the research	• Searching for and identifying professional conferences which may attract audiences focused on particular topics of interest	• Selecting relevant conferences with potential members interested in particular topics • Considering practicalities in the selection of conference	• Being open to a variety of conferences
	Prepare the presentations	• Knowing how to build professional presentations to standard	• Creating the presentation with proper substance, pacing, experiential elements, and other relevant aspects	• Valuing the sharing of information and shared experiences through presentation

continued on following page

Table 1. Continued

Performance-Level Learning Objectives	Competency / Targeted Capability	Knowledge	Skills	Attitudes ("Abilities" in some KSAs)
	Title the presentation	• How to title presentations in representative ways • How to title presentations in attention-getting ways	• Writing a title that is representative of the presentation and eye-catching and memorable simultaneously	• Valuing accuracy • Considering the strategy aspects of naming presentations
	Write a short description of the presentation per the requirements of the conference organizers	• Knowing how to write abstracts describing a presentation in an informative way • Knowing how to write abstracts describing a presentation in attention-getting ways	• Creating an abstract about the proposed presentation in alignment with the conference standards	• Valuing concision • Valuing informativeness in abstracts
	Create relevant queries to respective conference organizers	• Knowing how to interact with conference organizers to retrieve the necessary information and responses	• Interacting with organizers of conference to achieve professional aims	• Valuing the importance of intercommunications • Valuing the importance of accurate representations
	Follow through on the presentations (if accepted…or if invited)	• Understanding the presentation deliverables for professional conference	• Following through on the presentations to the standards of the conference organizers and the conference attendees	• Upholding the professional standards of participants in professional conferences
(13) Identify venues to publish the work	Identify potential publishers of interest	• Understanding one's own needs and preferences in a publisher • Understanding when there is a match between the self (or authoring team) and the publisher • Labeling the areas of focus for respective publishers	• Locating and identifying publishers of interest for particular projects	• Understanding the importance of alignments between researcher-authors and publishers (based on shared interests)
	Identify potential periodicals of interest	• Knowing how to search through academic periodicals	• Applying a rational selection method for academic periodicals	• Having an articulate-able set of standards for the selection of potential academic periodicals for publishing
	Review the respective publishing guidelines	• Understanding of publishing practices and guidelines	• Reading the respective publishing guidelines of publishers	• Valuing the expectations of target publishers • Valuing the common social norms and practices of publishers
	Create relevant queries to the respective publishers (but not simultaneously)	• Proper querying of respective publishers	• Creating proper queries of respective publishers	• Eliciting responses from respective target publishers
	Create manuscripts to quality	• Meeting manuscript standards	• Meeting manuscript standards	• Valuing the manuscript standards of the respective publishers
	Submit the drafted manuscripts within deadline	• Meeting deadlines	• Meeting deadlines	• Valuing the time deadline rules of the respective publishers
	Revise appropriately to double-blind peer critiques	• Being receptive to double-blind (single-blind, non-blind) peer critiques	• Responding appropriately to double-blind (single-blind, non-blind) peer critiques	• Valuing the feedback and critiques of double-blind (single-blind, non-blind) reviewers

continued on following page

Designing Integrated Learning Paths for Individual Lifelong Learners and/or Small Groups

Table 1. Continued

Performance-Level Learning Objectives	Competency / Targeted Capability	Knowledge	Skills	Attitudes ("Abilities" in some KSAs)
	Respond appropriately to editor critiques and suggestions	• Being receptive to editor critiques and suggestions	• Responding appropriately to editor critiques and suggestions	• Valuing the professional responses of editors, based on their professional expertise and experiences
	Follow all applicable laws and policies for publishing	• Awareness of applicable laws and policies for publishing	• Adhering to applicable laws and policies for publishing	• Valuing the shared rules surrounding publishing to protect people's reputations, effort, and other aspects
(14) Continue to hone research and related skills	Maintain self-confidence and self-efficacy	• Understanding personal value and capabilities	• Practicing awareness of personal value and capabilities • Behaving in alignment with a high sense of personal value and capabilities	• Understanding the importance of self-value and awareness of personal/professional capabilities
	Stay engaged in the work	• Understanding the importance of persistence in pursuing work	• Persisting in work • Engaging in the work with the application of various skills • Maintaining resilience in the face of difficulties in the work	• Valuing professional engagement
	Have a social support group	• Socializing with others to provide mutual support	• Socializing with others to provide mutual support	• Valuing others' ideas, thoughts, personalities, and other aspects
	Read new research regularly	• Engaging in the information space	• Consuming new research, information, and knowledge regularly	• Valuing new information and turning that into knowledge
	Publish regularly (through peer-reviewed publication channels)	• How to publish in professional peer-reviewed periodicals	• Sharing quality research through peer-reviewed publication channels	• Valuing the sharing of new research with peers through publishing
	Attend competitive professional conferences regularly (through vetted channels)	• How to secure spaces in professional conferences	• Sharing quality research through professional conferences	• Valuing the sharing of new research with peers through presenting
	Learn new technologies	• Exploration of new technologies	• Harnessing new technologies for research	• Valuing the potential affordances and enablements of new technologies in a research context
	Maintain healthy habits and lifestyles	• Knowing how to maintain healthy habits and lifestyles	• Maintaining health in order to be able to focus on work	• Valuing healthy lifestyles
	Stay inspired, and feed curiosity	• Knowing how to stay inspired about particular research topics and work	• Expressing inspiration and curiosity about particular fields	• Valuing ongoing curiosity about a particular field or domain, and related ones
	Practice resilience	• Knowing how to come back from hardship and challenges and discouragements	• Practicing resilience in the world	• Valuing persistence in the face of hardship and other challenges
(15) Expand the ranges of research and related skills	Learn continuously	• Applying methods for learning continuously • Creating a strong knowledge base on which to build learning	• Acquiring new knowledge continuously • Exploring new potential areas of interest	• Engaging the world with curiosity • Seeing the benefits of acquiring broad knowledge

continued on following page

Designing Integrated Learning Paths for Individual Lifelong Learners and/or Small Groups

Table 1. Continued

Performance-Level Learning Objectives	Competency / Targeted Capability	Knowledge	Skills	Attitudes ("Abilities" in some KSAs)
	Explore broadly, even outside areas of current expertise and familiar domains	• Being comfortable outside one's domain • Being comfortable taking risks	• Exploring broadly • Investigating the world outside of conventional tracks and paths	• Encouraging a self-sense of curiosity
	Take risks	• Awareness of risks	• Gauging risk • Harnessing risk for particular positive aims	• Understanding risk-taking as a necessary step to advancing professional and other aims • Being comfortable having an original voice and / or point-of-view
	Form and maintain professional relationships outside the bounds of current comfort	• Knowing how to form and maintain professional relationships	• Forming and maintaining professional relationships	• Valuing other people for their professional interests
	Form and maintain personal relationships outside the bounds of current comfort	• Knowing how to form and maintain personal relationships	• Forming and maintaining personal relationships	• Valuing other people for their personal dimensions
	Participate in professional gatherings outside areas of familiar expertise	• Background in a variety of domain areas • Exposure to various disciplinary and interdisciplinary areas	• Participating in professional gatherings beyond direct expertise	• Appreciating learning in others' areas of direct expertise
	Engage in interdisciplinary work	• Interest in other fields • Knowledge of other fields	• Ability to learn about other fields, including peripheral ones • Collaborating with others in other fields	• Respecting work achieved in other fields • Considering contributing work to other fields

Figure 3. 1 Identify space for new research (mind map)

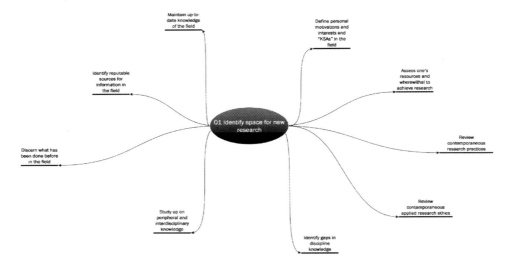

Figure 4. 2 Design Research (mind map)

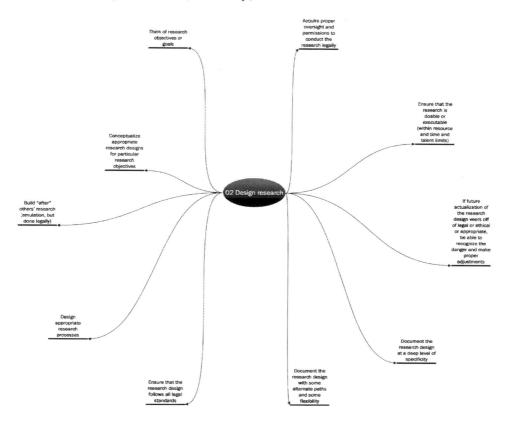

This backwards curriculum design (CD) is only partial and limited. The high-level objective of the learning is a major delimiter. Also, the mind maps should be defined out another orbit or two, with specific learning objects defined to inform the learning sequences. For example, what technology tools should be acquired? What simulations should the learner explore? What learning videos should be engaged? What articles should be read? What notes should be taken? What conferences should be attended? What publications should be contacted? What assignments should be included in the sequence? In terms of how this design in experienced, what order of the learning might be most effective for the particular individual?

The use of one rather-elaborate case to explore the backwards curriculum design of nonformal and informal learning for an individual or group serves as a kind of proof of concept. The approaches here are certainly non-definitive, and many other paths to creating such designs are available. Another part that was left off was the closing of the loop of the learning, with the target learner and target learner groups

Designing Integrated Learning Paths for Individual Lifelong Learners and/or Small Groups

Figure 5. 3 Create a research instrument (mind map)

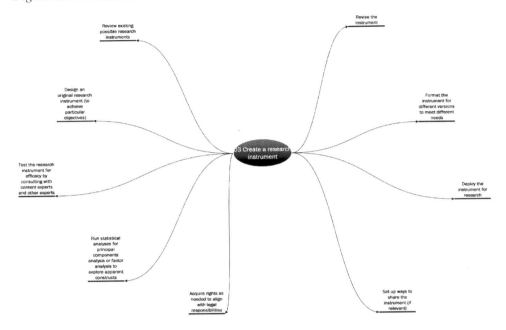

likely assessing the efficacy of the learning and their abilities during the sequences. Certainly, learners may strive to back-trace what they found to be most effective. And they can explore to see what parts of the proposed curricular designs may be most effective.

With the advent of massive open online courses (MOOCs) funded by leading universities and major thinkers in their respective fields, more complex skillsets may be attainable. MOOCs may provide more structured and designed curriculums. Beyond MOOCs, though, there are many other complex skillsets of interest, and backwards curriculum design may offer a way forward to harness more scattered learning for upskilling, for career ambitions, for new skillset acquisitions, and other learning endeavors. This approach of backwards design from targeted complex skill sets may apply to formal learning in some contexts but may have to build on some extant CD sequences, at least in part.

FUTURE RESEARCH DIRECTIONS

From this work, there are a number of potential future research directions. Some of these approaches may involve "design research" about design methods, efficacies/inefficacies, and other approaches.

Designing Integrated Learning Paths for Individual Lifelong Learners and/or Small Groups

Figure 6. 4 Follow research design and processes (mind map)

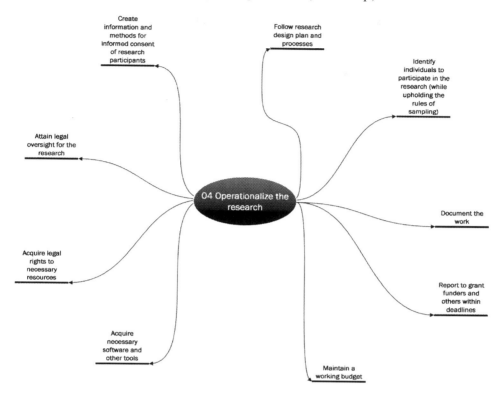

Figure 7. 5 Collect data (mind map)

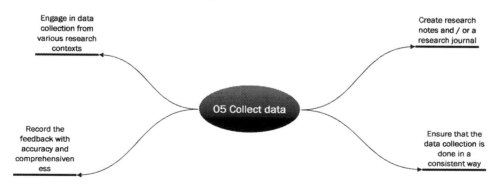

One core question is whether backwards curriculum design is the right approach for individual self-learning and group self-learning? What are other valid options? What are the strengths and weaknesses of these respective options? Are some learning trajectories more effective than others, and why or why not?

Designing Integrated Learning Paths for Individual Lifelong Learners and/or Small Groups

Figure 8. 6 Document and record research data (mind map)

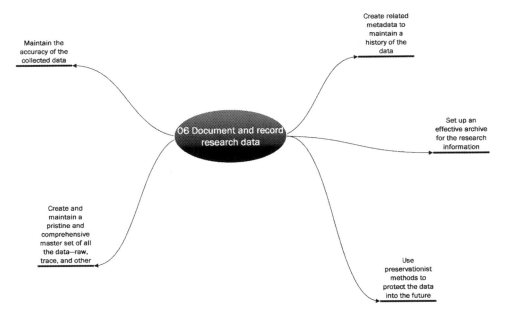

Figure 9. 7 Clean and pre-process the research data (mind map)

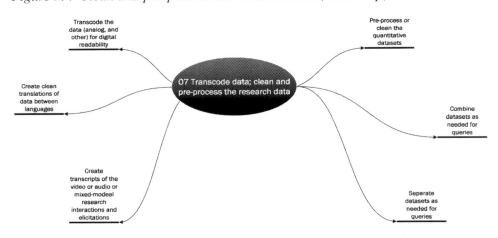

Does this approach work better on nonformal learning (structured but non-accredited) or on informal learning (learning as a byproduct of living)? Or does this backward CD work equally fine no matter the type of learning? What parts of traditional CD (on formal learning) seem to apply to the nonformal and informal approaches?

Designing Integrated Learning Paths for Individual Lifelong Learners and/or Small Groups

Figure 10. 8 Create a codebook (mind map)

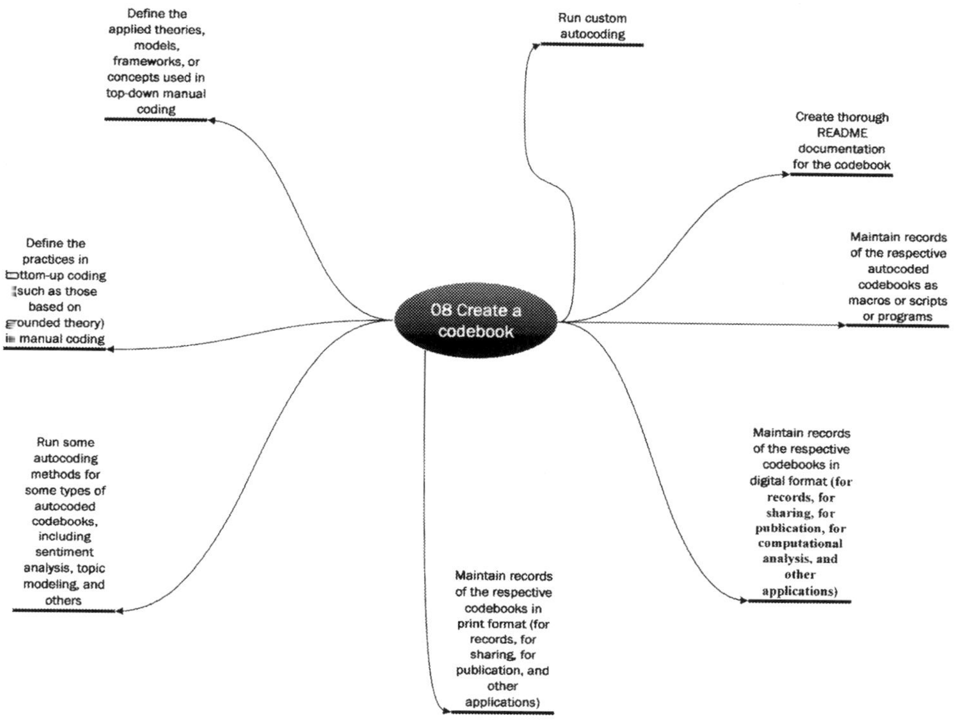

- Define the applied theories, models, frameworks, or concepts used in top-down manual coding
- Run custom autocoding
- Create thorough README documentation for the codebook
- Maintain records of the respective autocoded codebooks as macros or scripts or programs
- Define the practices in bottom-up coding (such as those based on grounded theory) in manual coding
- 08 Create a codebook
- Run some autocoding methods for some types of autocoded codebooks, including sentiment analysis, topic modeling, and others
- Maintain records of the respective codebooks in print format (for records, for sharing, for publication, and other applications)
- Maintain records of the respective codebooks in digital format (for records, for sharing, for publication, for computational analysis, and other applications)

Closer in, what are some of the methods to backwards design in this contemporaneous open-shared learning context? Is it possible to map all approaches? Based on the particular complexity of learning outcomes, what patterns of curricular design are there? Is it possible to generally describe these patterns?

In terms of simpler learning outcomes, from which backwards designs might originate, what is meant by "simpler"? Do these involve different types of curriculum development patterns?

How dependent is this approach on having access to available open-shared learning contents? Is there room for the self-development of learning contents, self-development of assignments, self-development of assessments? Is there traction for such approaches?

Are there differences between such CDs for individuals (micro level) and groups (meso level)? If so, what are these differences, and why? Are there particular approaches that work better for individuals vs. groups? And vice versa?

Closing the loop would also be important in these learning contexts by ensuring that there is some form of evidentiary feedback to learners, maybe even some objective and evidentiary feedback. After all, in terms of backward design, Wiggins (Feb.

95

Designing Integrated Learning Paths for Individual Lifelong Learners and/or Small Groups

Figure 11. 9 Analyze the collected data (mind map)

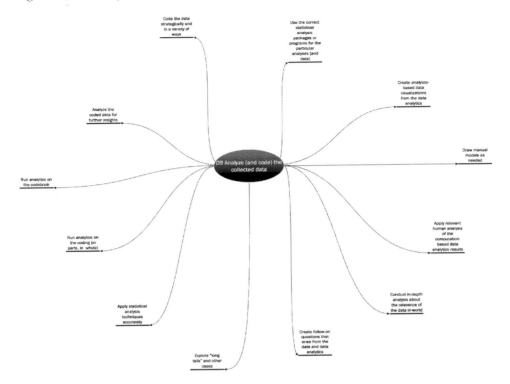

2012) has observed that the learning activities "have to yield successful performance" related to the goals, based on the defined "assessment evidence" (in Stage 2 of the three-step backward design approach) (Slide 60). (Certainly, this information would be useful at the top level of the goal-based objectives.) What are some practical ways to enable self-assessment and other-assessment of learning at the individual level? At group level? Are there ways to harness external assessments for reliable feedback to the respective individual and group learners? Or perhaps the feedback should merely be whatever the learner finds in engaging in the world, based on what they experience (although this would require emotional toughness.)

In such contexts, how do curricular designs change and evolve? What are some standards to apply before changes are made, such as the removal of particular learning sequences or the adding of others? How rigidly or flexibly should the designs be taken?

What about the design of social aspects to the self-learning approaches? The making of communities of practice for groups? How can such entities provide mutual support for enhanced learning? Would it benefit the learner to have a larger sense of a learning context?

Figure 12. 10 Create relevant data visualizations and diagrams (mind map)

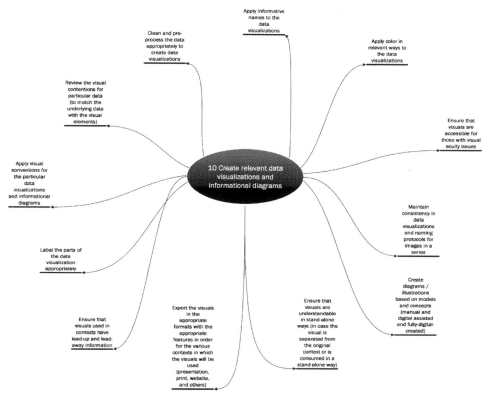

And then, given the importance of learner agency, how can that agency be supported, so that individuals and groups may show their initiative to benefit the learning and the KSA development. How can learners engage in collaborative curriculum design? If the CD is not a once-and-done but an evolving design, how can that evolution be scaffolded and supported?

What are ways to enable the learners to experience "significant learning experiences"? What are "significant learning experiences" in these contexts, and do they vary by learner…or by item in a learning sequence (or experience in a learning sequence)?

People have varying levels of self-awareness of their learning, their learning preferences, their prior knowledge, and their actual capabilities (which is probably higher than they assume). Are there instruments that would be useful for self-assessment of themselves, scaled to one or a small group?

It would seem that this work can go towards less structure and more informality, on the one hand…or it can go towards formality, structure, increased organization,

Designing Integrated Learning Paths for Individual Lifelong Learners and/or Small Groups

Figure 13. 11 Write up the research for presentation (mind map)

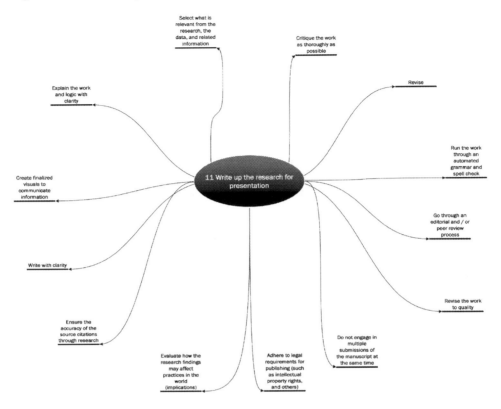

Figure 14. 12 Identify venues to present work (mind map)

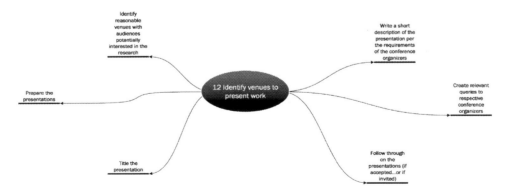

and other aspects, on the other hand. In the first approach, learners will have to take

Designing Integrated Learning Paths for Individual Lifelong Learners and/or Small Groups

Figure 15. 13 Identify venues to publish work (mind map)

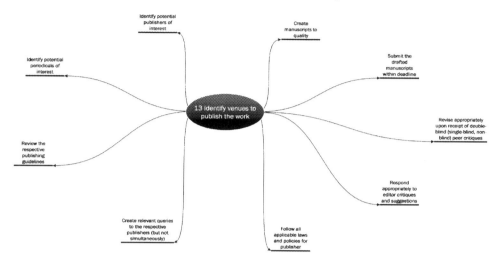

Figure 16. 14 Continue to hone research and related skills (mind map)

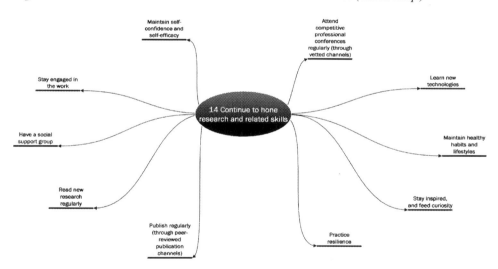

leading roles in their own learning; in the latter, there can be more supports for the learners in their learning.

Another research direction involves how an individual or learning group changes through this experience. What do they learn of themselves as learners? How do they maintain motivation? How can they advance their work and strengthen their learning into new topics into the future? Some of the skill sets assume years and years of

Designing Integrated Learning Paths for Individual Lifelong Learners and/or Small Groups

Figure 17. 15 Expand the ranges of research and related skills (mind map)

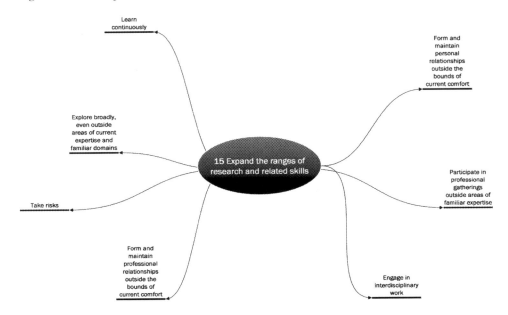

investment, and the longitudinal time angle may be of interest. An assumption here is that there may be time intensifications when a learner may focus larger amounts of time and effort to the work and times when there may be almost no activity towards the ends of building the target complex skillset. [Certainly, complex skill sets may be acquired in the short-term, the middle-term, and the long-term, but the ability to design these into the long-term and the far future extends the work.]

Such designs may be created by single curriculum designers or cross-functional teams, and perhaps studying the respective designs from such teams may be helpful.

The social dimensions of such learner groups may also be explored. How do they interact? How do they benefit and / or hinder each other in their learning? What unique contributions do the members bring to their groups?

No matter what the various research threads, this is an under-explored area (and there may be an actual gap with no research in this area). It does seem that some practice such skill acquisition, but they have not written about these experiences in the academic literature space.

CONCLUSION

When people go to acquire skills, many can find their way to relevant learning resources and discipline themselves sufficiently to develop high levels of expertise—if they

Designing Integrated Learning Paths for Individual Lifelong Learners and/or Small Groups

Figure 18. Complex Whole-Set Learning in Varying Potential Sequences

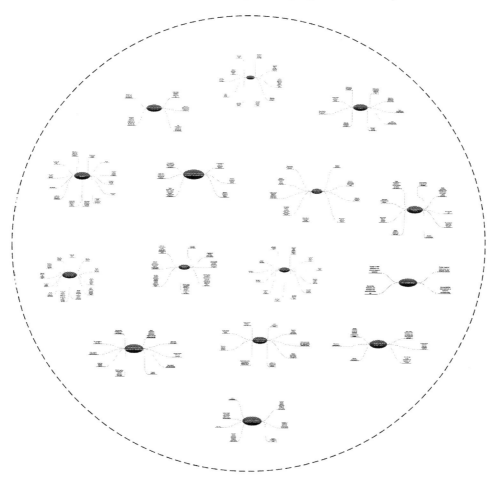

Complex Whole-Set Learning in Varying Potential Sequences

are disciplined and resilient. Otherwise, learner commitments can be quite fragile, especially as the learning becomes more complex and challenging, and "costs" rise, and support (social, financial, and other) dwindles. The work of capturing the learning also applies to transfer, or applying the learning to new contexts—ranging from near-transfer to far-transfer, depending on the closeness (similarity) of the learning contexts. In each new application context, additional effort will be required to harness the learned skills and to apply them elsewhere.

REFERENCES

Acedo, C., & Hughes, C. (2014). Principles for learning and competences in the 21st-century curriculum. *Prospects, 44*(4), 503–525. doi:10.100711125-014-9330-1

Choppin, J. (2011). Learned adaptations: Teachers' understanding and use of curriculum resources. *Journal of Mathematics Teacher Education, 14*(5), 331–353. doi:10.100710857-011-9170-3

Choppin, J., McDuffie, A. R., Drake, C., & Davis, J. (2018). Curriculum ergonomics: Conceptualizing the interactions between curriculum design and use. *International Journal of Educational Research, 92*, 75–85. doi:10.1016/j.ijer.2018.09.015

Conole, G., Dyke, M., Oliver, M., & Seale, J. (2004). Mapping pedagogy and tools for effective learning design. *Computers & Education, 43*(1-2), 17–33. doi:10.1016/j.compedu.2003.12.018

Edström, K., Gunnarsson, S., & Gustafsson, G. (2007). Integrated curriculum design. In *Rethinking Engineering Education* (pp. 77–101). Boston, MA: Springer. doi:10.1007/978-0-387-38290-6_4

Grant, J. (2010). Principles of curriculum design. *Understanding medical education: Evidence, theory and practice*, 1-15.

Hendrickson, S. (2006, January). Backward approach to inquiry. *Science Scope, 29*(4), 30–33.

Kelting-Gibson, L. M. (2005). Comparison of curriculum development practices. *Educational Research Quarterly, 29*(1), 26–36.

Knowledge, skills, and abilities. (2018, Nov. 17). In *Wikipedia*. Retrieved May 5, 2019, from https://en.wikipedia.org/wiki/Knowledge,_Skills,_and_Abilities

Lightfoot, J. M. (1999, September/October). Fads versus fundamentals: The dilemma for information systems curriculum design. *Journal of Education for Business, 75*(1), 43–50. doi:10.1080/08832329909598989

McKenney, S., Nieveen, N., & van den Akker, J. (2002). Computer support for curriculum developers: CASCADE. *Educational Technology Research and Development (ETR&D), 50*(4), 25 – 35.

McTighe, J., & Thomas, R. S. (2003, February). Backward design for forward action. *Educational Leadership, 60*(5), 52–55.

Nation, I. S. P., & Mcalister, J. (2010). Approaches to curriculum design. In *Language Curriculum Design* (pp. 136–148). New York: Routledge, Taylor & Francis Group.

Prideaux, D. (2003). ABC of learning and teaching in medicine: Curriculum design. *BMJ (Clinical Research Ed.)*, *326*(7383), 268–270. doi:10.1136/bmj.326.7383.268 PMID:12560283

Tangworakitthaworn, P., Gilbert, L., & Wills, G. B. (2013). A conceptual model of intended learning outcomes supporting curriculum development. In W. Ng., V.C. Storey, & J. Trujillo (Eds.), *International Conference on Conceptual Modeling*. Springer. 10.1007/978-3-642-41924-9_15

Wiggins, G. (2012, Feb.). *Understanding by Design slideshow*. UNC Greenboro Library. Retrieved Mar. 28, 2019, from http://library.uncg.edu/info/distance_education/wiggins.pdf

Wiggins, G., & McTighe, J. (1998). What is backward design? Understanding by Design, 1 – 11.

Xie, Y., Bai, J., Li, G., & Yin, R. (2014, Aug.). Research and application on Web 2.0-based sharing models of curriculum resources. In *International Conference on Hybrid Learning and Continuing Education* (pp. 129-139). Springer.

Zitter, I., Howeve, A., & de Bruijn, E. (2016). A design perspective on the school-work boundary: A hybrid curriculum model. *Vocations and Learning*, *9*(1), 111–131. doi:10.100712186-016-9150-y

ADDITIONAL READING

Joseph, P. B., Bravmann, S. L., Windschitl, M. A., Mikel, E. R., & Green, N. S. (2000). *Cultures of Curriculum*. Mahwah, NJ: Lawrence Erlbaum Associates, Publishers.

KEY TERMS AND DEFINITIONS

Backwards Curriculum Design: Structuring a curricular sequence with contents based on the desired observable learning outcomes.

Curriculum Design: The formal and systematic setup of learning sequences in blocks and paths for learning in accredited schools (pre-K12) and higher education (from freshman learning to doctoral and post-doctoral studies).

Formal Learning (or Structured Learning): Accredited learning involving defined learning objectives, learning outcomes, standardized measures of learning, syllabi, certification standards, and other elements.

Informal Learning: Pervasive incidental learning from everyday life.

Nonformal Learning: The learning that occurs in structured learning contexts (which do not involve accreditation, certification, and credits), such as organized but informal hobbyist cooking courses.

Self-Directed Learning: Independent learning, self-education, autodidacticism, self-learning.

Chapter 6
Recognizing Curricular Infusions in Extant Online Learning Contents by Types and at Varying Scales

Shalin Hai-Jew
https://orcid.org/0000-0002-8863-0175
Kansas State University, USA

ABSTRACT

Online learning exists in a dynamic environment, with changing research, applicable laws and policies, pedagogical approaches, and technologies. The changing external environment necessarily informs the curriculum given the need for learning relevance. Curricular infusions (CIs) occur as a practical method of integrating new elements into extant learning: values, ethics, thinking, knowledge, worldviews, practices, tools and technologies, and other elements. These infusions may occur at the most granular level of the learning object all the way to learning disciplines and domains. The method of curricular infusion enables adaptivity to occur with online learning without having to rebuild learning from scratch, so infusions could be additive to particular learning sequences or integrated with the learning objects, and other aspects of designed online learning. This work explores some of the prior research into curricular infusions and introduces some basic ways to reverse engineer curricular infusions in extant online learning.

DOI: 10.4018/978-1-5225-9833-6.ch006

INTRODUCTION

The moment an online learning object or module or course or program or discipline is created, it starts to date out, sometimes gradually, sometimes precipitously. Parts of the learning contents become less relevant to contemporaneous learners. The pedagogical approaches leave a feeling that the learning is designed for other learners, maybe those of a different generation or background or culture. New ethical guidelines in the domain go unaddressed. The technologies start to show their age, or they fail to function altogether. "Curricular infusion" (CI), integrating new learning contents into existing learning contents, programs, and practices, may be a fairly low-cost way to revise and update such contents, without requiring fundamental redesigns. These are popular approaches because of the lighter footprint and lesser costs for such piecemeal updating. CI enables working through campus politics and "presents a viable, cost effective method because it obviates obstacles and limitations inherent in the creation, approval, and implementation of new courses of purely international focus" (Guerin, 2009, p. 613).

The idea of curricular infusions had its apparent heyday back in the 1960s (Figure 1), but it's a concept and a practice whose time has arrived again. The rising line graph presages a powerful future for this practice in addition to the efficiencies of this approach.

Curricular infusions are seen as practical in enabling "a viable, cost effective method because it obviates obstacles and limitations inherent in the creation, approval, and implementation of new courses" focused on the topic (Guerin, 2009, p. 613). This cost savings also extends to institutional levels, such as the infusing of international perspectives across a range of core curriculums, disciplines, and

Figure 1. "Curricular Infusion" in Google Books Ngram Viewer

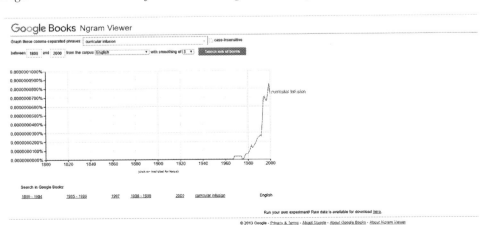

institutions, enabling broad reach but without "drastic change" in an environment of "dwindling electives and greater focus on the core courses" in community college learning (Raby, Summer 2007, p. 60). An earlier work made this point as well: "Infusion has the advantage of reaching all students, of conserving curriculum space, and of offering more opportunity for integration of the domestic with the international, although it is not without its challenges as a model of curriculum enrichment." (Healy, Fall 1988, p. 227)

A simple continuum related to updating online learning designs and contents may have piecemeal updates at one end to a total from-scratch redesign and re-development on the other (Figure 2). In between may be the inclusion of new learning modules, sequences, assignments, experiences, and other aspects. In most cases, the updates will likely be either piecemeal ones or redesigns of parts of an online learning sequence; in the more rare cases where the learning is designed from scratch, these entail higher costs, resources, time investments, and human resources investments.

In institutions, curricular infusions are often highly distributed, with various staff with responsibilities for this effort beyond faculty (Skidmore, Marston, & Olson, Aug. 2005, p.190). Instead of creating a discrete and alternative "add-on," infused learning contents may supplement existing interrelated curricular contents in a flexible way (Helge, Nov. 1981, p. 11). Further, this work will explore ways to analyze and extract infused curricular elements through either (1) a direct object / sequence / course / curricular analysis, or (2) a before-after comparison of those elements. The analysis of infused contents may inform on how successfully infused curriculums are, or may inform retrofitting and redesign efforts. (For example: What are the infused values in this learning module, and how may these be more effectively updated? Or what research instruction is integrated in this learning sequences, and what aspects of research should be changed, and what new aspects should be included?) In the same way that researchers suggest the presence of "hidden curriculums" based on informing cultures (Joseph, Bravmann, Windschitl, Mikel, & Green, 2000), infused elements may be subtle in their presence, requiring sophisticated insider knowledge as

Figure 2. A continuum of approaches for updating online learning designs and contents

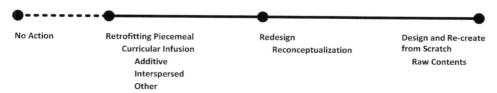

A Continuum of Approaches for Updating Online Learning Designs and Contents

well as close human reading. Curricular infusions do not necessarily retract into the background but may have contents and practices foregrounded as "first imperative" concerns (Puk & Behm, Spring 2003, p. 217), based on exigencies (like the health of the planet or ecosphere).

Some infused ideas and practices may occur at a subconscious level of awareness by the instructional designer/developer or instructional design/development team. A design hand can be subtle and indirect. Learning design, for example, may involve creating conditions in which particular types of social interactions may happen, with learners introducing issues or taking the lead or asking particular questions. For example, it is possible to reverse engineer and extract some of the authorizing documents, laws, content sources, and other influential informing contents behind online learning resources, with some level of confidence.

In an earlier work, the author suggested that online course updates benefitted from focusing on four main areas (in descending order, but with all parts generally relevant): "(1) Legal Guidelines and Relevant Policies, (2) Progress / Change in the Domain Field (and in related cross-disciplinary or multi-disciplinary fields), (3) The Course Curricular Strategies / Teaching and Learning Methodologies, and (4) Relevant Updated Technologies" (Hai-Jew, Dec. 15, 2010). The predicates for updating online learning contents are likely broader than even those mentioned in this earlier work although the four elements mentioned likely still apply. In many cases, though, curriculums are lagging indicators of what is actually occurring in a field, except possibly in graduate-level research work. To speed updates to learning materials, curricular infusions may be one applicable tool.

REVIEW OF THE LITERATURE

Curricular infusion (CI) is defined formally as the integration of new learning contents to an existing curriculum. It has been referred to as "nesting," in which "teachers target content from other courses within their own courses (Brauer & Ferguson, 2015, p. 315). The work of infusing new learning requires prioritization and sequencing to "position" the learning contents and the experienced learning sequence (maybe with knowledge first before application) or an "immersion experience" first before direct teaching (Torres, Ottens, & Johnson, Sept. 1997, p. 10). Another definition of an infusion method is as "direct, explicit, interactive, and parallel teaching" of the target infused learning and the core contents (de Acedo Lizarrag, de Acedo Baquedano, Mangado, & Cardelle-Elawar, 2009, p. 31). As part of "integrated instruction," infusion "involves taking the existing curriculum and content and infusing other subject area content or skills into it (Kataoka & Patton, 1996, as cited in Reisberg, May 1998, p. 273). If "Fusion design of curriculum integration" is about the merging of "related subjects into a new subject" built around a unified idea, then "infusion" involves having "aspects of one subject area… inserted or infused into a second to help the learner gain deeper understanding of the second" with "one subject area…the helper of another" (Parker 2005, as cited in Hinde, May/June 2005, pp. 106 - 107). Curricular infusion is a tool to address learning specializations with specific content areas and to extend learning to specific non-traditional target groups of learners (Kopels & Gustavsson, Winter 1996, p. 124). There is the sense that an infusion approach has elements "which are general and some that are content specific" (Zohar & Schwartzer, 2005, as cited in Kadir, 2017, p. 84). These dynamics may be seen in some of the research. Professional collaboration and intercommunications skills are infused in a hard science (Cheah, 2009), and such "soft skills" may apply to a range of professions broadly. There is the infusion of women's voices in "middle and senior high school history curriculum" (Cruz & Groendal-Cobb, Nov./Dec. 1998, p. 271), and women's perspectives are relevant generally and specifically.

In some conceptualizations, infusion is a more advanced step in learning depth:

…DePauw and Karp (1994) proposed a model similar to Kowalski's disability-infusion model, structured in three levels: The first level, additive, includes the addition of general disability-related information into the content of the general curriculum courses and aims at initial familiarization of the students with disability-related topics. The second level, inclusion, includes the integration of more advanced disability-related information into the content of the general curriculum courses and aims at stimulating students to think, hypothesize and search into questions that relate disability with sports and exercise. The third level, infusion, includes the merging of disability-related information within the general curriculum content and requires the commitment and cooperation of all the academic stuff (sic) and the students…to help professors and students to develop critical thinking and be able to evaluate with equal competence topics related to sports and exercise of all individuals, regardless of their disabilities." (Kalyvas, Koutsouki, & Skordilis, July 2011, pp. 24 - 25)

In the literature, curricular infusions are sometimes closely related to particular learning contents and topics; however, the generic and basic definition does not necessarily involve any particular content per se.

Curricular Infusions in Learning Contexts

The research literature has a number of different topics to which CI has been applied. Technological issues appear with regularity in the research, in part because technologies are constantly updating and changing. In an information technology curricula, recurring concepts were infused dealing with "problem solving, interplay between theory and practice, project experience in software system development, project experience in software system integration, system management, end user support, (and) fundamental principles of science and mathematics" (Alford, Carter, Ragsdale, Ressler, & Reynolds, 2004, p. 263). Infusion has been applied to computer technology integration in teacher education (Toledo, 2005). Cybersecurity lessons have been infused into computer science for transfer to university (Tang, Tucker, Servin, & Geissler, 2018) and to a computer science curriculum (Cao & Ajwa, 2016). Various technologies have been infused in work places (Hinchey, Pressburger, Markosian, & Feather, 2006). Educational robotics have been introduced into a course on road safety (Ioannou, Socratous, & Nikolædou, 2018). Critical thinking has been integrated in "computer-mediated history learning" (Yang, 2007). E-commerce has been infused in information systems curriculum (Moshkovich, Mechitov, & Olson, Fall 2005). Massive multiplayer online games (MMOGs) have been introduced into classrooms for the learning motivation and realism value (Bawa, Watson, & Watson, 2018). Another effort involved infusing technologies for teachers (Rowley, Dysard, & Arnold, 2005). There are mixed topics as well. There has been the simultaneous infusion of "emerging technologies" and complementary teaching methods in mechanical engineering at a university (Delale, Liaw, JiJi, Voiculescu, Summer 2011). Technology and "21st century skills" have been infused into school librarians' instruction (Hanson-Baldauf & Hassell, 2009, p. 10). In the aftermath of Hurricane Andrew in 1992, a government grant (Project Infusion) focused on training personnel in instructional technology along with rebuilding schools destroyed by the extreme weather (Leblanc, 1996, p. 25). Another work described the infusion of technology in schools, even with predictable resistances (Demetriadis, et al., 2003).

    Curricular infusions have been applied in various forms of health applications. One example involves "disability sport" in a sport management curriculum (Shapiro, Pitts, Hums, & Calloway, 2012). Nursing practicums have been enriched with gerontological nursing content (Kohlenberg, Kennedy-Malone, Crane, & Letvak, 2007), to enhance health care for the elderly. Likewise, there have been infused geriatrics studies in baccalaureate nursing curricula (Latimer & Thornlow, 2006). Others have reported the infusion of "gerontology content in nongeriatric undergraduate nursing courses" (Hancock, Helfers, Cowen, Letvak, Barba, Herrick, Wallace, Rossen, & Bannon, 2006, p. 103). There are gerontology competencies in graduate nursing programs (Kennedy-Malone, Penrod, Kohlenberg, Letvak, Crane, Tesh, Kolanowski, Hupcey, & Milone-Nuzzo, Mar. – Apr. 2006). Some of the CI strategies include requiring "readings that pertain to geriatric nursing" and creating assessments with a percentage of questions related to gerontological nursing and requiring an amount of clinical time "devoted to caring for older adults in all clinical settings" (Kennedy-Malone, Penrod, Kohlenberg, Letvak, Crane, Tesh, Kolanowski, Hupcey, & Milone-Nuzzo, Mar. – Apr. 2006, p. 124). Systems thinking, interprofessional education and practice, and other methods, have been harnessed to support healthcare graduates in understanding healthcare holistically (Clark & Hoffman, 2018). Aging and multigenerational practice (with a focus on gerontology) have been included in social work education (Fredriksen-Goldsen, Hooeyman, & Bonifas, Winer 2006), and gerontology concerns have also been infused into social work (Cummings, Cassie, Galambos, & Wilson, 2006; Holody & Kolb, 2011). Learning content about aging has been interspersed in undergraduate social work education (Lee & Waites, Winter 2006). There has been infused learning contents to raise awareness "older people with chronic mental illness" in social work (Cummings & Kropf, Spring 2000) and of "older people with developmental disabilities" in social work curriculum (Kropf, Spring/Summer 1996). Counselor education has been infused with multiculturalism learning (Ametrano, Callaway, & Stickel, 2002). One project aimed to eliminate "behavioral health disparities for racial and ethnic minority populations" (Salas & Altamirano, June 2012), which suggests long-term and ongoing efforts. Diversity curriculum has been disseminated across a campus (Ukpokodu, Winter 2010).

Some of the infused contents relate to the creation of more civil societies, with improved understandings of peace-building (Bickmore, Fall 2005) and human rights (du Preez, Simmonds, & Roux, 2012). Another involved the teaching of skills for violence prevention in social and behavioral spaces (Williams & Reisberg, March 2003). Cultural diversity infusion enables learners to develop their empathy and understanding of others (Carrell, 1997). Multicultural learning enables people to adapt to a complex and pluralistic world and introduces them to "under-represented ideas and points of view" (Obiakor, Nov. 1994, Abstract, n.p.). There are infusions of "LGBT perspectives and representations" ("lesbian, gay, bisexual, and transgender") in a 9th grade history class to enable the creation of safe spaces for learners (Helmsing, 2016, p. 175). CI was used to help mainstream learners with disabilities in regular classrooms, and this effort was advanced through an adaptive curriculum for preservice student teachers (Aksamit & Alcorn, 1988). CI efforts supported European Union citizenship education, with themes shared "across" or "through" curriculums for learners from two different EU countries (Carvalho, Salema, Stanciugelu, Martins, Iorga, & Puscas, 2014, p. 154). The hard work of introducing "cultural others" in infused curriculums (Shujaa, Summer 1995) has been ongoing for decades. Ethics have been infused in public administration curriculum (Hejka-Ekins, 1998). Subculture materials are infused for "heritage speakers" of Spanish in higher education (Gonzalez-Pino, 2000).

There are ecological efforts. Teachers infuse aquaculture to agriscience learners (Conroy, 1999). Ecological literacy is taught broadly (Puk & Behm, Spring 2003).

Sustainability and environmental concerns are taught in higher education (Jankowska, Smith, & Buehler, 2014). Applied and practical math has been infused in agricultural education and career and technical education in rural schools (Anderson, Fall 2008). One ambition is to achieve internalization of values and practices to ensure an environmentally friendly society (Hassan & Ismail, 2011). One infusion served to inculcate "environmental knowledge, awareness, positive attitudes and behavior in long term" (Zohir, 2009, as cited in Hassan & Ismail, 2011, p. 3404).

In curricular infusions, the learners are not only the students, but the teachers, too. After all, the learning contents may be cutting edge (and unrefined and undeveloped even) in contemporaneous ways. For example, global awareness was infused for agriculture faculty (King, 1991) and critical thinking for teachers (Swartz, May 1986), to enable their ultimately sharing with their students. Global citizenship education was infused in teacher trainings (Yemini, Tibbitts, & Goren, 2019). To activate children's thinking skills, thinking methods were taught to "both children and teachers" (Dewey & Bento, 2009, p. 344). CIs enable teachers to design learning to be receivable by people with a range of differing abilities (Kowalski, April 1995).

Infused topics also go beyond courses, as a basic unit for curricular infusion. There has been work to formalize ethics teaching throughout the legal profession, through designed infusion for pervasive ethics teaching (Menkel-Meadow &b Sander, Summer-Autumn, 1995, p. 129). Legal issues have been applied to the field of social work (Kopels & Gustavsson, Winter 1996), with various applied and practical considerations. In another, multicultural awareness was infused into existing coursework, independent courses, and university-wide activities (Torres, Ottens, & Johnson, Sept. 1997, pp. 11-12). The work of internationalizing a curriculum is infused beyond stand-alone courses to enable reaching out to a majority of students instead of those who might take an elective (Guerin, 2009, p. 613). Information literacy has been distributed across various curriculums (Harris, Mar. 2013). Social justice pedagogies have been infused, including "social justice content, context, and outcomes," and without sufficient success (Garii & Appova, 2013, p. 206). Cultural competency was infused in courses and also across courses (Osteen, Vanidestine, & Sharpe, 2013).

Many CI endeavors involve extending learner capabilities. "Content literacy" is introduced into a number of subjects, with their own respective languages and applications of reading and writing (O'Brien, Stewart, & Moje, Jul.-Aug.-Sep., 1995) and the need for transferability to a variety of applied contexts. Teachers work to strengthen learner self-efficacy and agency through the development of metacognition, with the instructor infusing "ideas about how one learns (multiple intelligences) and aids to learning (technology" (Kysilka, Summer 1998, p. 200). Reading is infused to increase science literacy in middle school students (Fang & Wei, 2010); evaluative research found that even small amounts of reading infusion with high "positive impact on middle school students' science literacy" (Fang & Wei, 2010, p. 262). CI was found to be efficacious in changing classroom climate to be a safe learning environment (Jones & Sanford, Fall 2003, p. 126). In one case, research and creative learning was infused for undergraduate scholarship advances across the curriculum at an institution of higher education (Davis & Jacobsen, 2014). In an earlier work, creativity was infused into student classrooms in the Far East as part of educational reform (Cheng, 2011), involving some cultural changes in collectivist- and consensus-based societies. CI training has involved methods to incorporate critical thinking in high school biology (Zohar & Tamir, Mar. 1993). Another study involved teaching "thinking skills (comparison, classification, analysis, synthesis, seriation, interpreting causes, predicting effects, and analogical reasoning), creativity, and self-regulation of learning simultaneously along with the syllabus content of Sciences, Language, Mathematics, and Social Sciences" (de Acedo Lizarrag, de Acedo Baquedano, Mangado, & Cardelle-Elawar, 2009, p. 34). In this case, teachers explained the skill and then stimulated student production of new ideas (de Acedo Lizarrag, de Acedo Baquedano, Mangado, & Cardelle-Elawar, 2009, p. 34). Another CI involved math infusion in middle school technology education classes (Burghardt, Hecht, Russo, Lauckhardt, & Hacker, Fall 2010).

When applied to research education, CIs have involved the integration of social constructivist theories and practices into multicultural science education research (Atwater, 1996). In this and other cases, the research outcomes may not be fully clear even at the moment of infusion.

The "whole learner" approach in teaching and learning extends to health issues, with health issues into academic courses "through readings, guest speakers and discussions, and class assignments" (Riley & McWilliams, Summer 2007, p. 14). CI has been harnessed to address the risks of binge drinking (Flynn & Carter, 2015, p. 324). In this study, two approaches were applied: "information only" and "service learning":

SL (service learning) is a unique form of curriculum infusion that refers to a pedagogical method in which students apply course concepts to real life situations (Furco, 2003). SL differs from curriculum infusion approaches that rely on one-time information-based lecture/discussion sessions by immersing students in the subject matter over a period of time (Eyler & Giles, 1999, as cited in Flynn & Carter, 2015, pp. 325 - 326).

The service learning approach enables learners to apply their theoretical knowledge to the real world and to bring back outside knowledge to the classroom to enable "reciprocal learning" and potential deep learning (Flynn & Carter, 2015, p. 326). In other CI work, there are explicit efforts to extend the transferability of the learning to different locales (Whitcomb, Sept. 2009). Some infused curriculums train nurses to be more resilient through their own self-care (for "psychological, physical, and emotional well-being"), so they can provide quality healthcare to their patients (Riley & Yearwood, 2012, pp. 364 - 365).

Some CIs bridge between various entities. Infused service learning serves as a bridge between higher education and society (Hlengwa, 2010). Industry segments in an academic course bridge between industry and higher education (Pitts & Shapiro, 2017, p. 44). Career trainings overlap with school studies (Millar, 1995). Global learning enriches learner perspectives across a range of fields (Hendrix, 1998). Some types of infusions—like popular culture in educational discourses—have mixed results (Duff, 2004), but they enable the bridging of peoples by interests and cultural influences.

Infused internationalization enhances global awareness in terms of trade to enable smoother commercial engagements with a particular country (Jin, Swinney, Cao, Muske, Nam, & Kang, May 2011). The rationale for internationalization has been around for decades:

In an age of ever-deepening global interdependence, it is not difficult to demonstrate that knowledge about the cultures, economies, governments and values of the ninety-five percent of the world's population that live beyond US borders can enrich understanding in almost any field of study. From a career standpoint, professionals in any field will be more successful to the extent that they can view problems from multiple cultural perspectives, can understand the local consequences of global interdependence and can draw upon comparative knowledge about how other societies address similar issues (Skidmore, Marston, & Olson, Aug. 2005, p.190)

The infusion has to successfully show learners the relevance of the related KSAs to motivate their engagement, so the designed approaches cannot be one-size-fits-all (Skidmore, Marston, & Olson, Aug. 2005, p.190). To be effective, this authoring team suggests that the "infusion model vests responsibility for internationalization neither with a particular major nor with a general education program, but with the institution as a whole." (Skidmore, Marston, & Olson, Aug. 2005, p.190) Global education is advanced using multiple methods (Hendrix, 1998, p. 306), given that the pedagogical designs are not mutually exclusive. The values of social justice and research curriculums are melded, with complex implications (Longres & Scanlon, Fall 2001).

Curricular infusions involve hard design, development, and deployment work. These difficulties have been described in some of the case-based research. One example involves the complex nuances and implications of the infusing of culture in curriculums (Nobles, 1990). For many, the work is continuing and not a one-off.

Researchers have observed that there are barriers to the adoption of curricular infusion, by practitioners and learners. One has observed resistances in secondary schools:

The current model for infusing content literacy into the secondary schools oversimplifies the complexities of secondary-school curriculum, pedagogy, and culture. Infusion is based on the assumption that content literacy practices, values, and philosophy, packaged in textbooks, courses, and inservice activities, can be integrated into schools using a logical, technical rationality within which schools are viewed as neutral settings...What the model fails to consider is that the secondary school is a socially and culturally constructed institution and that teachers and students are social and cultural beings who, thorough their interactions, continually create new contexts. (O'Brien, Stewart, & Moje, Jul.-Aug.-Sep.,

This research team proposes an alternative to infusion which sensitizes "university, inservice, and preservice teachers to the complexities of school curriculum, pedagogy, and culture" may be more efficacious to infuse content literacy (O'Brien, Stewart, & Moje, Jul.-Aug.-Sep., 1995, p. 454). CIs may be applied in politically fraught environments (LeBlanc & Dyer, Dec. 2004).

Evaluations of Curricular Infusions

In evaluating the relative success of curricular infusions, those that do evaluate seem to do so along two tracks: the learner experience from their point of view, and the objectively measurable learning outcomes. For the first, there have been elicitations of learner perspectives (Anderson, MacPhee, & Govan, Fall 2000; Beyerbach, Walsh, & Vannatta, 2001). In the latter condition, there are measures of the efficacy of infusion (and immersion) teaching methods as compared to general teaching of critical thinking (Angeli & Valanides, 2009). The infusion approach was found to result in positive learning of critical thinking in mathematics (Aizikovitsh & Amit, 2010). A research team applied post-test only experimental design to education about college students' alcohol consumption. Their findings: "curriculum infusion" may be "effective in reducing negative drinking consequences in college students despite not affecting drinking behaviors" (White, Park, & Cordero, 2010, p. 515). In other cases, the changes to learners seem somewhat limited, with infusion preparation programs resulting in more "positive beliefs and intentions than skills" (Cameron & Cook, 2007, p. 353). Another type of assessment is an ongoing one, such as a regular logging of activities (Jones & Sanford, Fall 2003, pp. 119 - 120). One study explored the effectiveness of infusing collaborative inquiry approaches in labs to enhance student learning (Luckie, Maleszewski, Loznak, & Krha, 2004).

One study suggests that smaller course sizes may result in more effective curricular infusions (Cordero, Israel, White, & Park, 2010, p. 79). Educational infusions are more effective when applied "in a consistent, routine manner" (Bergen-Cico, Razza, & Timmins, 2015, p. 3457).

RECOGNIZING CURRICULAR INFUSIONS FOR CURRICULAR INFUSION DESIGN ANALYSIS (1) AND LEARNING CONTENT REDESIGN AND RETROFITTING (2)

Curricular infusions may be created in any number of ways. A formal and fully explicated design approach may include the following base elements for their design, development, deployment, evaluation, and revision (Table 1).

A general sequence to design curricular infusions may be seen in Figure 03, starting with the left sequence focused on the design/development/deploying of curricular infusions (1). To the right (2) is the sequence of reverse-engineering curriculum infusions based on an extant curriculum or other learning contents (from granular to large-scale sized learning contents).

1. Designing / Developing / Deploying Curricular Infusion

One approach to curricular infusion is to identify the elements to be infused based on authorizing documents and concepts. Those learning objectives and learning outcomes should be defined, and a plan may be made about where it should be infused and how. Should the new learning be integrated into existing contents? Should the new learning be componentized as learning objects or modules or assignments or activities, or some mix of the prior? Should there be an interactive social element in the learning? Should the learning be required or optional? Will the learning be explicit (learning by being told and performing and practicing) or implicit (learning by osmosis)?

2. Extraction of Curricular Infused Elements and Messaging

In one conceptualization, the CI is built, and then it is assessed to make sure that the intended learning actually occurs (thus, the circular arrow back to redesign). In terms of reverse engineering CI, it can be applied in a stand-alone way to a curriculum to see what threaded or interwoven themes and pattern are present. In another type, one can compare a pre- and a post- curricular infusion curriculum to identify the differences. As to the efficacy of the CI for learning, multiple methods have been identified—based on learner experiences (learner surveys, learner interviews) and

Table 1. General elements to designing, developing, deploying, evaluating, and revising curricular infusions (CIs) in various contexts

General Elements in Designing, Developing, Deploying, Evaluating, and Revising Curricular Infusions (CIs)	Specific Contextual Details
CI Design	
Rationale(s)	
Objective(s)	
Stakeholder(s)	
Pedagogical Method(s)	
Programmatic Method(s)	
Learning Contents	
• Learning Assignments	
• Learning Activities	
• Team Learning / Social Learning	
• Learning Assessments	
• Modules	
• Examples	
• Learning Sequences	
• Cognitive Scaffolding Supports	
Respective Timelines of Efforts (Pacing)	
Assessment(s)	
CI Development	
Pedagogical Resources (raw files, digital contents, interactive learning objects, multimedia contents, digitally-enabled experiences, augmented reality, virtual reality, and others)	
Technologies	
CI Deployment	
Instructor Roles	
Learner Roles	
Other Roles	
CI Evaluation	
Learner Experiences	
Learning Efficacy Measures	
Content Analysis	
CI Revision	
Revision Plan(s)	

Figure 3. (1) Designing / developing / deploying curricular infusion; (2) extraction of curricular infused elements and messaging

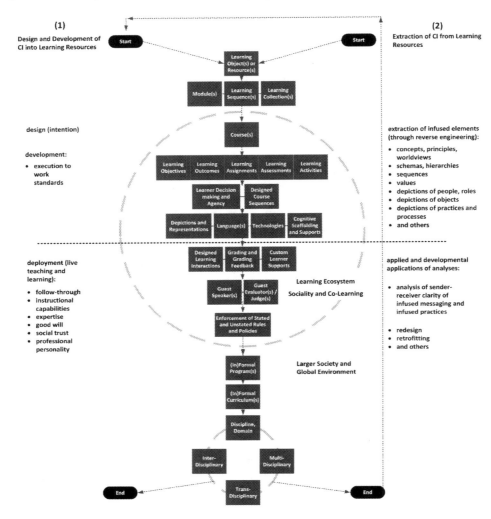

(1) Designing / Developing / Deploying Curricular Infusion; (2) Extraction of Curricular Infused Elements and Messaging

learning efficacy (learner post-test, pre-and-posttest, experimental designs with experimental/treatment/intervention groups vs. control groups, and others).

Essentially, this work entails going through designed learning contents, learning assignments, learning data, and other learning artifacts (submitted learner assignments, discussion boards, and others) in order to identify themes, patterned practices, and other aspects, to understand intended and unintended curricular infusions.

Understanding curricular infusions may benefit from some simple categorizations. One approach may be to differentiate between CIs by apparent CI target learning objectives and related learning outcomes. For example, the main focuses of the learning may be related to defined "knowledge, skills, and abilities" (KSAs); another version is "knowledge, skills, and attitudes." The U.S. Office of Personnel Management defined KSAs as "the attributes required to perform a job and are generally demonstrated through qualifying service, education, or training" ("Knowledge, skills, and abilities," Nov. 17, 2018). "Knowledge" points to the necessary information to perform a function; "skill" refers to "an observable competence to perform a learned psychomotor act," and an "ability" is "competence to perform an observable behavior or a behavior that results in an observable product" ("Knowledge, skills, and abilities," Nov. 17, 2018). These may be addressed at the "acquisition" of KSAs or their "maintenance" or achieving higher levels of expertise in these. Given the complexity of modern-day learning requirements, people likely have a wide range of KSAs in which they are experts, novices (new learners on track to acquire the full expertise), and amateurs (new learners who are only interested in partial skillsets in the area for non-professional aims).

There are limits, of course, because, a topic may apply to all three categories, such as global acculturation. In other cases, CIs may be targeted to an expansion of the traditional target learners. The CIs may be categorized by type of learning contents—whether informational, activity, social interactivity, project-based, case-based, or other pedagogical aspect. The scope of the CIs may be helpful, whether the focus is at micro, meso, or macro scale. Perhaps a mixed combination of approaches may be most effective in the descriptions, given the complexities in this space. Table 2 combines scale and the concept of "designed" and incidental "non-designed" types of curricular experiences, mitigated by instructor interventions and supports. This table considers curricular infusions in a dynamic context—based on live "high-tech high-touch" interactive online learning contexts (most typical in higher education).

The design of online learning is informed by a mix of perspectives: the content expert, the instructional designer, the developer, the writer, the photographer, the graphic artist, and others. In highly formalized instructional design, theories and models of learning may underlie the design work. As such, the resulting learning will be informed by deep thinking about the following:

- Learning objectives
- Learning outcomes
- Learning assignments
- Learning activities
- Learning assessments
- Social interactivity

Table 2. Micro-, meso-, and macro-scale learning elements and levels of control over the learning

Designed Learner-Facing Learner Contents and Activities (from Curricular Infusions)	Non-Designed or Incidental Wildcard Learner-Facing Learning Contents and Activities / Events	Instructor Interventions and Supports
Micro		
Learning objects and resources (lectures, slideshows, videos, games, simulations, notes, books, maps, datasets, data visualizations, and others)		
Modules, learning sequences, learning collections		
	Social commentary on open learning resources	
	Formal reviews on open learning resources	
		Monitoring of social commentary
		Monitoring of formal reviews
		Counter-vailing commentary
		Redesigns and retrofitting
Meso		

continued on following page

There will be considerations of which technologies would be most effective for the learning experiences and what data should be collected for learning analysis. The developed learning contents to enable the various aspects of the learning will be nuanced, with tradeoffs between the various considerations. In every design context, there should be a checkoff to make sure that the critical elements in the learning have all been included appropriately and to proper measure. With so many moving parts, sometimes, learning elements get left out and have to be purposefully introduced. In other cases, subtle messaging may be introduced unawares and have to be ferreted out through analysis.

DISCUSSION

In learning sequences built through design, there are numerous choices made at every level—in terms of content for teaching and learning, language nuances, image nuances, included data, cases shared, assigned work, assessments, and other aspects. In contrast to whatever is included, much is left out in the revision process. Given the limited time, attention, fiscal, space, and other resources for learning, a heavy selection process occurs to actualize a learning sequence. In courses, the learning contents and activities and assessments are held in fine interdependence and balance; the elements inform each other for an overall learning experience.

Table 2. Continued

Designed Learner-Facing Learner Contents and Activities (from Curricular Infusions)	Non-Designed or Incidental Wildcard Learner-Facing Learning Contents and Activities / Events	Instructor Interventions and Supports
Course(s) (learning objectives, learning outcomes, learning assignments, learning assessments, learning activities, learner agency, course sequence options, depictions and representations, languages, technologies, cognitive scaffolding and supports, and others)		
Teaching and Learning (designed learning interactions, grading and grading feedback, custom learner supports, guest speaker(s), guest evaluator(s), policy enforcement, and others)		
	Comments and representations by co-learners in discussions, in collaborative work, in assignment submittals, and others	
	Comments and representations by guest speakers in pre-recorded or live events, in learning contents, in panel discussions, and others	
	Comments and representations by third-party content creators (in learning objects, in published works, and others)	
	Live events (including virtual world simulations)	
	Field trips (both virtual and real-space)	
	Social media commentary on online social platforms used for teaching and learning	
		Debriefings and reframings
		Follow-on studies (in-depth or otherwise)
		Redesigns and retrofitting
Programs (informal and formal)		
	Comments and representations by colleagues	
	Comments and representations by administrators	
		Debriefings and reframings
		Follow-on studies (in-depth or otherwise)
		Professional conversations
		Redesigns and retrofitting
Curriculums (informal and formal)		
	Comments and representations by colleagues	
	Comments and representations by administrators	
		Professional conversations
		Redesigns and retrofitting
Macro		

continued on following page

Table 2. Continued

Designed Learner-Facing Learner Contents and Activities (from Curricular Infusions)	Non-Designed or Incidental Wildcard Learner-Facing Learning Contents and Activities / Events	Instructor Interventions and Supports
Disciplines		
Interdisciplinary studies		
Multi-disciplinary studies		
Institutional		
Multi-institutional		
Societal		
Global		
	External policymaking decisions	
	New technologies	
	New paradigm shifts	
	New leaders	
	New resources	
	New ethics practices	
	New professional practices	
		Professional conversations
		Shared resources
		Redesigns and retrofitting

A curricular infusion (CI) introduces a new element into specific learning in a particular curricular context. The introduction may be light-handed or heavy-handed in its diffusion (based on design and development and the teaching). As noted, the impacts may be far-reaching and may impact a wide range of stakeholders to the learning, and some impacts may be intended and others incidental and maybe not even anticipated.

In the research literature, various types of curricular infusions have been created based on different and mixed "authorities": new laws, new models, new pedagogical methods, new technologies, new policies, new required knowledge/skills/abilities (KSAs), and others. These originating animating authorities can apply at any level of learning contents, micro, meso, and macro. The intensity of the curricular infusions also may vary. Various technologies may be harnessed to achieve these works.

Also, it is possible to analyze extant curriculums and curricular contents for purposeful and unintentional curricular infusions, to analyze the efficacy of instructional designs (1) and / or to inform redesigns and retrofitting (2). In this latter case, the assumption is that if there is sufficient evidence for a case of an infusion (through the identification of themes, patterns, and such, in the digital and analog learning contents, the assignments, the assessments, the actual teaching, and other aspects), then the observed infusions should be addressed as a present phenomenon, even if the original content experts, designers and developers, did not intend those outcomes.

To be clear, curricular infusions may be highly useful in particular contexts, but these approaches are not applicable in all contexts. In some cases, perhaps a stand-alone module may better address learner needs in the particular learning context. Or perhaps the online learning needs to be rebuilt from ground-up because the required changes are so fundamental, such as a shift from one focal technology as learning content to another.

FUTURE RESEARCH DIRECTIONS

This work summarized the available literature on curricular infusions and introduced a simple listing of types by the contents being introduced (for what learning ends, and whether conceptual or analog) and by real-world examples. Follow-on research may add to the typology, with other classifications and curricular infusion (CI) types.

The literature would benefit from information on which online learning contexts, what scales of online learning, what time-lengths of learning, which learners, and other aspects of learning are relevant when deciding to choose curricular infusion or larger-scale redesign and redevelopment of online learning.

Also, while the research literature does have cases of when curricular infusions may be efficacious or inefficacious, more general insights about that phenomenon would be helpful. (The recorded research suggests that the studies are of learner experiences and learner academic performances, but other approaches would be helpful to explore as well, such as a basic content analysis for efficacy.)

CONCLUSION

What is taught directly and indirectly has far-reaching impacts on each new generation of learners. There are constructive human interests in terms of updating curriculums as soon as reasonably possible to ensure accurate and relevant learning. It is important to analyze learning contents at micro, meso, and macro levels to understand what is being taught through subtle curricular infusions for hidden curriculums, so learning efficacy may be studied…and appropriate revisions and retrofits may be achieved. This chapter provides some light approaches to both of these efforts—the original design, development and deployment…and then the reverse engineering of curricular infusions for practical analysis and design insights.

REFERENCES

Aizikovitsh, E., & Amit, M. (2010). Evaluating an infusion approach to the teaching of critical thinking skills through mathematics. In the proceedings of WCES-2010. *Procedia: Social and Behavioral Sciences, 2*(2), 3818–3822. doi:10.1016/j.sbspro.2010.03.596

Aksamit, D. L., & Alcorn, D. A. (1988). A preservice mainstream curriculum infusion model: Student teachers' perceptions of program effectiveness. *Teacher Education and Special Education, 11*(2), 52–58. doi:10.1177/088840648801100202

Alford, K. L., Carter, C. A., Ragsdale, D. J., Ressler, E. K., & Reynolds, C. W. (2004). Specification and managed development of information technology curricula. *Proceedings of SIGITE '04*, 261 – 266. 10.1145/1029533.1029598

Ametrano, I. M., Callaway, Y. L., & Stickel, S. A. (2002). Multicultural infusion in the counselor education curriculum: A preliminary analysis. *Proceedings of the annual meeting of the Eastern Educational Research Association*, 1 – 17.

Anderson, S. (2008, Fall). Math infusion in agricultural education and career and technical education in rural schools. *Rural Research Brief*, 1 – 4.

Anderson, S. K., MacPhee, D., & Govan, D. (2000, Fall). Infusion of multicultural issues in curricula: A student perspective. *Innovative Higher Education, 25*(1), 37–57. doi:10.1023/A:1007584318881

Angeli, C., & Valanides, N. (2009). Instructional effects on critical thinking: Performance on ill-defined issues. *Learning and Instruction, 19*(4), 322–334. doi:10.1016/j.learninstruc.2008.06.010

Atwater, M. M. (1996). Social constructivism: Infusion into the multicultural science education research agenda. *Journal of Research in Science Teaching, 33*(8), 821–837. doi:10.1002/(SICI)1098-2736(199610)33:8<821::AID-TEA1>3.0.CO;2-Y

Bawa, P., Watson, S. L., & Watson, W. (2018). Motivation is a game: Massively multiplayer online games as agents of motivation in higher education. *Computers & Education, 123*, 174–194. doi:10.1016/j.compedu.2018.05.004

Bergen-Cico, D., Razza, R., & Timmins, A. (2015). Fostering self-regulation through curriculum infusion of mindful yoga: A pilot study of efficacy and feasibility. *Journal of Child and Family Studies, 24*(11), 3448–3461. doi:10.100710826-015-0146-2

Beyerbach, B., Walsh, C., & Vannatta, R. (2001). From teaching technology to using technology to enhance student learning: Preservice teachers' changing perceptions of technology infusion. *Journal of Technology and Teacher Education, 9*(1), 105–127.

Bickmore, K. (2005, Fall). Foundations for peacebuilding and discursive peacekeeping: Infusion and exclusion of conflict in Canadian public school curricula. *Journal of Peace Education, 2*(2), 1–17.

Brauer, D. G., & Ferguson, K. J. (2015). The integrated curriculum in medical education: AMEE Guide No. 96. *Medical Teacher, 37*(4), 312–322. doi:10.3109/0 142159X.2014.970998 PMID:25319403

Burghardt, M. D., Hecht, D., Russo, M., Lauckhardt, J., & Hacker, M. (2010, Fall). A study of mathematics infusion in middle school technology education classes. *Journal of Technology Education, 22*(1), 58–74. doi:10.21061/jte.v22i1.a.4

Cameron, D. L., & Cook, B. G. (2007). Attitudes of preservice teachers enrolled in an infusion preparation program regarding planning and accommodations for included students with mental retardation. *Education and Training in Developmental Disabilities, 42*(3), 353–363.

Cao, P. Y., & Ajwa, I. A. (2016). Enhancing computational science curriculum at liberal arts institutions: A case study in the context of cybersecurity. In the proceedings of the International Conference on Computational Science. *Procedia Computer Science, 80*, 1940–1946. doi:10.1016/j.procs.2016.05.510

Carrell, L. J. (1997). Diversity in the communication curriculum: Impact on student empathy. *Communication Education, 46*(4), 234–244. doi:10.1080/03634529709379098

Carvalho, C., Salema, M. H., Stanciugelu, I., Martins, D., Iorga, E. M., & Puscas, M. (2014). The impact of differences in curriculum on knowledge related to European Citizenship: A comparative analysis in the case of Portuguese and Romanian pupils. *Procedia: Social and Behavioral Sciences, 149*, 152–157. doi:10.1016/j.sbspro.2014.08.179

Cheah, S.-M. (2009). Using CDIO to revamp the chemical engineering curriculum. *Proceedings of the 5th International CDIO Conference*, 1 – 12.

Cheng, V. M. Y. (2011). Infusing creativity into Eastern classrooms: Evaluations from student perspectives. *Thinking Skills and Creativity, 6*(1), 67–87. doi:10.1016/j.tsc.2010.05.001

Clark, K., & Hoffman, A. (2018). Educating healthcare students: Strategies to teach systems thinking to prepare new healthcare graduates. *Journal of Professional Nursing*, 1–6. PMID:31126396

Conroy, C. A. (1999). Identifying barriers to infusion of aquaculture into secondary agriscience: Adoption of a curriculum innovation. *Journal of Agricultural Education*, *40*(3), 1–10. doi:10.5032/jae.1999.03001

Cordero, E. D., Israel, T., White, S., & Park, Y. S. (2010). Impact of instructor and course characteristics on the effectiveness of curriculum infusion. *Journal of American College Health*, *59*(2), 75–81. doi:10.1080/07448481003705917 PMID:20864432

Cruz, B. C., & Groendal-Cobb, J. L. (1998, November/December). Incorporating women's voices into the middle and senior high school history curriculum. *Social Studies*, *89*(6), 271–275. doi:10.1080/00377999809599869

Cummings, S., & Kropf, N. P. (2000, Spring). An infusion model for including content on elders with chronic mental illness in the curriculum. *Advances in Social Work*, *1*(1), 93–105. doi:10.18060/105

Cummings, S. M., Cassie, K. M., Galambos, C., & Wilson, E. (2006). Impact of an infusion model on social work students' aging knowledge, attitudes, and interests. *Journal of Gerontological Social Work*, *47*(3-4), 173–186. doi:10.1300/J083v47n03_11 PMID:17062529

Davis, S. N., & Jacobsen, S. K. (2014). Curricular integration as innovation: Faculty insights on barriers to institutionalizing change. *Innovative Higher Education*, *39*(1), 17–31. doi:10.100710755-013-9254-3

de Acedo Lizarraga, M. L. S., de Acedo Baquedano, M. T. S., Mangado, T. G., & Cardelle-Elawar, M. (2009). Enhancement of thinking skills: Effects of two intervention methods. *Thinking Skills and Creativity*, *4*(1), 30–43. doi:10.1016/j.tsc.2008.12.001

Delale, F., Liaw, B. M., Jiji, L. M., Voiculescu, I., & Yu, H. (2011, Summer). Infusion of emerging technologies and new teaching methods into The Mechanical Engineering Curriculum at The City College of New York. *Advances in Engineering Education*, 1–36.

Demetriadis, S., Barbas, A., Molohides, A., Palaigeorgiou, G., Psillos, D., Vlahavas, I., ... Pombortsis, A. (2003). 'Cultures in negotiation': Teachers' acceptance / resistance attitudes considering the infusion of technology into schools. *Computers & Education*, *41*(1), 19–37. doi:10.1016/S0360-1315(03)00012-5

Dewey, J., & Bento, J. (2009). Activating children's thinking skills (ACTS): The effects of an infusion approach to teaching thinking in primary schools. *The British Journal of Educational Psychology*, *79*(2), 329–351. doi:10.1348/000709908X344754 PMID:19224679

Du Preez, P., Simmonds, S., & Roux, C. (2012). Teaching-learning and curriculum development for human rights education: Two sides of the same coin. *Journal of Education, 55*, 83–104.

Duff, P. A. (2004). Intertextuality and hybrid discourses: The infusion of pop culture in educational discourse. *Linguistics and Education, 14*(3-4), 231–276. doi:10.1016/j.linged.2004.02.005

Fang, Z., & Wei, Y. (2010). Improving middle school students' science literacy through reading infusion. *The Journal of Educational Research, 103*(4), 262–273. doi:10.1080/00220670903383051

Flynn, M. A., & Carter, E. (2015). Curriculum infusion of the social norms approach: Information only vs. service learning. *Communication Education, 65*(3), 322–337. doi:10.1080/03634523.2015.1107112

Fredriksen-Goldsen, K. I., Hooyman, N. R., & Bonifas, R. P. (2006, Winter). Multigenerational practice: An innovative infusion approach. *Journal of Social Work Education, 42*(1), 25–36. doi:10.5175/JSWE.2006.200400420

Garii, B., & Appova, A. (2013). Crossing the great divide: Teacher candidates, mathematics, and social justice. *Teaching and Teacher Education, 34*, 198–213. doi:10.1016/j.tate.2012.07.004

Gonzalez-Pino, B. (2000). An infusion curriculum for the heritage speaker of Spanish. *Texas Papers in Foreign Language Education, 5*(1), 93 – 109.

Guerin, S. H. (2009). Internationalizing the curriculum: Improving learning through international education: Preparing students for success in a global society. *Community College Journal of Research and Practice, 33*(8), 611–614. doi:10.1080/10668920902928945

Hai-Jew, S. (2010, Dec. 15). An instructional design approach to updating an online course curriculum. *Educause Review.* Retrieved Mar. 2, 2019, from https://er.educause.edu/articles/2010/12/an-instructional-design-approach-to-updating-an-online-course-curriculum

Hancock, D., Helfers, M. J., Cowen, K., Letvak, S., Barba, B. E., Hewrrick, C., ... Bannon, M. (2006). Integration of gerontology content in nongeriatric undergraduate nursing courses. *Geriatric Nursing, 27*(2), 103–111. doi:10.1016/j.gerinurse.2006.02.002 PMID:16638481

Hanson-Baldauf, D., & Hassell, S. H. (2009). The information and communication technology competencies of students enrolled in school library media certification programs. *Library & Information Science Research, 31*(1), 3–11. doi:10.1016/j.lisr.2008.03.003

Harris, B. R. (2013, March). Subversive infusions: Strategies for the integration of information literacy across the curriculum. *Journal of Academic Librarianship, 39*(2), 175–180. doi:10.1016/j.acalib.2012.10.003

Hassan, A., & Ismail, M. Z. (2011). The infusion of Environmental Education (EE) in chemistry teaching and students' awareness and attitudes towards environment in Malaysia. *Procedia: Social and Behavioral Sciences, 15*, 3404–3409. doi:10.1016/j.sbspro.2011.04.309

Healy, L. M. (1988, Fall). Curriculum building in international social work: Toward preparing professionals for the Global Age. *Journal of Social Work Education, 3*(3), 221–228. doi:10.1080/10437797.1988.10671256

Hejka-Ekins, A. (1998). Teaching ethics across the public administration curriculum. *Journal of Public Affairs Education, 4*(1), 45–50. doi:10.1080/15236803.1998.12022009

Helge, D. (1981, November). Increasing preservice curriculum accountability to rural handicapped populations. *Teacher Education and Special Education, 6*(2), 137–142.

Helmsing, M. (2016). Becoming-American: Experiencing the nation through LGBT fabulation in a ninth grade U.S. history class. *Journal of Social Studies Research, 40*(3), 173–186. doi:10.1016/j.jssr.2016.02.001

Hendrix, J. C. (1998). Globalizing the curriculum. *The Clearing House: A Journal of Educational Strategies, Issues and Ideas, 71*(5), 305–308. doi:10.1080/00098659809602732

Hinchey, M. G., Pressburger, T., Markosian, L., & Feather, M. S. (2006). The NASA Software Research Infusion Initiative: Successful technology transfer for software assurance. Proceedings of TT'06, 43 – 47.

Hlengwa, A. (2010). Infusing service-learning in curricula: A theoretical exploration of infusion possibilities. *Journal of Education, 48*, 1–14.

Holody, R., & Kolb, P. (2011). 10 steps to sustain infusion of gerontology across the social work curriculum. *Educational Gerontology, 37*(9), 791–808. doi:10.1080/03601271003780974

Ioannou, A., Socratous, C., & Nikolædou, E. (2018). Expanding the curricular space with educational robotics: A creative course on road safety. In *EC-TEL. European Conference on Technology Enhanced Learning* (pp. 537–547). Springer. 10.1007/978-3-319-98572-5_42

Jankowska, M. A., Smith, B. J., & Buehler, M. A. (2014). Engagement of academic libraries and information science schools in creating curriculum for sustainability: An exploratory study. *Journal of Academic Librarianship, 40*(1), 45–54. doi:10.1016/j.acalib.2013.10.013

Jin, B., Swinney, J., Cao, H., Muske, G., Nam, J., & Kang, J. H. (2011, May). Doing business with China: Curriculum internationalisation (sic) through an infusion method. *Innovations in Education and Teaching International, 48*(2), 171–181. doi:10.1080/14703297.2011.564012

Jones, T. S., & Sanford, R. (2003, Fall). Building the container: Curriculum infusion and classroom climate. *Conflict Resolution Quarterly, 21*(1), 115–130. doi:10.1002/crq.52

Joseph, P. B., Bravmann, S. L., Windschitl, M. A., Mikel, E. R., & Green, N. S. (2000). *Cultures of Curriculum*. Mahwah, NJ: Lawrence Erlbaum Associates, Publishers.

Kadir, M. A. A. (2017). What teacher knowledge matters in effectively developing critical thinkers in the 21st century curriculum? *Thinking Skills and Creativity, 23*, 79–90. doi:10.1016/j.tsc.2016.10.011

Kalyvas, V. A., Koutsouki, D., & Skordilis, E. K. (2011, July). Attitudes of Greek physical education students towards participation in a disability-infusion curriculum. *Education Research Journal, 1*(2), 24–30.

Kennedy-Malone, L., Penrod, J., Kohlenberg, E. M., Letvak, S. A., Crane, P. B., Tesh, A., ... Milone-Nuzzo, P. (2006). Integrating gerontology competencies into graduate nursing programs. *Journal of Professional Nursing, 22*(2), 123–128. doi:10.1016/j.profnurs.2006.01.010 PMID:16564479

King, D. R. (1991). *Perceptions regarding the infusion of a global perspective into the curriculum as identified by the faculty of the College of Agriculture at Iowa State University*. Iowa State University Digital Repository.

Knowledge, Skills, and Abilities. (2018, Nov. 17). In *Wikipedia*. Retrieved May 5, 2019, from https://en.wikipedia.org/wiki/Knowledge,_Skills,_and_Abilities

Kohlenberg, E., Kennedy-Malone, L., Crane, P., & Letvak, S. (2007). Infusing gerontological nursing content into advanced practice nursing education. *Nursing Outlook*, *55*(1), 38–43. doi:10.1016/j.outlook.2006.09.006 PMID:17289466

Kopels, S., & Gustavsson, N. S. (1996, Winter). Infusing legal issues into the social work curriculum. *Journal of Social Work Education*, *32*(1), 115–125. doi:10.1080/10437797.1996.10672289

Kowalski, E. M. (1995, April). The infusion approach to teacher development. *Journal of Physical Education, Recreation & Dance*, *66*(4), 49–54. doi:10.1080/07303084.1995.10608141

Kropf, N. P. (1996, Spring/Summer). Infusing content on older people with developmental disabilities into the curriculum. *Journal of Social Work Education*, *32*(2), 215–226. doi:10.1080/10437797.1996.10778452

Kysilka, M. L. (1998, Summer). Understanding integrated curriculum. *Curriculum Journal*, *9*(2), 197–209. doi:10.1080/0958517970090206

Latimer, D. G., & Thornlow, D. K. (2006). Incorporating geriatrics into baccalaureate nursing curricula: Laying the groundwork with faculty development. *Journal of Professional Nursing*, *22*(2), 79–83. doi:10.1016/j.profnurs.2006.01.012 PMID:16564471

LeBlanc, M. D., & Dyer, B. D. (2004, December). Bioinformatics and computing curricular 2001: Why computer science is well positioned in a post-genomic world. *Inroads: The SIGCSE Bulletin*, *36*(4), 64–68.

Leblanc, P. (1996). Project Infusion: Teachers, training, and technology. *Journal of Information Technology for Teacher Education*, *5*(1-2), 25–34. doi:10.1080/0962029960050104

Lee, E.-K. O., & Waites, C. E. (2006, Winter). Infusing aging content across the curriculum: Innovations in baccalaureate social work education. *Journal of Social Work Education*, *42*(1), 49–66. doi:10.5175/JSWE.2006.042110002

Longres, J.F., & Scanlon, E. (2001, Fall). Social justice and the research curriculum. *Journal of Social Work Education*, (373), 447 – 463.

Luckie, D. B., Maleszewski, J. J., Loznak, S. D., & Krha, M. (2004). Infusion of collaborative inquiry throughout a biology curriculum increases student learning: A four-year study of 'Teams and Streams.' *Advances in Physiology Education –. The American Journal of Physiology*, *287*, 199–209.

Menkel-Meadow, C., & Sander, R. H. (1995, Summer – Autumn). The 'infusion' method at UCLA: Teaching ethics pervasively. *Law and Contemporary Problems, 58*(3/4), 129–138. doi:10.2307/1192025

Millar, G. (1995). *Helping schools with career infusion.* Eric Clearinghouse on Counseling and Student Services. ERIC Digest.

Moshkovich, H., Mechitov, A., & Olson, D. (2005, Fall). Infusion of electronic commerce into the information systems curriculum. *Journal of Computer Information Systems, 46*(1), 1–8.

Nobles, W. (1990). The infusion of African and African American content: A question of content and intent. *Infusion of African and African American content in the school curriculum,* 5-26.

O'Brien, D. G., Stewart, R. A., & Moje, E. B. (1995, July-August). Why content literacy is difficult to infuse into the secondary school: Complexities of curriculum, pedagogy, and school culture. *Reading Research Quarterly, 30*(3), 442–463. doi:10.2307/747625

Obiakor, F. E. (1994, Nov.). Multiculturalism in the university curriculum: Infusion for what? *The Regents Conference on Diversity and Multiculturalism in the University Curriculum,* 1 – 23.

Osteen, P., Vanidestine, T., & Sharpe, T.L. (2013). *Multicultural curriculum and MSW students' attitudes about race and diversity.* Faculty publications. Florida State University Libraries.

Pitts, B. G., & Shapiro, D. R. (2017). People with disabilities and sport: An exploration of topic inclusion in sport management. *Journal of Hospitality, Leisure, Sport and Tourism Education, 21,* 33–45. doi:10.1016/j.jhlste.2017.06.003

Puk, T., & Behm, D. (2003, Spring). The diluted curriculum: The role of government in developing ecological literacy as the first imperative in Ontario secondary schools. *Canadian Journal of Environmental Education, 8,* 217–232.

Raby, R. L. (2007, Summer). Internationalizing the curriculum: On- and off-campus strategies. *New Directions for Community Colleges, 138*(138), 57–66. doi:10.1002/cc.282

Reisberg, L. (1998, May). Facilitating inclusion with integrated curriculum: A multidisciplinary approach. *Intervention in School and Clinic, 33*(5), 272–277. doi:10.1177/105345129803300503

Riley, J. B., & McWilliams, M. (2007, Summer). Engaged learning through curriculum infusion. *Peer Review: Emerging Trends and Key Debates in Undergraduate Education, 9*(3), 14–17.

Riley, J. B., & Yearwood, E. L. (2012). The effect of a pedagogy of curriculum infusion on nursing student well-being and intent to improve the quality of nursing care. *Archives of Psychiatric Nursing, 26*(5), 364–373. doi:10.1016/j.apnu.2012.06.004 PMID:22999032

Rowley, J., Dysard, G., & Arnold, J. (2005). Developing a new technology infusion program for preparing tomorrow's teachers. *Journal of Technology and Teacher Education, 13*(1), 105–123.

Salas, L.M., & Altamirano, B.N. (2012, June). *A behavioral health disparities curriculum infusion initiative: Eliminating behavioral health disparities for racial and ethnic minority populations: Workforce development to mobilize social work as a resource.* U.S. Department of Health and Human Services, Office of Minority Health and the National Association of Deans and Directors of Schools of Social Work.

Shapiro, D. R., Pitts, B., Hums, M. A., & Calloway, J. (2012). Infusing disability sport into the sport management curriculum. *Sport Management International Journal, 8*(1), 101–118.

Shujaa, M. J. (1995, Summer). Cultural self meets cultural other in the African American experience: Teachers' responses to a curriculum content reform. *Theory into Practice, 34*(3), 194–201. doi:10.1080/00405849509543679

Skidmore, D., Marston, J., & Olson, G. (2005, August). An infusion approach to internationalization: Drake University as a case study. *Frontiers: The Interdisciplinary Journal of Study Abroad, 11,* 187–203. Retrieved from https://eric.ed.gov/?id=EJ891469

Swartz, R. J. (1986, May). Restructuring curriculum for critical thinking. *Educational Leadership, 43*(8), 43–44.

Tang, C., Tucker, C., Servin, C., & Geissler, M. (2018). Computer science curricular guidance for associate-degree transfer programs. *Proceedings of SIGCSE '18*, 435–440. 10.1145/3159450.3159536

Toledo, C. (2005). A five-stage model of computer technology integration into teacher education curriculum. *Contemporary Issues in Technology & Teacher Education, 5*(2), 177–191.

Torres, S. Jr, Ottens, A. J., & Johnson, I. H. (1997, September). The multicultural infusion process: A research-based approach. *Counselor Education and Supervision, 37*(1), 6–18. doi:10.1002/j.1556-6978.1997.tb00526.x

Ukpokodu, O. N. (2010, Winter). How a sustainable campus-wide diversity curriculum fosters academic success. *Multicultural Education*, 27–36.

Whitcomb, S. A. (2009, Sept.). *Strong start: Impact of direct teaching of a social-emotional learning curriculum and infusion of skills on emotion knowledge of first grade students* (Doctoral dissertation). University of Oregon.

White, S., Park, Y. S., & Cordero, E. D. (2010). Impact of curriculum infusion on college students' drinking behaviors. *Journal of American College Health, 58*(6), 515–522. doi:10.1080/07448481003621726 PMID:20452927

Williams, G. J., & Reisberg, L. (2003, March). Successful inclusion: Teaching social skills through curriculum integration. *Intervention in School and Clinic, 38*(4), 205–210. doi:10.1177/105345120303800402

Yang, S. C. (2007). E-critical/thematic doing history project: Integrating the critical thinking approach with computer-mediated history learning. *Computers in Human Behavior, 23*(5), 2095–2112. doi:10.1016/j.chb.2006.02.012

Yemini, M., Tibbitts, F., & Goren, H. (2019). Trends and caveats: Review of literature on global citizenship education in teacher training. *Teaching and Teacher Education, 77*, 77–89. doi:10.1016/j.tate.2018.09.014

Zohar, A., & Tamir, P. (1993, March). Incorporating critical thinking into a regular high school biology curriculum. *School Science and Mathematics, 93*(3), 136–140. doi:10.1111/j.1949-8594.1993.tb12211.x

ADDITIONAL READING

Joseph, P. B., Bravmann, S. L., Windschitl, M. A., Mikel, E. R., & Green, N. S. (2000). *Cultures of Curriculum*. Mahwah, NJ: Lawrence Erlbaum Associates, Publishers.

KEY TERMS AND DEFINITIONS

Curricular Infusion: The inculcation of ideas, values, practices, worldviews, or technologies into an existing learning object, sequence, course, or discipline.

Chapter 7
Optimizing Static and Dynamic Visual Expressions of Time-Based Events, Processes, Procedures, and Future Projections for Instructional Design

Shalin Hai-Jew
https://orcid.org/0000-0002-8863-0175
Kansas State University, USA

ABSTRACT

Time-based visuals are used to depict time-based events, processes, procedures, and future projections, among others. These come in 2D, 3D, and 4D types, and they may be static or dynamic, non-interactive, or interactive. A simple process or procedure may be expressed visually as a timeline, a flowchart, a stacked diagram, a node-link game tree, a workflow diagram, dedicated-type sequence diagrams, or some other sequence-based visual. With the proliferation of more complex time-based sequences—with multiple paths, multiple actors, decision junctures, conditionals, and other forms of dimensionality, and with multimodal expressions and interactive digital interfaces, with processes as descriptions, theorized steps, directional procedures, projections, and other types—the visual depictions of processes and procedures have become much more complex and layered. This work describes some efforts to optimize these visual expressions through proper design, development, testing, and revision.

DOI: 10.4018/978-1-5225-9833-6.ch007

INTRODUCTION

Scenario 1: The faculty-client wants a designed visual that depicts multiple interrelated historical events (complexes of phenomena) on a basic timeline, with collected events from multiple countries. She wants the macro-level information to be presented as factually as possible without any suggestions of event-based associations, but rather, she wants the focus to be on unfolding time.

Scenario 2: Here, the faculty-client has requested a time-based documentation of an experimental laboratory procedure. He has requested a visit to his laboratory for the observation of the procedure, and he wants a digital sequencing depicted in multiple ways. He wants representations of what would happen at various decision junctures, such as what will happen if there is a misstep or an inappropriate decision. He also wants a clean flowchart showing the proper decisions and the respective decision junctures for this procedure.

Scenario 3: The research team has been out in their respective field sites for many months. They have been posting their notes to a shared site. They are requesting a descriptive process diagram of a particular observed phenomenon based on their collective notes, which include scanned (digitized) handwritten notes, filled data tables, audio files, photos, video files, and other data. Whatever is created will be added to a continuing web log of the research team's experiences and some initial findings and some early hypothesizing.

Scenario 4: A research team is conducting the subjective perceptions of time passage in sleep experiments. They have collected data from the respective experiment participants, and they have found subjective variances in experienced time. They want to combine the different time estimates of the participants with their respective narratives of their experiences during the sleep sessions.

The sparsely-described prior instructional design challenges all converge on the expression of time-based visualizations, which are a key part of instructional designs. For an instructional designer, in each scenario, there are understood contexts, understood representations of time, a sense of the target learners and time-based messaging, and potential conventional visualizations and related technologies. The likely resulting visuals are likely canonical ones: multiple co-related timelines (1), tabbed descriptions of the experiment, simulations, and flowcharts (2), informational graphics, time-based slideshows, multimodal time-based visualizations, and a process diagram (3), and summary timelines, individual annotated timelines with narrations

(4). (Note: The respective faculty-clients and teams may have different visions of what they want, however.)

This chapter explores some visual expressions of time-based phenomenon from an instructional design view. This does not aspire to include every possible type of time-based visualization, of which there are potentially hundreds, and time is a dimension in various data visualizations and informational graphics, even when it is not forefronted. In the learning context, time-based data visualizations, whether static or dynamic, have to meet several common requirements:

- They have to be recognizable and accurately interpretable by learners and users.
- They often integrate other informational dimensions beyond time (like space, and / or other factors).
- They promote visual learning.
- They are memorable (and serve as visual mnemonics or "aids to memory").
- They may have clear start-and-end points, or multiple start and multiple end points.
- They may be understood as a sequence or as multiple sequences.
- There may be interaction effects between various phenomenon in the visual.
- The underlying data may stem from the imagination, from data, from in-world observations, or some combination of the prior. Imaginary time-based visuals may be fanciful and fantastical, or they may aspire to reality (such as projections into the future). In general, time-based visualizations are fact-based and built off of in-world data.
- They are (informationally) accessible to those even with visual acuity, color-blindness, light-contrast, and other visual challenges. They are designed to human perception (and its limits).

This work highlights some methods for optimizing time-based visuals, from the design phase to development to the launch. This work covers both static and dynamic time-based visuals, available through commercial authoring tools. This also covers time-based visuals in multiple dimensions: 2D, 3D, and 4D.

REVIEW OF THE LITERATURE

Time is a critical aspect of virtually all research because human endeavors exist in time, even as the actual nature of time is up for debate (What is "time-space"? What is "punctuated equilibrium"?). In all domain fields, there are histories. There are critical moments when particular discoveries were made. There are birth dates and death dates of contributors to various fields. Lifespan-based phenomena inform time-based analyses, such as survival analyses and time-to-event analyses (Hosmer, Lemeshow, & May, 2008). There are time sequences for particular procedures. There are described time sequences for particular processes. There is anticipated time, the sense of predictive futures for particular fields and the open questions which are set up to help direct the field towards particular problem solving and targeted discovery. There are intervals between particular events. There are particular time periods or phases of particular interests. There is simultaneous time in the world, with co-occurring events. There are different ways to slice continuous time. There are intensifications of time, with heightened frequencies of particular behaviors. There is latent time, with hidden occurrences that may affect particular phenomenon but which is not seen yet.

As a construct, time may be fairly ephemeral and abstract. In a simplified sense, it may be conceptualized as monotemporal with everyone existing in one standard time. A more nuanced sense of time is as a "pluritemporal" concept based on people's different culturally informed sense of time (Nowotny, 1992, as cited in Yakura, Oct. 2002, p. 956). Biologically, people may experience time differently, based on "several complementary systems" in the human brain that enable the subjective perception of time ("Time perception," Dec. 9, 2018). Various research suggests that people experience distortions in time perception or "temporal illusions." The importance of time in virtually all learning domains means that conveying its impact is important in learning. Of particular application is "visual learning," which refers to "the use of illustrations, photographs, diagrams, graphs, symbols, icons, and other visual models that allow individuals to quickly make sense of complex information" (O'Bannon, Puckett, & Rakes, 2006, p. 126).

In any number of visualizations, there are common elements, such as particular "frame(s) of reference" and "variables" from the data for the respective visuals (Aigner, Miksch, Schumann, & Tominski, 2011, pp. 149 - 151). Time is a common aspect of visualizations, with its arrangement as either "linear" or "cyclic," and "time primitives" as "instant" or "interval" in one research team's conceptualization (Aigner, Miksch, Schumann, & Tominski, 2011, pp. 149 - 151). In some cases, time is main focal point of the visual.

Early time visuals may have been text ones, described by words. One of the most basic time-based visuals is a linear timeline, with a start point at the left and an arrow into the future to the right, with events listed in chronological order ("Timeline," Dec. 7, 2018). As represented, time runs from left to right (with the infinite future depicted to the right). Particular selected events are marked out on the line, with labels for the events. The lengths of the respective segments represent discrete time durations, or the underlying timeline just represents continuous time. Some timelines have arrows at both the left and the right, with the present as one discrete slice-in-time in the middle. A simple timeline may represent overlapping time, with multiple events co-occurring simultaneously. There may be multiple start- and end- points, for one or multiple events. Periodic events may be depicted with some set intervals. Traditional timelines were built "on the assumption that time can be represented in standardized, invariable, context-free units (Adam, 1990, as cited in Yakura, Oct. 2002, p. 956).

Based on these simple models, there can be particular types of timelines. For example, "event timelines" showcase particular related events or events of a type (Biswas, Sagar, & Srinivasan, 2008). An "event is defined as an "occurrence of an incident at a particular instant of time with a set of attributes describing it" (Biswas, Sagar, & Srinivasan, 2008, p. 604). Identifying the relevant "schematic attributes" to an event (Biswas, Sagar, & Srinivasan, 2008, p. 604) is important in creating a coherent event-mapping timeline. For every event, there may be lead-up precursors, and there may be lead-away events, too; identifying what is relevant of the main and subevents and treating them with the proper proportion is important. The challenge is to formally define when an event has started (maybe t_1 as "time 1" and follow-on relevant events as t_2 and so on), when it continues, and when it ultimately and definitely ends. Operationalizing the time-based visual will be important for the defensibility and informativeness of the visual. Chronological events may be collated to form a sense of history. The past is explored for lessons and for their "moral utility" (Meacham, 2018), to inform on present-day decisions and ways of being.

While timelines are still in use today, often with multimodal dimensions (text, imagery, audio, video, hyperlinks, simulations, and others) and narrative overlays, there are a number of additional types of time-based visuals. In two dimensions, there are time-based visualizations as concept maps, flowcharts, vertical bar charts, line graphs, scattergraphs (with time as the x-axis), tables, causal chains, game trees (for probabilities of likely futures) and others. A time-based visual may be something as simple as pre- and post- side-by-side (or top and bottom) images. Or there can be a sequence of images in time lapse, or in forwards sequential order or backwards sequential order. Entire graphs may be depicted in sequences to capture a sense of the macro. Time can be represented in data changes over time. Another approach is a non-linear one, such as the "pebble-in-the-pond" approach for process (Merrill, Aug. 2002), which is comprised of concentric circles beginning with a central phase in the middle and expanding out. In 3D, there are 3D versions of the 2D diagrams, and unique expressions such as bubble representations over time. In 4D, there are (2D and 3D-based) simulations, videos, slideshows, drawings, and other expressions with the 4th dimension (time) directly written into the visuals and embedded in keyframes.

Learners may engage with visual imagery in interactive ways based on computational enablements. Building to human visual analysis requires understanding of human learners and also proper visual messaging:

A single image, however, typically provides answers to, at best, a handful of questions. Instead, visual analysis typically progresses in an iterative process of view creation, exploration, and refinement. Meaningful analysis consists of repeated explorations as users develop insights about significant relationships, domain-specific contextual influences, and causal patterns. Confusing widgets, complex dialog boxes, hidden operations, incomprehensible displays, or slow response times can limit the range and depth of topics considered and may curtail thorough deliberation and introduce errors. To be most effective, visual analytics tools must support the fluent and flexible use of visualizations at rates resonant with the pace of human thought (Heer & Schneiderman, 2012, p. 1)

Interactive imagery enables a variety of interaction types, in three main categories: "data & view specification," "view manipulation," and "process & provenance" (Heer & Schneiderman, 2012, p. 1). In their taxonomy of "interactive dynamics for visual analysis," the authors define 12 task types in three high-level categories: "(1) data and view specification (visualize, filter, sort, and derive); (2) view manipulation (select, navigate, coordinate, and organize); and (3) analysis process and provenance (record, annotate, share, and guide)" (Heer & Schneiderman, 2012, p. 2). How these interactions may be defined depend on the underlying technologies. Other visuals may be built based on the formal grammars of high-level computer languages "for succinctly describing how data should be mapped to visual features" (Heer & Schneiderman, 2012, p. 3). (Given how common dates and times are for structured data, the applied rules of programs for visual layouts can offer competitive advantage in visual depictions.)

Then, too, time may be expressed in cumulative compound data, such as represented in dashboards, which include mash-ups of data from various sources. Some aspects may be shown in real-time and others in lagged historical time, and so on. There may be elements that point to projected future time (but usually not too far out from the current present.)

Processes are commonly depicted in time as flowcharts, with particular processes (depicted in convention-defined shapes) occurring in certain orders and with critical decision making periods. When processes break down, analysts can backtrack to see where there may have been problems. Lines with arrows may indicate directionality. Other dimensions of data may be overlaid with line width, dash patterns, colors, and labels, among others. At various points in the branching logic sequences (or tracks), there may be "triggers" to activate particular behaviors.

Depending on the particular learning domain, there may be various visual depictions that are common to the field. For example, in reading, "visual organizers" are harnessed as "graphic representations of different kinds of thinking processes" (Clarke, Apr. 1991, p. 526).

VISUALIZED TIME FOR EVENTS, PROCESSES, PROCEDURES, AND FUTURE PROJECTIONS FOR INSTRUCTIONAL DESIGN

Social imagery provides some examples of extant time-based visuals. An extracted related tags network from Flickr for "time" as a tag shows ties to various visual descriptors: bw, exposure, reflective, tempo, shadow, hour, tiempo, blackandwhite, timelapse, and others. (Figure 1) (By convention, tags are written in the lower case, and multiple languages are referenced, given the global aspects of the Social Web.)

These visual senses of time may be expanded further with a 1.5 deg. related tags network of "time" on Flickr (Figure 2). In this follow-on graph, three groups were

Figure 1. Visual senses of "time" via related tags network on Flickr (1 deg.)

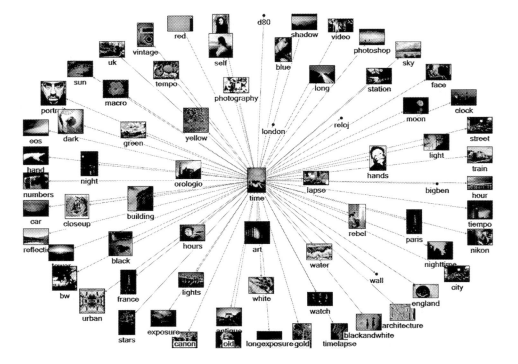

Optimizing Static and Dynamic Visual Expressions for Instructional Design

Figure 2. Visual senses of "time" via related tags network on Flickr (1.5 deg.)

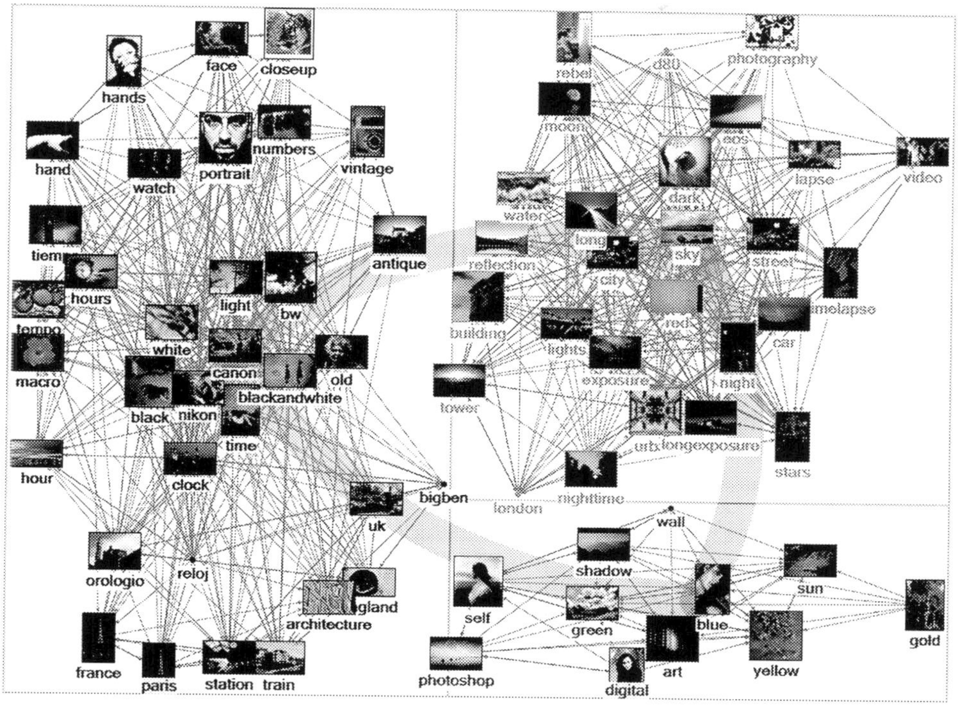

extracted, focused on people in time (Group 1), photography in time and location (Group 2), and abstractions of photography (Group 3).

A scraping of social imagery based on "time diagram" and "timeline" from social imagery also revealed some exemplars (Figure 3). The "time diagram" imagery show various types of work-based visuals: a Sankey flow diagram of building maintenance amounts over time, a military time clock linked to work schedules, diagrams of past present and future time (with present time as a "hypersurface" and past and future time as light cones, various line graphs, bubble diagrams, bar graphs, scattergraphs, game trees, and others. The "timeline" imagery reveals a number of different informational graphics based on time: a spiral of Earth on geologic time, train tracks representing the history of train travel, board game visualizations of various sequences, and others. One informational graphic depicts "descent into credit card debt" as a depicted descent into a dark mine (with the visual as a side cross-section of an underground space).

In terms of more formal references to time diagrams, visualizations, and maps, the Google Books Ngram Viewer offers some insights about the most common terms used in books, with "time diagram" coming to the fore (Figure 4).

Figure 3. A sampling of "time diagram" and "timeline" social imagery from Google Images

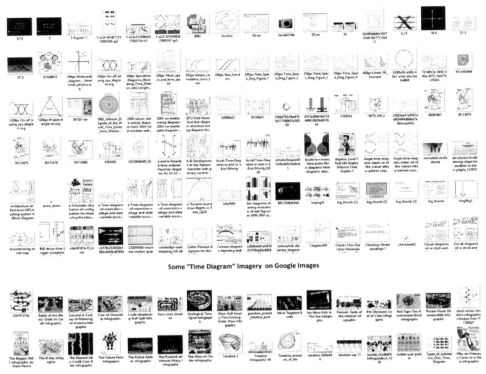

Table 1 sets up the concept of time-based visuals as built around time as past, present, future, and mixed (including all three categories) and informed by concepts (and the imagination), observations, and applied practices. These types of time conceptualizations are applied in different ways, listed in noun phrases prefaced by bullet points. The idea here is that the time-based visuals serve as jumping-off points for various types of learning, problem-solving, decision making, project planning, and others, in addition to being visual mnemonics or visual memory-enhancers. The sourcing of the time information, based on the context, will have varying fidelity or accuracy to the actual in-world events. (Definitive timelines are those well backed up by objective facts and / or solid proofs. Everything else may be understood as more subjective and interpretive.) The level of time precision may also vary. (Anything less than atomic time may be considered less precise.) Some of the time-based data may be more predictive of the future than others. The

Optimizing Static and Dynamic Visual Expressions for Instructional Design

Figure 4. Time diagram, time visualization, time map in the Google Books Ngram Viewer

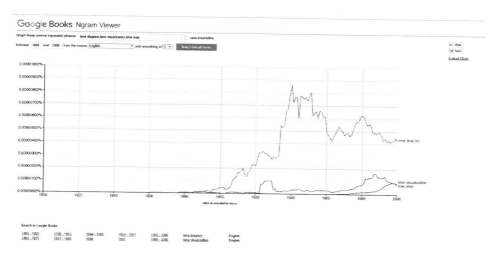

applications of the time-based visuals may be descriptive, normative, prescriptive, proscriptive, predictive, and others.

DISCUSSION

Instead of having a go-to for time-based visuals, a more creative approach may involve harnessing a collection of freeform "doodles" as a starting point, where possible. Those who are using content management systems and have built-in data dashboards may not have the option of creating their own designs, or if so, only within a narrow range of visual features. (Some systems may enable downloading the data and using other tools to create the time-based visuals.) Regardless, there is a benefit to avoiding pre-designed visuals and thinking about the design from the data and a blank screen.

Time-based visualizations come in a variety of forms, with different enablements. To be effective, those who would design focal-time-based visuals may ask and answer the following questions (in the following general order) to optimize their work:

The Nature of Time and the Target Phenomena (Dimensions Underlying the Events)

- What is the nature of time in this visual? Is time monotemporal or pluritemporal, and why? If it is pluritemporal, what are the underlying causes for the pluri-

Table 1. Some types of sequences by time and by origin types

Mixes of Time	Data Sourcing / Inspiration for Time-Based Visuals		
	Conceptualized, Theorized, Imagined (in Mind)	**Observed, Described (In-World)**	**Practiced, Applied (In-World)**
Past (including Near-, Mid-, and Far-) Time	• Fictionalized histories and stories • Interpretive histories and stories • Mythmaking	• Historical interpretation • Mythmaking	• Learned processes • Decision making sequences and junctures
Present, Contemporaneous Time	• Fictionalized stories • Interpreted events	• Documentation of described events • Analyses • Diagnostics • Problem-solving • Decision making • Comparisons • Action-taking • Research • Project planning	• Processes • Procedures • Decision making sequences and junctures • Experimental sequences • Improvised sequences
Future (including Near-, Mid-, and Far) Time	• Planning • Designs • Projections	• Anticipated futures from observed present • Nascent and near-term future observations	• Anticipated or projected futures • Anticipated decisions • Actions taken in anticipation of…
Mixed (Continuous and Phased) Times (past, present, and future)	• Fictionalized past, present, and futures	• Fact-based observed trajectory paths • Fact-based projections or trends • Decision making • Project planning	• Experiential sequence (in past, present, and anticipated future time) • Predictivity based on time sequences for resource allocation, for project planning, and others

aspects? What are the other dimensions of time which are relevant for the particular context?

- What are the assumptions underlying the time-based visuals? How clear are these assumptions to users? (Is it spelled out somehow?)
- Is there a clear start point and end point? Is this a one-time pass-through or a multiple pass-throughs phenomenon?
- In terms of the egos, entities, and variables depicted, what are the interrelationships? In the next time interval, and the next and the next, how do these interrelationships change? What is the influence of time on the depicted egos, entities, and variables, and the interrelational dynamics? The context?

Optimizing Static and Dynamic Visual Expressions for Instructional Design

Figure 5. Simplified elements of some common time-based diagrams

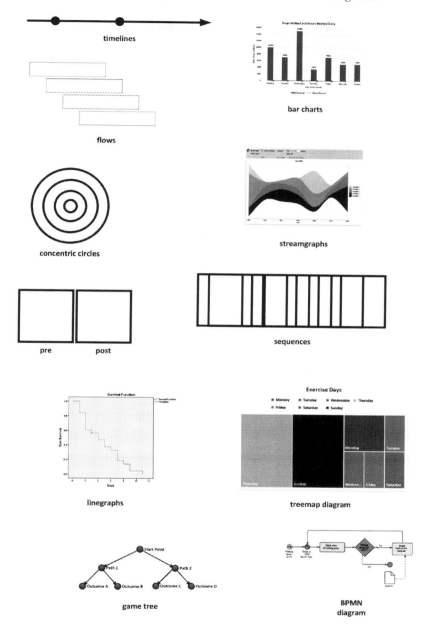

Simplified Elements of Some Common Time-Based Diagrams

- If time is mixed with other dimensions (like space or funding or technologies), how well are the other dimensions depicted? How clear are they?

The Informing Data

- Where does the underlying data come from for the time-based visuals? How confident can learners be of the underlying data? How valid are the imagination-based time-based visuals? What has been left out, and is that "silence" appropriate?

The Interpretive Lens

- What theoretical model or framework of point-of-view informed the time-based visual? What was the learning context of the time-based phenomena?
- How are start and end times understood and defined? What is left off of the time aspect?
- How were time patterns extracted?
- How were cause-and-effect relationships understood?
- How were critical time periods (if any) identified? How were events (if any) identified?
- Is the learning purpose of the time-based visual defined within the visual? Around the visual? Is the learning purpose clear to a majority of the target learners / users?
- Is the authorship of the time-based visual clear? And if not, is the author at least identifiable through reasonable online search? (Or is the timeline depicted as created by an omniscient narrator with an all-knowing mind?)

Types of Time-Based Visuals

- What are the optimal types of time-based visuals for the particular data? Which are most practical to use for the particular instructional design context? What are the pros and cons related to using particular time-based visuals? What are the tradeoffs?
    - What sorts of information is needed? What sort of artwork is needed?
- Does the format of the time-based visuals result in constraints to what may be expressed about time and the depicted phenomena and egos/entities? How may those be accommodated for?

Clarity and Coherence

- In static visuals, are all elements accurately and clearly labeled (words, symbols, numbers, text; legends; pullouts; leadup and lead away text) ? Are pullouts included to indicate where users should focus? Are the proper time measures used, and are they consistently applied? Is the context for the time-based visual clear? Are visual conventions generally followed? Does the visual design drive human attention to the correct parts?
- In dynamic visuals, are all elements clearly labeled (words, symbols, numbers, text; legends; pullouts; leadup and lead away text)? Are pullouts included to indicate where users should focus? Is the context for the time-based visual clear? Does the visual design drive human attention to the correct parts? Are the transitions informative? Are the changes over time clear? Are visual conventions generally followed? Is it clear how much time has transpired between states of equilibrium?
- In interactive visuals, re all elements clearly labeled (words, symbols, numbers, text; legends; pullouts; leadup and lead away text)? Are pullouts included to indicate where users should focus? Is the context for the time-based visual clear? Are the transitions informative? Are the changes over time clear? Does the visual design drive human attention to the correct parts? Are visual conventions generally followed? Is it clear how much time has transpired between states of equilibrium? Are there meaningful ways to engage with the time-based elements? Are there ways to coherently ask questions and discover answers? Are there ways to discover new insights through interacting with the visuals?
- If there are scripted actions for an interactive time-based visual, is the programming appropriate?
- In the time-based visuals, are there sufficient controls against misinterpretation and misunderstandings? Is it clear what has been left out? Is the informational data- or inspiration-sourcing clear?

Cultural Neutrality, Cultural Bridging

- If cross-cultural elements come to the fore of the time-based visuals, are there ways to be inclusive of users from different cultures? Are there ways to introduce more cultural neutrality? Are there ways to filter information based on cultural preferences?

Receptivity of Target Learners and Users

- Beyond the local troubleshooting of the time-based visuals, it may be beneficial to bring in people who represent target learners to better understand how they respond to the visuals and then to revise accordingly.

In addition to the quality considerations above, how a time-based visualization fits with the other learning resources used in the learning context would be important. Such objects also need to be able to stand alone, in a disaggregated way from the original learning contexts, because of how people use online learning resources by separating out pieces and sharing those. Online learners may spawn new and unintended uses of particular learning resources by sharing them broadly. The automated nature of search also enables objects to be disaggregated from the original context and treated as a separate entity in itself. All to say that the design of time-based visuals is not a non-thinking endeavor with equifinality (everything ending in only one type of representation).

FUTURE RESEARCH DIRECTIONS

The point of using time-based visuals in a learning context is achieve the following:

- introduce particular phenomenon (or related phenomena)
- indicate time patterns in in-world phenomena
- enhance human pattern recognition of complex phenomena
- improve human capabilities at analysis of time-based events
- advance decision making in complex environments
- enable some level of projection into the future, and so on.

What is most effective will depend on the learning domain, the focus of the learning, target learner backgrounds, and other factors. This research can be advanced by research based understandings of ways to improve such depictions in case-by-case bases and in generalizable ways. In the instructional design context, this work is under-studied. This work has offered only some preliminary approaches to improving time-based visuals, and follow-on works would contribute to this space.

It would be helpful to know what some of the more difficult challenges of depicting time in visuals may be. Some design elements of time-based visuals may muddy understandings and occlude insights, so those should be observed as well. Some visuals may mislead users as to predictivity, and those insights would also be of value.

CONCLUSION

The focal representation of time in informative visuals is important for (visual) learning. Their criticality suggests the importance of designing these coherently for proper messaging and interpretive depth.

REFERENCES

Aigner, W., Miksch, S., Schumann, H., & Tominski, C. (2011). Survey of visualization techniques. In *Visualization of Time-Oriented Data* (pp. 147–254). London: Springer. doi:10.1007/978-0-85729-079-3_7

Biswas, A., Sagar, B. V., & Srinivasan, J. (2008). Managing and correlating historical events using an event timeline datatype. LNCS, 4947, 604 – 612. doi:10.1007/978-3-540-78568-2_52

Clarke, J. H. (1991, April). Using visual organizers to focus on thinking. *Journal of Reading*, *34*(7), 526–534.

Heer, J., & Schneiderman, B. (2012). A taxonomy of tools that support the fluent and flexible use of visualizations. *ACM Queue; Tomorrow's Computing Today*, 1–26.

Hosmer, D. W., Lemeshow, S., & May, S. (2008). *Applied Survival Analysis: Regression Modeling of Time-to-Event Data* (2nd ed.). Hoboken, NJ: Wiley-Interscience. doi:10.1002/9780470258019

Meacham, J. (2018). *The Soul of America: The Battle for Our Better Angels*. New York: Random House.

Merrill, M. D. (2002, August). A Pebble-in-the-Pond Model for instructional design. *Performance Improvement*, *41*(7), 41–46. doi:10.1002/pfi.4140410709

O'Bannon, B., Puckett, K., & Rakes, G. (2006). Using technology to support visual learning strategies. *Computers in the Schools: Interdisciplinary Journal of Practice, theory, and Applied Research*, *23*(1-2), 125 – 137. doi:10.1300/J025v23n01_11

Time Perception. (2018, Dec. 9). In *Wikipedia*. Retrieved from https://en.wikipedia.org/wiki/Time_perception

Timeline. (2018, Dec. 7). In *Wikipedia*. Retrieved from https://en.wikipedia.org/wiki/Timeline

Yakura, E. K. (2002, October). Charting time: Timelines as temporal boundary objects. *Academy of Management Journal, 45*(5), 956–970. Retrieved from http://www.jstor.org/stable/3069324

KEY TERMS AND DEFINITIONS

2D Diagram: A figure involving two dimensions, on the x and y axes, on a flat plane.

3D Diagram: A figure involving three dimensions, on the x, y, and z axes, in three-dimensional space (with depth).

4D Diagram: A figure involving four dimensions, on the x, y, and z axes, and with changes over time (time as the fourth dimension).

Game Tree: A node-link diagram depicting various potential outcomes.

Monotemporal: A singular (objective) sense of standardized time.

Pluritemporal: A multiple subjective sense of subjective time.

Spatiality: Shape, size, and other space-based attributes.

Timeline: A depiction of time along the x-axis (may be linear or recursive or circular time).

Visual Transitions: The showing of changes over time (various "states") in a dynamic process, such as in slideshows, simulations, video, and other contexts.

Chapter 8
Defining Salient Features of "Boutique" Instructional Designs and Implications for Design, Development, and Deployment

Shalin Hai-Jew
https://orcid.org/0000-0002-8863-0175
Kansas State University, USA

ABSTRACT

"Boutique" instructional design (ID) projects are fairly common across verticals, especially in higher education, open shared learning, government, and some commercial enterprises. In general, boutique-designed learning is small-scale, with narrowly targeted learners, limited development funding/access to information/ development and deployment technology/human resources, and other aspects. The strategies and tactics for successful boutique projects differ in some ways than those used for mid-scale and full-scale/general ID projects. This work explores some of the dimensions of boutique ID projects and the implications of those dimensions on design, development, and deployment strategies and tactics. This work is informed by decades in the profession, a review of the literature, and analyses of related open-source and closed-source online learning objects.

DOI: 10.4018/978-1-5225-9833-6.ch008

INTRODUCTION

Boutique instructional design projects are of a particular but fairly common kind. To understand the background meanings of this term, it may help to first explore what a "boutique" is without any tie to instructional design.

Boutiques, in the real physical and online, are specialty shops that are organized around particular themes, brands, shopper experiences, services, and select products. Here, the personality of the shopkeeper or the brand (corporate or local) is important. A major selling point is that the shopping experience is one-of-a-kind and unavailable elsewhere. Boutique collections are tailored, selected, and curated, for particular aesthetics or other purposes, by a masterful hand. In general parlance, a "boutique" refers to a specialty store dealing in stylish luxury goods, with elite patronage; boutiques traffic in high cost products, typically clothing ("Boutique," June 13, 2019). A direct one-degree article-article network on Wikipedia, based on the "boutique" article page, the crowd-sourced encyclopedia, shows a variety of evocations at present, with fine art, clothing brands, shop brands, services, and other references (Figure 1).

Figure 1. "Boutique" article-article network on Wikipedia (1 deg.)

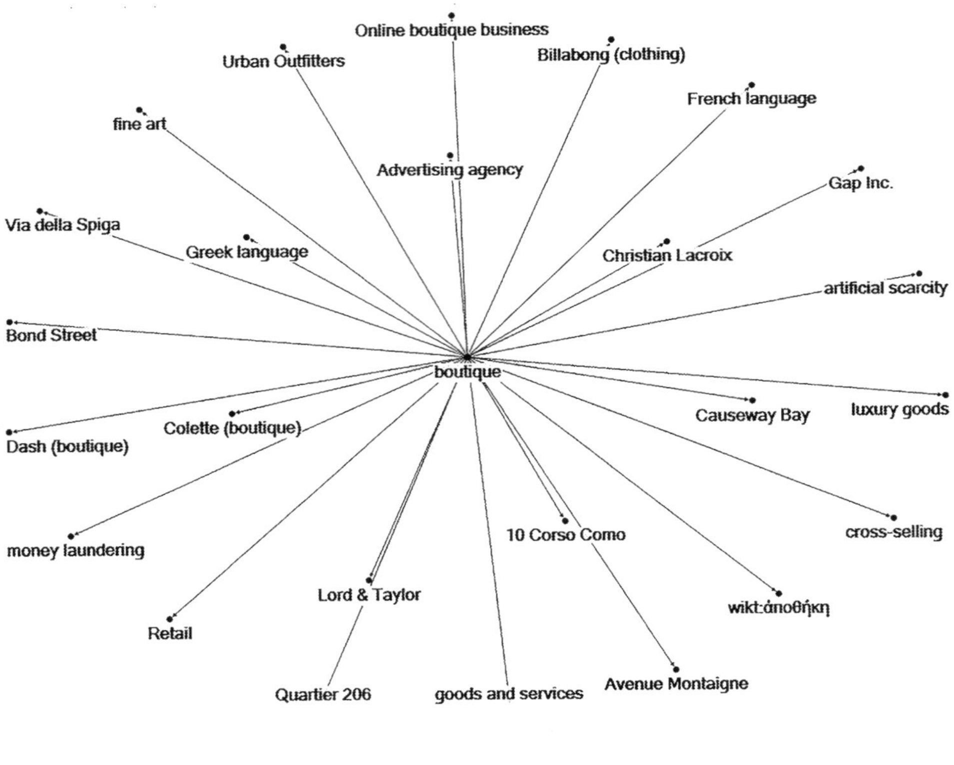

Defining Salient Features of "Boutique" Instructional Designs

In a direct one-degree related tags network on the Flickr social image-sharing site, based around "boutique," there are references to "handmade" products and social crowd-sale sales sites like Etsy (Figure 2). The global city references show something of the penetration of these practices in the world. Beyond clothes, there are references to art, gifts, baby products, and makeup.

This all begs the question of what "boutique" instructional design projects refer to, both formally and informally. Are boutique projects more or less expensive than non-boutique "big box" projects? Are boutique projects more stylish and stylized? Do they show a unique hand in the styling? Where are boutique projects most common (In terms of verticals? In terms of organizations?)? What are the implications of boutique-ness on instructional design, development, and deployment? This work explores these questions based on a review of the literature and decades in the instructional design field, in both public and private sectors.

Figure 2. "Boutique" related tags network on Flickr (1 deg.)

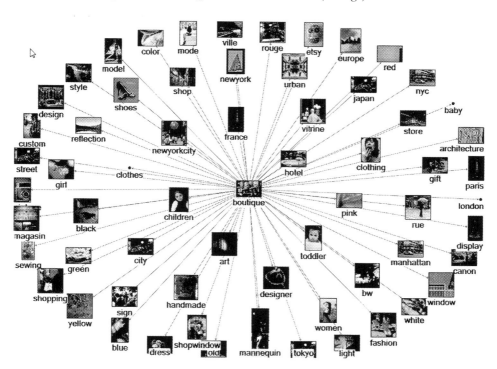

REVIEW OF THE LITERATURE

One of the earliest references to "boutique" in relation to distance education is of a business strategy, among several: 1) the distance education superstore; 2) the distance education chain store; 3) the distance education boutique; 4) the distance education cooperative; 5) corporate alliances; and 6) the distance education consultancy. (Moore, 1999, p. 1) The author elaborates:

In the distance learning boutique, teachers have to work on a wide range of tasks, tasks that in superstores and specialty stores are the work of specialists. These teachers must learn the many skills needed to design and produce distance learning materials, as well as manage interaction with learners as they work with those materials. This is more and different work than in conventional class teaching. At best, teachers have to be trained, paid, and administered differently than in their traditional teaching roles. At worst, in an effort to compete, institutions may put pressure on their labor—the faculty—to work longer hours and accept lower compensation. In other words, in time, boutiques may turn into sweatshops! (Moore, 1999, p. 3)

In higher education boutiques contexts, the subject matter experts (SMEs) or content experts do their own design, development, and deployment, potentially with some one-on-one support (Madden, 2016, p. 270) from instructional designers and digital content developers. Bates (2004) explains:

Hartman and Truman-Davis (2001) describe the boutique approach to e-learning course development. A teacher approaches an instructional support unit for professional assistance on an individual, one-to-one basis from an instructional designer or technology support person...However, the model starts to become unsustainable as demand increases because of the resources needed. It causes particular difficulties for the instructional support unit or person, as there is no obvious way to determine priorities between multiple requests for help, and there is no boundary around the support commitment. Furthermore, because the teacher usually initiates the process, the wrong kind of assistance may be requested. For instance, the request may be limited to purely technical assistance, when what may be required is a different approach to course design for the technology to be used effectively. Nevertheless, the boutique model can be useful in helping individual teachers to get started in using technology in a systematic and professional way. (Bates, 2004, pp. 285 - 286)

"Boutique instructional design" refers to one-on-one or customized support to SMEs, often based on the sense of needs as negotiated between the SME and the service provider. "Boutique course development" is described as a context in which "a professor works together with an instructional designer or technology support person (in) a one-on-one basis" (Rapanta, July 2011, p. 54). Boutique-level service is conceptualized as high level and supportive and unique (Shea, Fredericksen, Pickett, & Pelz, 2004, p. 350). A "boutique or craft" approach to creating learning is considered somewhat risky in terms of quality, with "faculty…working in isolation and without commonly shared tools" (Hartman, Dziuban, & Moskal, 2000, p. 157). Content experts may be experts in their respective fields but have no training on adult learning, instructional design, learner assessment, or multimedia design for learning, among others.

Moore (1999) suggests that the boutique strategy may not be sustainable because it has to capitalize on its name to be able to "charge prices comparable to those of the superstore and specialty store" (p. 4). It has to meet the quality of the learning product in a competitive environment but is at a disadvantage "since the boutiques and mom-and-pop stores do not have the technical systems, division of labor, or large investment sums available to their competitors" (Moore, 1999, p. 4). In challenging budget environments, universities developing resources with limited fee-for-service may work for "boutique course development" but not for the "large-scale course improvement model" (Barac, Davies, Duffy, Aitkin, & Lodge, Dec. 2013, pp. 77 – 78). Post-graduate courses are boutique ones in some cases because of the specialized focuses (Bright, 2012), with various pre-requisite learning. If higher education exists as a pipeline, with people dropping out at each stage, those who have survived into the present phase are fewer. "Boutique" has also been applied to some types of undergraduate research that has limited focus on "the most gifted or persistent students" and less so on "the wider student body" (Rowland, et al., Dec. 2014, p. 16). Boutique courses are associated with low enrollment (Andrade & Alden-Rivers, 2019, p. 13). The focus on such courses is about "a rich learning experience" foremost and "secondly on scaling the process" (Duffy & Kirkley, 2004, p. 18). Beyond dedicated purposes, "boutique education" may be adaptive to particular learners by taking "the characteristics of diverse learners into account" (Evans, 1992, as cited in Koçdar & Özdamar, 2010, p. 82). In terms of assessing for learning outcomes, "boutique models" may be applied course-by-course, but these approaches may be difficult to implement "despite being more accurate" (Gašević, Dawson, Rogers, & Gašević, 2016, p. 83). For learners, boutique "integrated semester" learning experiences are thought to enable the transfer of professors' passions for cohort learning experiences and small group learning (Slostad, Baloche, & Darigan, 2004, p. 139).

The "boutique" approach may be applied to massive open online courses (MOOCs), which are often open-source and supported by teaching assistants and artificial intelligence. A "boutique" massive open online course (MOOC) is a small one as compared to large-scale ones (Salmon, Pechenkina, Chase, & Ross, 2017, p. 1287). Open online courses have also been built on boutique models (known as "boutique open online courses" or BOOCs) for specialized small-scale learning and training (Hickey, 2013; Tattersall, 2013, as cited in Hood & Littlejohn, 2016, p. 5), which are open to the broad public but of specificity and requirements which enable usage by only a few.

Boutique Programs

In this space, "boutique" programs are those that are supported by "extra researchers and staff that have struggled to persist beyond researcher involvement" due to "a lack of available hardware and school policies…" (Martin, Dikkers, Squire, & Gagnon, Jan./Feb. 2014, p. 36). In one case, the work thrives only with the support of the original faculty and does not appear to have institutional buy-in which might ensure its longer term survival. Boutique courses do not result in "the large-scale dissemination and long-term sustainability necessary for truly bringing about educational change" (Barab & Luehmann, 2003, pp. 11 – 12).

Another team has observed that boutique programs have to "be worthy of continued investments over time" and to be sustainable once the resources are spent; they have to be adaptable in the local context (McLaughlin & Mitra, 2001, as cited in Whitcomb, Borko, & Liston, May/June 2009, p. 11). In alignment with the prior, "boutique projects" have been referred to as "showcase" ones that "were good for researcher vitas but did not have any wide-scale impact" (Barab, May-June 2004, p. 18; Barab & Squire, 2004, p. 12). Some boutique projects are vanity ones, good for professional self-promotion but not much else. Said another way, administrators and designer/developers require the ability to move from "boutique to big box" (Van Acker, 2013) and potentially the other way as well. In some other usages in the academic literature, "boutique" programming is isolated and disconnected and low-impact, with "little impact to the institution as a whole" (Gardner, 2019, p. 48). For sustainability, small "boutique" programs benefit from inter-institutional collaboration (Tynan, Dunne, & Smyth, 2007, as cited in Stewart & Davis, 2012, p. 496).

"Boutique studies" are labeled as those "which produce much excitement and knowledge about circumstances that defy replication" (Roschelle & Jackiw, Oct. 3, 1997, p. 3). In many senses, boutique approaches are seen as "isolates," without connectivity to other contexts.

Boutique Schools and Boutique Niches

"Boutique" is also used to describe specialty schools, such as those "that prioritize developing leaders (schools with an emphasis on civic engagement, early college high schools, STEM schools, some charter models), or frankly, public schools with enough parent demand and funding to make communication offerings a priority" (Hess, Taft, Bodary, Beebe, & Valenzano, 2015, p. 248). These do not provide general full-range all-purpose education, and the focus is on selectivity, focus, emphasis, and limits. There are "boutique" universities with singular or a few specializations only (Yahya, Hamzah, Mothar, & Dimyati, 2018, p. 4). Within universities, there are "boutique market niches" with learners developing various expectations through word of mouth (Church, 2009, p. 6).

Boutique Learning Development Conditions

"Boutique" may refer to development conditions. In higher education, this is where the SME may consult with instructional designers and developers in their work for the "boutique approach" which is "difficult to scale up for enterprise-wide delivery of services" (Hartman & Truman-Davis, 2001, p. 48). On campuses where the instructional design service is based on a rate card, the cost alone will mean that a wide swath of the campus has no access to the service. On a by-request model, though, a number of faculty and staff will make inordinate demands and outsized requests. One work points to "boutique and freelance designers, who work within time and budget limitations" (Karmokar, Singh, & Tan, Sept. 2016, p. 36).

If a boutique experience means that the client may have more customized attention, on the provider-side, designer/developers have the ability to select the projects that they will take on (Galagan, Salopek, & Barron, May 1999). Decisions can be made on a project-by-project basis, *ceteris paribus*. Another work described a locally created course built *without* instructional design support by the SME as a "boutique product" (Nation & Walker, 1992, p. 134). Boutique courses can be *ad hoc* products by SMEs (and non-SMEs) given the ease-of-use of many authoring tools. Boutique ID enterprises can focus on particular topics or curriculum or learner age groups. They can engage in divergent thinking and creativity. They can take on complex but limited jobs and design and build from scratch, or they can inherit projects and retrofit learning resources and build on what already exists. They can run custom shops.

"Boutique" has been applied to technologies as well. One research team has observed "the ongoing boutique approach to software development...at the heart of e-learning" in reference to the advances in "web-based technologies...digital storage; processing and media" (Koohang & Harman, 2005, p. 76). The confluence of those advances enable modern electronic learning. "Boutique software development" refers to smaller companies that focus on "the mid-market sector and small business companies" and offer custom coding to clients along with close-in support (Laptick, May 30, 2018). Also, learning management systems offer "boutique" versions as "LMS lite" versions (Bozarth, 2005, p. 20). The difference has to do with scale and purpose. In a research context, the boutique problem refers to the study of "only highly promising—and often unusual—programs" being the focus of study (Lynch, Hill, Gonzalez, & Pollard, 2019, p. 11), which takes attention away from research work with findings that may be more transferable.

IMPLICATIONS OF "BOUTIQUE" ON INSTRUCTIONAL DESIGN, DEVELOPMENT, AND DEPLOYMENT

So based on the descriptions of boutique designs and informed by decades in the teaching field, Table 1 offers some resource-based contrasts between boutique, mid-scale, and full-scale instructional design projects.

While Table 1 shows some of the contrasts between the boutique or specialty instructional design projects, mid-scale instructional design projects, and full-scale / general instructional design projects, these are general points of contrast based on resourcing (technological, informational, human resources, budgeting, etc.) and targeting and objectives. These are generalizations, which have their limits. Certainly, there are ways to push out the curve in terms of what is available to a boutique ID project team, such as partnerships, negotiated access to resources, and other approaches.

It can be difficult to generalize further about these three categorizing approaches. All three types may have a mix of co-located team members and physically distributed ones. Larger teams tend to use stylebooks, but boutique teams may as well. Any of the teams may use formalized approaches to the development work and have sequences of riffing or improvisation. A boutique work may start small and scale up (think Khan Academy), or it may start big and spin-off boutique pieces (think various Lynda.com trainings with open-source video snippets which are broadly available).

Also, practitioners in this space may express their personality and aesthetics more originally and powerfully. They may place their imprimatur on their work, and they may sometimes even apply their byline to it. There may be more space for collaborative exploration and expression of learning designs, in coordination with the client. The efficacy of the work may be measured in different ways than for large-scale projects (which use various types of learning analytics). Perhaps eye-catching set pieces may be designed for the custom learning developments, to make the learning experiences memorable.

Defining Salient Features of "Boutique" Instructional Designs

Table 1. Instructional design project scale and type and implications on design, development, and deployment

	Boutique / Specialty* Instructional Design Project(s)	Mid-Scale Instructional Design Project(s)	Full-Scale / General Instructional Design Project(s)
Design	• Have limited technological options (often through perennial licensure) • Have select access to informational content, including open-source content • Have limited internal and external feedback on the design • May have some localized templates • Based on legal requirements and standards • Informed by specific client requirements • Targeted to a thin-slice of learners (in the long tail)	• Have some technological options (through potentially both perennial licensure and subscription access) • Have access to informational content, both commercial and open-source • Have internal and external feedback on the design (beta testing), including professional • May have localized and professional templates • Based on legal requirements and standards • Informed by grant funder requirements • Targeted to a broad population of learners (in the middle of a normal curve, out two standard deviations)	• Have a wide range of technological options (often through subscription) • Have access to a wide range of informational content resources for research (commercial and open-source) • Have access to team feedback on the design; have access to external feedback on the design (beta testing); have access to professional feedback on the design • Have formalized structures and templates for the design • Based on legal requirements and standards • Informed by grant funder requirements • Targeted to a broad population of learners (in the middle of a normal curve, out two standard deviations)
Development	• Have some technological options for development • Have access to some of informational content resources for development • Have the capability to develop original contents • Generally lack a budget for specialty development (like animations, like games, like case studies, and others) • Have access to team feedback on development; have access to external feedback on development • May have access to user testing data on the draft developed resources • May have specialized technologies for learner analytics • Have formalized structures and templates for the development (**Note**: Access to technologies depends in part on their democratization, which suggests a broader range of usage, even for boutique instructional design projects. Some free accesses are for some limited usage, however.)	• Have some technological options for development • Have access to some informational content resources for development • Have the capability to develop original contents • May have a budget for specialty development (like animations, like games, like case studies, and others) • Have access to team feedback on development; have access to external feedback on development • May have access to user testing data on the draft developed resources • May have access to some specialized technologies (or services) for learner analytics • Have formalized structures and templates for the development	• Have a wide range of technological options for development • Have access to a wide range of informational content resources for development • Have the capability to develop original contents • Have a budget for specialty development (like animations, like games, like case studies, and others) • Have access to team feedback on development; have access to external feedback on development • Have access to user testing data on the draft developed resources • Have specialized technologies (or services) for learner analytics • Have formalized structures and templates for the development

continued on following page

In learning designs, "set pieces" are attention-getting and memorable aspects of a learning sequence (or course), with core learning value. Often, they are the focal points of a course. They add to the allure of taking a particular course. For example, this is the first course that…combines various interdisciplinary subjects… uses particular technologies…enables learners to meet with talent scouts…enables

Table 1. Continued

	Boutique / Specialty* Instructional Design Project(s)	Mid-Scale Instructional Design Project(s)	Full-Scale / General Instructional Design Project(s)
Deployment	• Have open-source or free or low-cost technologies for deployment • May or may not have access to user data (beyond frequency counts of the user accesses) • May / may not revise or update the learning contents • May / may not harness higher-tech like artificial intelligence and data analytics • May or may not generalize to a larger population of learners • May be relevant for a limited time to a limited audience	• Have a combination of open-source or free or low-cost technologies and formalized commercial technologies for deployment • May have some data collection on the usage of the learning resource (and other relevant information like learner data) • May / may not revise or update the learning contents • May harness higher-tech like artificial intelligence and data analytics • May or may not generalize to a larger population of learners • May be relevant for a period of time to a mixed audience	• Have formalized commercial technologies for deployment (with high control) • Have data collection on the usage of the learning resource (and other relevant information, like learner data) • May revise or update the learning contents • May harness higher-tech like artificial intelligence and data analytics • May or may not generalize to a larger population of learners • May be relevant for a period of extended time to a mixed audience

application for internships…enables world travel for project-based learning… The features are attractive and enable talking points (and publicity outreaches) about the formal learning to potential learners. The idea is to differentiate the boutique course based on particular set pieces.

Set pieces instantiate in different ways. They may be full sensory and interactive simulations, embedded serious games, culminating field trips, portfolios, collaborations, research work, interactions with in-field celebrities (or charismatic individuals), or some combination that is unique. Set pieces may integrate with other aspects of the learning, or they may be self-contained and stand-alone. Some set pieces may be co-created with learners. Others may be informed by professionals, such as those in-field who may evaluate learner projects and portfolios. Some may be the "hard fun" of learning competitions, design projects, development projects, and difficult challenges (something very lightly akin to "hell week" in the mainstream media sense of Navy SEAL training). There may be serendipity or chance elements at play, such as simulations informed by fast-moving real-world events. In some cases, style may come to the fore, with different atmospherics.

To be effective, learning set pieces need to be sufficiently substantive to get past the so-called "hype cycle" and through the "peak of inflated expectations, trough of disillusionment, slope of enlightenment" to the "plateau of productivity." In other words, it has to maintain the positive word of mouth while also enabling relevant learning. As yet, no taxonomy of online learning set pieces is available. A learning sequence may contain one or more set pieces, but these are generally thought to be few. And many learning sequences have no set pieces. (In accredited learning in higher education, the required or mandatory courses that have defined learners may have less incentive to create set pieces, which require some costly or effortful

Defining Salient Features of "Boutique" Instructional Designs

inputs. Required learning sequences tend to be more formulaic, in part because of the integration of the respective learning pieces into a coherent learning program. Many are based on textbooks or textbook series with pre-created contents, which further constrain the studies. Also, basic learning sequences have so many objectives to address that there may not be sufficient space for excessive innovation. Electives, whose survival requires attracting learners, may be more common candidates for the building of set pieces in the learning.)

DISCUSSION

What do these observations mean for the actual boutique instructional design work?

Design

1. Because of the limitations of resources, the instructional designer/developer (ID/D) needs to ascertain and understand the client vision for the project and the deliverables.
2. There should be early work in assessing what is already available in open shared learning resources, so wheels are not reinvented (unless the ID/D or team can do better).
    a. Reviewing what is available in the world may help the client better understand what is or is not possible.
3. The ID/D needs a clear sense of who the target learners are, the learning objectives, the learning outcomes, the technologies (and their desirable functionalities), and other aspects.
4. If a set piece or multiple set pieces are included, these should be designed with anticipation of learner needs, available resources and technologies, and fit with the overall learning design (whether the set piece is integrated or somewhat stand-alone).
5. The ID/D needs to understand the maintenance costs of the learning resources over time. Cost limits are present in every phase of the boutique instructional designs, including oftentimes, well into the future.
6. If there will be a set piece or multiple set pieces, those should be drafted out. Set pieces are attention-getting pieces that showcase the topic in powerful ways. If there are ongoing dependencies for maintenance of the set pieces, those should be considered in the work.
7. All learning contents should be heavily vetted in draft form, prior to development, before any development work is invested. Development work is costly in time and resources, and controlling for revisions will be important.

a. Aesthetic designs should be vetted heavily as well.

Development

8. Draft learning contents should be tested with live learners, to assess usability and user understanding and acceptance.
9. The learning contents should be revised based in part on the pilot testing in the prior step.
10. All digital and other contents should be kept in raw form (a pristine master set) to enable the widest flexibility (and the least digital obsolescence over time) in terms of development.
11. Accurate records should be kept of all learning resources in order to enable flexibility in future usage of the digital resources.
12. Original learning contents should be protected by copyright protections, technological protections, and others.

Deployment

13. During deployment of the learning resources, it would help to set up some learner assessment features to understand the efficacy of the teaching and learning.
14. Then, the observations of the learning efficacy may be applied to redesign, retrofitting, and redevelopment, as needed.

Boutique instructional design projects are common across verticals based on particular learner needs, particularly in the adult learning space. They are pervasive in higher education, government, open shared learning (Hai-Jew, 2019), and commercial enterprises. How these instantiate depends on the context, the clientele, the target learners, the target learning, the target skills, the learning objectives and related learning outcomes, the harnessed technologies, and others.

FUTURE RESEARCH DIRECTIONS

This is an early work on boutique instructional designs and their possible implications on design, development, and deployment. Future research may add to the number of implications for design, development, and deployment. There is room for case-based research on various "boutique" endeavors in the academic space: course development, MOOC / BOOC development, research work, boutique projects, and others. The lessons from those works may be unique to the context; others may be transferable.

CONCLUSION

This work explored "boutique" instructional designs and "boutique" applications in academia, with both positive and negative implications. This offered some general implications of how boutique-ness may affect the instructional design work on three phases: design, development, and deployment.

REFERENCES

Andrade, M. S., & Alden-Rivers, B. (2019). Developing a framework for sustainable growth of flexible learning opportunities. *Higher Education Pedagogies, 4*(1), 1–16. doi:10.1080/23752696.2018.1564879

Barab, S., & Squire, K. (2004). Introduction: Design-based research: Putting a stake in the ground. *Journal of the Learning Sciences, 13*(1), 1–14. doi:10.120715327809jls1301_1

Barab, S. A. (2004, May-June). Using design to advance learning theory, or using learning theory to advance design. *Educational Technology*, 16–20.

Barab, S. A., & Luehmann, A. L. (2003). Building sustainable science curriculum: Acknowledging and accommodating local adaptation. *Science Education, 87*(4), 454–467. doi:10.1002ce.10083

Barac, K., Davies, L., Duffy, S., Aitkin, N., & Lodge, J. (2013). Five stages of online course design: Taking the grief out of converting courses for online delivery. In *ASCILITE-Australian Society for Computers in Learning in Tertiary Education Annual Conference* (pp. 77-81). Australasian Society for Computers in Learning in Tertiary Education.

Bates, T. (2004). The promise and the myths of e-learning in post-secondary education. In *The Network Society: A Cross-cultural Perspective* (pp. 271–292). Cheltenham, UK: Edward Elgar Publishing Limited. doi:10.4337/9781845421663.00025

Boutique. (2019, June 13). In *Wikipedia*. Retrieved June 27, 2019, from https://en.wikipedia.org/wiki/Boutique

Bozarth, J. (2005). Shoestring E-learning. *Training-New York Then Minneapolis Then New York, 42*(9), 20–24.

Bright, S. (2012). *eLearning lecturer workload: working smarter or working harder?* Academic Press.

Church, J. T. (2009). Quality matters: Making commodities and manufacturing knowledge in the virtual university. *Enhancing Learning in the Social Sciences*, *1*(3), 1–14. doi:10.11120/elss.2009.01030003

Duffy, T. M., & Kirkley, J. (2004). *Designing Environments for Distributed Learning: Learning theory and practice*. Mahwah, NJ: Lawrence Erlbaum and Associates.

Galagan, P. A., Salopek, J. J., & Barron, T. (1999, May). Training's new guard: Here's a look at who's doing it differently. *Training & Development*, *53*(5), 27–36.

Gardner, D. (2019). Beyond the four levels: An evaluation model for growth and sustainability. Wayne State University.

Gašević, D., Dawson, S., Rogers, T., & Gasevic, D. (2016). Learning analytics should not promote one size fits all: The effects of instructional conditions in predicting academic success. *The Internet and Higher Education*, *28*, 68–84. doi:10.1016/j.iheduc.2015.10.002

Hai-Jew, S. (2019). *Designing Instruction for Open Sharing*. Springer Nature. doi:10.1007/978-3-030-02713-1

Hartman, J., Dziuban, C., & Moskal, P. (2000). Faculty satisfaction in ALNs: A dependent or independent variable. *Journal of Asynchronous Learning Networks*, *4*(3), 155–179.

Hartman, J. L., & Truman-Davis, B. (2001). Institutionalizing support for faculty use of technology at the University of Central Florida. *Teaching faculty how to use technology: Best practices from leading institutions*, 39-58.

Hess, J. A., Taft, B., Bodary, S. R., Beebe, S. A., & Valenzano, J. M. III. (2015). Forum: The common core. *Communication Education*, *64*(2), 241–260. doi:10.1080/03634523.2015.1014387

Hood, N., & Littlejohn, A. (2016). *Quality in MOOCs: Surveying the terrain*. Commonwealth of Learning.

Karmokar, S., Singh, H., & Tan, F. B. (2016, September). Using multidisciplinary design principles to improve the website design process. *Pacific Asia Journal of the Association for Information Systems*, *8*(3), 17–44. doi:10.17705/1pais.08302

Koçdar, S., & Özdamar, N. (2010). The Nature of Learning Theories and Their Effects on Distance Education Practices in Turkey. Educational Structures in Context: At the Interfaces of Higher Education, 77 - 91.

Koohang, A., & Harman, K. (2005). Open source: A metaphor for e-learning. *Informing Science Journal, 8*, 75–86. doi:10.28945/488

Laptick, S. (2018, May 30). What is a boutique software development company, and what are some examples? *Quora*. Retrieved June 26, 2019, from https://www.quora.com/What-is-a-boutique-software-development-company-and-what-are-some-examples?awc=15748_1561580967_474ff323dc4807%E2%80%A6

Lynch, K., Hill, H. C., Gonzalez, K., & Pollard, C. (2019, Mar.). *Strengthening the research base that informs STEM instructional improvement efforts: A meta-analysis.* Brown University Working Paper.

Madden, M. E. (2016). Planning for distance learning: Issues and strategies. *Journal of Behavioral and Applied Management, 4*(3), 255–286.

Martin, J., Dikkers, S., Squire, K., & Gagnon, D. (2014, January/February). Participatory scaling through augmented reality learning through local games. *TechTrends, 58*(1), 35–41. doi:10.100711528-013-0718-1

Moore, M. G. (1999). Editorial: Institutional restructuring: Is distance education like retailing?! *American Journal of Distance Education, 13*(1), 1–7. doi:10.1080/08923649909527010

Nation, D., & Walker, R. (1993). Course development without instructional design. In D. O. Courses (pp. 119–149). Centre for Distance Learning, Monash University.

Rapanta, C. (2011, July). *Communication processes in e-learning design and development: An interaction analysis approach* (Dissertation). Faculty of Communication Sciences Universrsità della Svizzera italiana.

Roschelle, J., & Jackiw, N. (1997, Oct. 3In press). Technology design as educational research: Interweaving imagination, inquiry, and impact. In A. Kelly & R. Lesh (Eds.), *Research Design in Mathematics & Science Education*. Amsterdam: Kleuwer.

Rowland, S., Green, M., Lawrie, G., Myatt, P., Pedwell, R., Wang, J., ... Zimbardi, K. (2014, December). The ALLURE of massified undergraduate research. Showcase on Education. *Australian Biochemist, 45*(3), 15–19.

Salmon, G., Pechenkina, E., Chase, A.-M., & Ross, B. (2017). Designing Massive Open Online Courses to take account of participant motivations and expectations. *British Journal of Educational Technology, 48*(6), 1284–1294. doi:10.1111/bjet.12497

Shea, P. J., Fredericksen, E. E., Pickett, A. M., & Pelz, W. E. (2004). Faculty development, student satisfaction, and reported learning in the SUNY learning network. *Learner-Centered Theory And Practice In Distance Education: Cases From Higher Education,* 343-377.

Slostad, F., Baloche, L., & Darigan, D. (2004). The integrated semester: Building preservice teachers' commitments to the use of cooperative learning as essential pedagogy. In E. G. Cohen, C. M. Brody, & M. Sapon-Shevin (Eds.), *Teaching Cooperative Learning: The Challenge for Teacher Education. State University of New York Press.*

Stewart, S., & Davis, D. (2012). On the JUVE or in decline: Reflecting on the sustainability of the Virtual Birth Centre developed in *Second Life. Australasian Journal of Educational Technology, 28*(3), 480–503. doi:10.14742/ajet.846

Van Acker, T. A. (2013). From Boutique to big box: A case study concerning teacher change transitioning to a public Montessori elementary school. The University of North Carolina at Greensboro.

Whitcomb, J., Borko, H., & Liston, D. (2009, May/June). Growing talent: Promising professional development models and practices. *Journal of Teacher Education, 60*(1), 207–212. doi:10.1177/0022487109337280

Yahya, A. H., Hamzah, M., Mothar, M., & Dimyati, N. I. (2018, June 1–2). Predicting the future of MOOCs implementation in redesigning higher education of a mega university. In *Proceedings of the International Scientific Conference Blue Economy and Blue Growth.* Burgas, Bulgaria: Burgas Free University.

ADDITIONAL READING

Hai-Jew, S. (2019). *Designing Instruction for Open Sharing.* Springer Nature. doi:10.1007/978-3-030-02713-1

KEY TERMS AND DEFINITIONS

Boutique: A specialty shop or establishment.
Instructional Design: The purposeful design and creation of learning experiences and related resources.

Section 3
Data for Design

Chapter 9
The Respective Roles of Broad and Deep Research in Instructional Design and Development Work

Shalin Hai-Jew
https://orcid.org/0000-0002-8863-0175
Kansas State University, USA

ABSTRACT

The work of instructional design (ID) requires new content learning, which often requires various types of published or secondary research as well as direct elicitations from the cooperating subject matter experts (SMEs) about the topic. For instructional design projects, both design and development, a range of information is required: who the target learners are; what content knowledge is required (as knowledge, skills, and abilities); what pedagogical designs may be most effective; what technologies will be required for the build; what learning sequences, objects, assignments, and assessments are needed; what legal and technological standards need to be abided by. This work describes research strategies for instructional design, research documentation, research citations, and applying the many acquired research insights to the instructional design and development work.

INTRODUCTION

Typical professional job descriptions for instructional designers may list some of the following features: needs assessment, outlining, writing, learning object

DOI: 10.4018/978-1-5225-9833-6.ch009

development, and teamwork. A critical capability involves the ability to conduct both direct primary and indirect secondary research and analyze the results for application to the work. "Broad" research is generally conceptualized as easily accessible and lightly applied research; it is conducted in a quick and efficient way. "Deep" research involves effortful primary research. Deep research may include access to protected information. Both broad and deep research are applied to the actual instructional design and the related digital learning objects for the project. "Instructional design," defined generally, refers to the systematic work of building learning experiences for effective learning. Some of the informing data and information may be part of ongoing research regimens related to the teaching and learning context. Some of the research, of course, may not apply directly to the work at hand but may be kept in a formal or informal "knowledge base" to inform other work projects. (Figure 1)

This chapter explores some of the required types of research for instructional design projects in higher education (public sector) and in private industry.

REVIEW OF THE LITERATURE

A variety of theories / models / frameworks / research inform the design of instruction. There have been decades of research on how people learn at different life stages, a variety of human intelligences, people's different learning preferences, and different teaching and learning methods. With the advent of online learning, these research studies have been applied to that space as well. Indeed, the research literature has long informed instructional designs (McLoughlin, 1999). There are some understood "givens" on how multimedia may be packaged for learning effects based on human cognition, whether in print or digital formats and "different media environments" (Mayer, 2003, p. 132).

"Design experiments" have enabled the "engineering" of learning, with domain-specific theories informing respective designs in different fields (Cobb, Confrey, diSessa, Lehrer, & Schauble, Jan.-Feb. 2003, p. 9). Some approaches focus on the importance of cultural competence on instructional design in order to better connect with target learners, especially for online learning designed for export (Rogers, Graham, & Mayes, 2007, p. 197). Some research is engaged to assess instructional content prototypes (Tripp & Bichelmeyer, 1990). "Developmental research" in the field of instructional design and development is inclusive of "the study of the process and impact of specific instructional design and developmental efforts; or a situation in which someone is *performing* instructional design, development, or evaluation activities and *studying* the process at the same time; or the study of the instructional design, development, and evaluation process as a whole or of particular process components" (Richey, Klein, & Nelson, 2004, p. 1099). "Design research"

Figure 1. Various applications of research related to instructional design

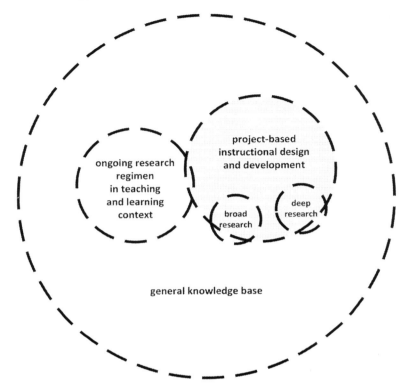

**Various Applications of Research
Related to Instructional Design**

involves harnessing research to inform instructional designs and methods by reflecting "on the process to reveal design principles that can inform other instructors and researchers, and future development projects" (Reeves, Herrington, & Oliver, Spring 2005, pp. 109 – 110). Some research focuses on how to enhance the online learning technologies and ecosystems.

The published research suggests a piecemeal sense of the role of research in the design of instruction. There are some case-based studies related to particular technologies, types of learning, particular learners, and learning contexts. The instructional design challenges range from well-structured problem solving to ill-structured and complex problem solving. In general, the design should be informed by the optimal known-knowns.

So far, the role of research in the applied and direct work of an instructional design project has not been addressed, not from a line developer view, and not in application to the holistic sequence. This chapter looks at how research is a necessary and central part of instructional design and development work.

RESPECTIVE ROLES OF BROAD AND DEEP RESEARCH IN INSTRUCTIONAL DESIGN AND DEVELOPMENT WORK

In the abstract, a short list of content was suggested as important to answer for any particular instructional design and development sequence.

- Who the target learners are
- What content knowledge is required (as knowledge, skills, and abilities)
- What pedagogical designs may be most effective
- What technologies will be required for the build
- What learning sequences, objects, assignments, and assessments are needed
- What legal and technological standards need to be abided by

The sources for the data may stem from secondary research (prior published sources, content analysis, document analysis, and others) as well as primary research (interviews from the subject matter experts, focus groups, interviews, observation research, and others). There are usually some professional standards used to vet the data and to understand their sufficiency. By common practice, there are various ways that the research may be documented and recorded. The research informs informational content inclusion, project-based decision making, technology selection and use, design and development work, and adherence to legal requirements, among others.

It is possible to segment the research content list into either "broad" or "deep" research (Table 1). Broad research tends to be fairly easy to access and applied in a light way; by contrast, deep research tends to be somewhat more effortful, may include protected information, and may require a fair amount of sophistication to analyze and use.

A typical sequence of an instructional design and development project is shown in Figure 2. This is based on the author's decades of work experience in this field as college faculty and as an instructional designer/developer. The sequence begins with project planning, which may occur synchronously with the creation of a work proposal for funding the work. Next is design of instruction, content development, alpha testing (in-house testing of the learning resources to ensure technological functionality and adherence to legal standards, among others), beta testing (user-based testing of the learning contents with members of the public who are standing

The Respective Roles of Broad and Deep Research in Instructional Design and Development Work

Table 1. Required broad and deep research for instructional design and development

	Broad Research	**Deep Research**
Types of Instructional Design and Development Information Required	• Who the target learners are	• What content knowledge is required (as knowledge, skills, and abilities) • What pedagogical designs may be most effective • What technologies will be required for the build • What learning sequences, objects, assignments, and assessments are needed • What legal and technological standards need to be abided by
Some Features of the Respective Research Types	• Is easily accessible • Is applied lightly	• Involves effortful primary research • May include some protected information • May require sophistication to analyze and use
	• Is applied to the actual instructional design • Is applied to the actual digital learning objects	

in for the target learners to understand their receptivity to the learning objects and potential revision needs), technological deployment, public launch, the monitoring of the learning object's usage, and then updates as needed. Sometimes in alignment with assessing the effect of the learning resources, an in-house project post-mortem may be conducted to analyze what went well and what didn't.

Research is part and parcel of the work. In Figure 3, primary and secondary research are differentiated. Published research is easy to access, in general, but it may not be sufficiently focused for the needs of the instructional design project. This is where firsthand or primary research comes in to inform the work. Also, while there may be discrete time periods for research work in the lifespan of an instructional design and development project, instructional designer/developers actually engage this in a recursive way and will conduct work as needed. Rarely is a project fully linear without returning to particular steps as needed. The figures have double-headed arrows to reflect this reality. Sometimes, research is conducted in a just-in-time way to meet particular needs. How issues are handled can be very project dependent.

In actual practice, the amount of effort spent on the respective research work may differ. One reason for this is that a lot of information is already internalized and understood by practice. Some general tendencies percentage-wise may be seen in Figure 4 and Table 2. Notice the scale in the spider chart runs from 0 to 30 in the

The Respective Roles of Broad and Deep Research in Instructional Design and Development Work

Figure 2. General work sequences with instructional design projects

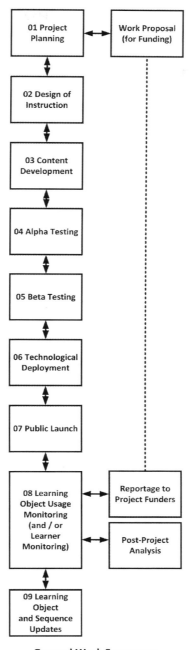

**General Work Sequences
with Instructional Design Projects**

Figure 3. General research-integrated work sequences with instructional design projects

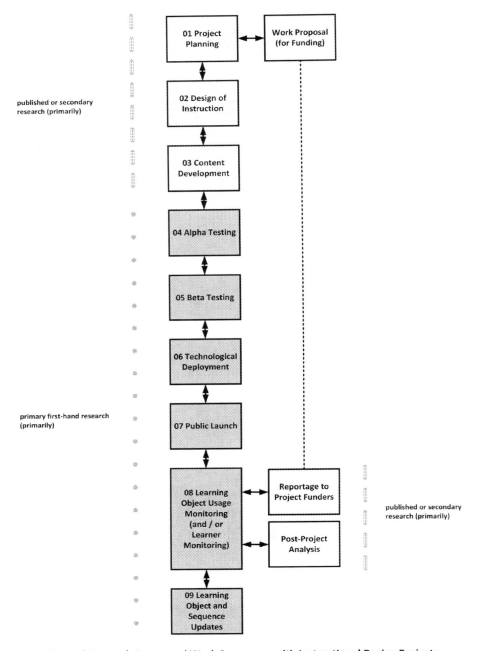

General Research-Integrated Work Sequences with Instructional Design Projects

spider chart in Figure 4. In both, select sub-elements of some of the work steps have been added for clarity. In virtually all cases of research, individuals and teams need some standards to vet he findings, to validate or invalidate the captured data and information. They also need to consider how to use the information in their work.

What might some of these research capabilities include? As expressed in verb phrases, they may include some (or all) of the following:

- Identify and locate relevant information from libraries, the Web and Internet, public and private collections, and other sources
- Elicit and collect relevant information from primary sources using multiple means, including online survey ones
- Comprehend collected information and understand the design and pedagogical and other implications of the information
- Set up a practical research design to collect accurate information about target learners
- Vet collected information for accuracy (including by separating fact from fiction)
- Conduct alpha tests (to standard) and understand revision implications from the data

Figure 4. General areas and related cumulative percentages for applied research for instructional design projects

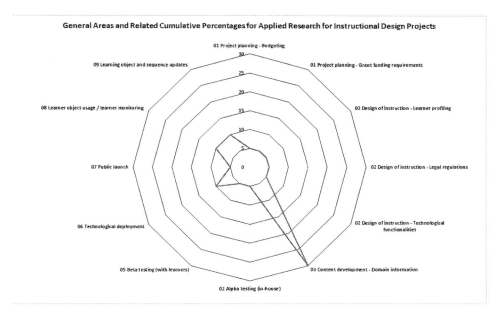

Table 2. General areas and related cumulative percentages for applied research for ID projects

01 Project planning - Budgeting	5
01 Project planning - Grant funding requirements	5
02 Design of instruction - Learner profiling	5
02 Design of instruction - Legal regulations	5
02 Design of instruction - Technological functionalities	5
03 Content development - Domain information	30
02 Alpha testing (in-house)	5
05 Beta testing (with learners)	5
06 Technological deployment	10
07 Public launch	5
08 Learner object usage / learner monitoring	10
09 Learning object and sequence updates	10

- Conduct beta tests (to standard) and understand revision implications from the learner data
    - Conduct beta tests with highly diverse learners in a sensitive and neutral way
- Acquire knowledge about how to use a variety of new technologies
    - Troubleshoot challenges with relevant technologies
- Conduct public launches of the learning resources to the proper audiences and for the desired outcomes
- Capture learner behavioral and performance data from the learning platforms (and in other ways)
- Discern when to update the learning contents and how (based on updated knowledge of pedagogical practices, updated domain knowledge, legal requirements for the learning, and other relevant factors
- Communicate research data findings in coherent ways through multiple means—verbal, visual, textual, multimodal, and others

These capabilities are not ones that can be trained fully through a master's or even doctoral program of study but will require growing into the skill set through mentorship and hard work. To maintain them over time will also require focus and dedicated hard work.

Different instructional design projects may have different research needs. The work of instructional design does not often result in one effective learning design ("equifinality") but may result in multiple effective designs. In this complex space, there is not one right answer but likely multiple effective designs and learning sequences.

Another way to think about the role of research in instructional design is to consider rookie mistakes in instructional design and whether or not research can help mitigate those errors. (Table 3) These show the importance of using research skills to solve practical issues in instructional design for novices and even some experts. After all, experts do have weak points in their professional work.

About Notetaking From ID Research

Concomitant with research for ID is "notetaking" from the research. The notes should include the following at minimum:

- High-fidelity and accurate representation of the research (with disambiguation as needed)
- Readability
- Citation of source(s) of the research
- Date when the notes were taken
- Author of the notes
- Planned usage of the notes

On a team, optimally, the respective members would benefit from each other's expertise and knowledge. These factors may be enhanced with the sharing of research notes. [Some team members may be more private than others, though, and if notes are seen as in the purview of individual employees, then perhaps there can be a shared online work space where relevant data may be shared without having people's full sets of notes available to all.]

The recorded information may be set up for use on a public or a private in-house track, oftentimes. If the information will be used for content with a public facing side, there should be highly rigorous source citations and legal rights releases (as needed). Certainly, notes and research sources may be multi-use. The team may discover new uses over time. New uses may require revisiting the idea of legal releases. For example, if a web meeting with a content expert is recorded for in-house use, to shape a learning object, but then, it is thought that a snippet of the video may be helpful for a learning object, the content expert needs to be contacted to sign a rights release for use of his or her likeness in a public-facing learning resource. If the expert declines to release those rights, then that video cannot be used for the learning resource.]

The Respective Roles of Broad and Deep Research in Instructional Design and Development Work

Table 3. Common rookie mistakes of novice instructional designers and the potential mitigating roles of research

Phases	Common Rookie Mistakes in Instructional Design	Potential Mitigating Role of Properly Applied Research
01 Project Planning	• Taking on a project outside one's capability	• Researching the actual required work and the standards
	• Mis-assessing of target learners	• Learning more about the target learners • Interacting with target learners • Studying the other created contents for target learners
	• A lack of knowledge of the target learners' backgrounds and cultures (or going with erroneous stereotypes)	• Studying the target learners' backgrounds • Studying the target learners' cultures
	• A lack of respect for learner needs	• (see above) • Empathy for learners and their needs
	• Mis-estimation of necessary inputs (time, resources, energy, skills, and others)	• Reviewing prior projects and input time • Engaging with experts for more accurate sense of necessary inputs
	• Insufficient inputs and available resources for the project	• (see above)
02 Design of Instruction	• Misinterpretation of learners' prior knowledge	• Application of assessment to target learners • Interview of target learners to understand prior knowledge • Discussions with informed clients about learners' prior knowledge
	• Inaccurate sense of target learners	• Affirmation of who the target learners are and what their actual needs are (based on evidence) • Testing prototype learning objects with target learners (or stand-ins for target learners) • Testing of prototype learning objects with SMEs and content experts
	• Lack of clarity about how to create effective learning objectives and related learning outcomes	• Study on how to create effective learning objectives and related learning outcomes

continued on following page

The maintenance of the notes and the raw sources should be done in light of data integrity (data are verifiable and unchanged from whomever shared the information) and digital preservation (data are accessible and available well into the future, optimally, without proprietary or closed software required). Sometimes, information is used on background, just to inform some of the work, without any obvious citations. Still, for the design and development team, it may help to know what ideas, sources, and notes informed particular work. [A common example of this latent influence may be that of formal research influence on questions asked in interviews or Q&As, with subject matter experts or "SMEs".]

Table 3. Continued

Phases	Common Rookie Mistakes in Instructional Design	Potential Mitigating Role of Properly Applied Research
03 Content Development	• Insufficient understanding of the learning contents	• Studying of the related discipline and target learning contents • Studying of related discipline information • Engaging with subject matter experts (SMEs) and content experts in the relevant domains
	• Designing learning contents in unconventional formats	• Experiencing learning objects in the particular target discipline • Acquiring learner expectations in the particular discipline
	• Inappropriate technology selection	• Familiarity with the technology • Knowledge of the underlying code and script • Learning how to test for technological functionality • Understanding all the required technological functions and capabilities • Understanding how to transcode
	• A lack of understanding of technological tradeoffs	• Ability to research and test quick-and-dirty digital learning objects • Ability to read technological documentation
	• Overconfidence in oneself (and resulting lack of openness to others' feedback and insights and critiques)	• Study of human cognitive biases • Study of human cognitive limits • Study of the deceptiveness of human ego
04 Alpha Testing	• Judgment of alpha testing to be irrelevant	• Study of the documented research on the relevance of alpha testing • Study of the learning resources for a variety of shortcomings and failures to meet defined standards • Study of alpha testing methods
	• Insufficient or inaccurate knowledge for legal requirements	• Study of legal requirements in all jurisdictions where the learning may be applied • Knowledge of intellectual property requirements • Knowledge of necessary documentation for copyright pursuit and acquisition • Knowledge of media law • Knowledge of privacy rights • Knowledge of requisite media releases • Knowledge of determining provenance of digital and other resources • Knowledge of effective documentation and record-keeping
	• Insufficient or inaccurate knowledge for accessibility requirements	• Study of accessibility requirements in all forms (web accessibility and others) • Study of human accessibility challenges (in all the respective forms)
	• Insufficient or inaccurate knowledge for technological standards	• Study of technological standards for all (digital and other) forms that the learning will take
05 Beta Testing	• Judgment of beta testing to be irrelevant	• Study of the relevance of learner acceptance in a learning sequence • Study of beta testing methods

continued on following page

Table 3. Continued

Phases	Common Rookie Mistakes in Instructional Design	Potential Mitigating Role of Properly Applied Research
06 Technological Deployment	• Inappropriate technological settings	• Study of the technology documentation
	• Inability to troubleshoot technology issues	• Study of the technology documentation • Ability to respond to exception errors based on the messaging
07 Public Launch	• Confusion about target learners to reach out to	• Exploration of the learner space to understand how to acquire stand-ins for target learners
08 Learning Object Usage Monitoring (and / or Learner Monitoring)	• Inefficacious harnessing of the learning system	• Ability to acquire and understand learning system documentation • Ability to acquire data • Ability to read a data dictionary • Ability to analyze data • Ability to launch learner surveys and other direct elicitations to understand learner usage of the learning resources
09 Learning Object and Sequence Updates	• Lack of clarity about how to update learning resources	• Ability to acquire recent knowledge in the learning domain • Ability to update knowledge of applicable laws related to the learning resources • Ability to review the project documentation related to the learning resources (and the continuing requirements for the learning resources) • And others

DISCUSSION

Instructional design work does require a wide range of skills, and one of the more critical ones involves the ability to conduct primary and secondary research and to apply those findings to their design and development work. Instructional design demands adaptivity, and part of that adaptivity requires continuous learning and the ability to acquire new information and to respond to that information appropriately, to optimize the learning designs and development. As such, "research" should be one of the listed capabilities for instructional designers, and it should be honed as a critical part of the professional skill set.

FUTURE RESEARCH DIRECTIONS

This work proposes a higher level of attention paid to research for those working in instructional design. In terms of future research, it would help to identify research and data analytics methods that enhance each of the nine steps in the instructional design sequence. It would be helpful to know how professionals in the field apply the research to their decision making and actions in respective projects, in cases, for example. Researchers may shed light on ways to be more accurate, efficient, effective, and relevant in the applied research work. They may inform ways to efficiently validate or invalidate data, or harness multiple trusted sources for richer data.

In terms of collaborative projects, it may help to understand how the research may be captured, documented, archived (and retrieved), and shared among team members, to advance the work.

Also, it may help to know how the research may be harnessed for more thorough project post-mortems (to ultimately improve future instructional design work).

Where continuing data collection is possible, such as on online learning platforms' dashboards and back-end data portals, learning from these would be helpful.

Given the focus on subjectivities of instructional designers and the sense of unique signatures, how do these idiosyncrasies affect the harnessing of research?

When the research dates out and is no longer relevant or is no longer *as relevant*, how should learning objects and sequences be updated?

CONCLUSION

This brief chapter uses an action research frame to suggest that research is important in instructional design and development projects. It offered a basic work sequence and highlighted some of the types of research conducted at each phase to advance the work.

Some may argue that research is the responsibility of principal investigators or dedicated researchers or content creators. In well funded teams with fully seated teams, that may be possible; in most cases, the ID stands in for researchers and will do critical work to support the instructional design and development.

REFERENCES

Cobb, P., Confrey, J., diSessa, A., Lehrer, R., & Schauble, L. (2003, January – February). Design experiments in educational research. *Educational Researcher*, *32*(1), 9–13. doi:10.3102/0013189X032001009

Mayer, R. E. (2003). The promise of multimedia learning: Using the same instructional design methods across different media. *Learning and Instruction*, *13*(2), 125–139. doi:10.1016/S0959-4752(02)00016-6

McLoughlin, C. (1999). The implications of the research literature on learning styles for the design of instructional material. *Australian Journal of Educational Technology*, *15*(3), 222–241.

Reeves, T. C., Herrington, J., & Oliver, R. (2005, Spring). Design research: A socially responsible approach to instructional technology research in higher education. *Journal of Computing in Higher Education, 16*(2), 96–115. doi:10.1007/BF02961476

Richey, R. C., Klein, J. D., & Nelson, W. A. (2004). Developmental research: Studies of instructional design and development. Handbook of research for educational communications and technology, 2, 1099 – 1130.

Rogers, P. C., Graham, C. R., & Mayes, C. T. (2007). Cultural competence and instructional design: Exploration research into the delivery of online instruction cross-culturally. *Educational Technology Research and Development, 55*(2), 197–217. doi:10.100711423-007-9033-x

Tripp, S. D., & Bichelmeyer, B. (1990). Rapid prototyping: An alternative instructional design strategy. *Educational Technology Research and Development, 38*(1), 31–44. doi:10.1007/BF02298246

ADDITIONAL READING

Clark, R. C., & Mayer, R. E. (2016). e-Learning and the Science of Instruction: Proven Guidelines for Consumers and Designers of Multimedia Learning (4th ed.). Hoboken, NJ: John Wiley & Sons.

KEY TERMS AND DEFINITIONS

Alpha Testing: In-house analysis of how well learning resources function technically and how closely they adhere to legal requirements and other standards (for revision purposes before public release).

Beta Testing: Formal analysis of how users (stand-ins for target learners) of learning resources respond to those resources in order to revise the draft learning contents.

Instructional Design: Systematic work of designing and building learning experiences for effective and efficient learning.

Conclusion

This book offered a range of insights from a diverse group of authors. The authors offered insights about salient educational theories, fresh conceptualizations of learners and the meeting of learner needs, mass-scale differences in terms of generational learning styles, building serialized online learning, designing learning paths for lifelong learners and learner groups, recognizing curricular infusions (from others' designs), expressing static and dynamic time for instructional designs, and considering the critical role of research for instructional design. I would like to express my gratitude to the respective authors in this work: Ouhao Chen, Slava Kalyuga, Rebecca M.L. Curnalia, Amber L. Ferris, Michael G. Strawser, Marjorie M. Meier, and Renee Kaufman. The respective authors capture well how instructional design is practiced: the thinking, the assessment, the decision making and design, the development, the research, and the focus on learners and the social good.

This edited text, *Form, Function, and Style in Instructional Design: Emerging Research and Opportunities,* has only touched on some limited approaches. It may be helpful to review the list of possible topics conceptualized for the initial call for chapter proposals. If I were checking off topics, it would seem that few of these would be removed.

INITIAL CONCEPTUAL RANGE AND DEPTH

Originally, it was thought that this edited collection might engage some topics such as the following suggested topics.

- Identifying Form, Function, and Style from Others' Designs
- Effective Instructional Designs based on Form, Function, and Style
- Elements of Form
- Related Techniques and Technologies to Form (in ID) (Structures in Time, Structures in Space)
- Elements of Function

Conclusion

- Related Techniques and Technologies to Function (in ID) (Enablements, Interactions, Experiential Sequences, User Role Designs)
- Elements of Style
- Related Techniques and Technologies to Style (in ID) (Interface Designs, Color Palettes, Players, Designed Interaction, Sound Design, Visual Design)
- Techniques and Technologies for Form/Function/Style in ID
- Technological Enablements of Form/Function/Style for Instructional Designs
- Form/Function/Style in Information Selection and Filtering
- Fictional Character Development
- Packaging Online Learning
- Styling Imagery and Image Sets
- Data Sets
- Artwork Sets
- Video Sets
- Freeform Design
- Design for Boutique (One-off, Custom) Instructional Design Projects
- Style in Writing
- Style in Voice
- Style in Humor
- Style in Tone
- Style in Cases
- Style in Skits
- Style in Problem Solving
- Going with Non-style
- Simplicity as Style
- Designing Tone
- Cultural Form/Function/Style
- Distinctive Instructional Design Styles and Signatures
- Personality Frame in Instructional Design Styles
- Instructional Design Style and Learning Efficacies
- Research into the Effects of Instructional Design Styles
- Cases of Instructional Design (ID) Styles
- Assessing Style Efficacy with Research
- Gender Considerations for Style
- Alternative Styles
- Style for Messaging
- Instructional Design Style and Persuasion
- Instructional Design Style and Branding
- Instructional Design Style and Trust Building
- Historical Style

Conclusion

- Regional Style
- Organizational Style
- Custom One-off Styles
- Styles for Long-Term Projects
- Inherited Designs of Style (for Instructional Designs)
- Instructional Design Stylebooks
- Form/Function/Style for Accessibility
- Others

This edited collection would have included a few additional works had prospective potential authors not run out of runway. At some point, the impending deadlines prevent potentially fine works from making it into the publishing light-of-day. Part-works revert to zero.

Instructional design is a dynamic field, with constant advancements in understanding how people effectively teach and learn, the available technologies in the field, effective methods to designing for effective teaching and learning, and other aspects. It is not likely that learners will be expected to learn from raw data and raw information, without the soothing hand of instructional design to ease the learning.

Shalin Hai-Jew
Kansas State University, USA
August 2019

Related Readings

To continue IGI Global's long-standing tradition of advancing innovation through emerging research, please find below a compiled list of recommended IGI Global book chapters and journal articles in the areas of digital learning, student engagement, and learning outcomes. These related readings will provide additional information and guidance to further enrich your knowledge and assist you with your own research.

Acquatella, F., Fernandez, V., & Houy, T. (2019). The Coursera Case as the Prefiguration of the Ongoing Changes on the MOOC Platforms. In J. Pelet (Ed.), *Advanced Web Applications and Progressing E-Learning 2.0 Technologies in Higher Education* (pp. 20–34). Hershey, PA: IGI Global. doi:10.4018/978-1-5225-7435-4. ch002

Al-Furaih, S. A. (2019). Smart Lesson Planning Environments for Deeper Learning: A Kuwaiti Case Study in Teacher Education. In A. Darshan Singh, S. Raghunathan, E. Robeck, & B. Sharma (Eds.), *Cases on Smart Learning Environments* (pp. 142–163). Hershey, PA: IGI Global. doi:10.4018/978-1-5225-6136-1.ch009

Alawani, A. S. (2019). Wamda: A Smart Mobile Learning System for UAE Teachers. In A. Darshan Singh, S. Raghunathan, E. Robeck, & B. Sharma (Eds.), *Cases on Smart Learning Environments* (pp. 203–226). Hershey, PA: IGI Global. doi:10.4018/978-1-5225-6136-1.ch012

Almarzooqi, S. S. (2019). Sa'i Smart Library Learning Lab: Disruptive Learning. In A. Darshan Singh, S. Raghunathan, E. Robeck, & B. Sharma (Eds.), *Cases on Smart Learning Environments* (pp. 299–329). Hershey, PA: IGI Global. doi:10.4018/978-1-5225-6136-1.ch017

Related Readings

Alqurashi, E. (2019). Technology Tools for Teaching and Learning in Real Time. In J. Yoon & P. Semingson (Eds.), *Educational Technology and Resources for Synchronous Learning in Higher Education* (pp. 255–278). Hershey, PA: IGI Global. doi:10.4018/978-1-5225-7567-2.ch013

An, Y., & Cao, L. (2017). Examining the Characteristics of Digital Learning Games Designed by In-service Teachers. *International Journal of Game-Based Learning*, 7(4), 73–85. doi:10.4018/IJGBL.2017100104

Andujar, A. (2019). Shaping the Future of Telecollaboration: WebRTC. In J. Yoon & P. Semingson (Eds.), *Educational Technology and Resources for Synchronous Learning in Higher Education* (pp. 151–172). Hershey, PA: IGI Global. doi:10.4018/978-1-5225-7567-2.ch008

Araújo, R. D., Ferreira, H. N., Cattelan, R. G., & Dorça, F. A. (2018). A Hybrid Architecture for Adaptive, Intelligent, and Ubiquitous Educational Systems. In R. Zheng (Ed.), *Digital Technologies and Instructional Design for Personalized Learning* (pp. 120–144). Hershey, PA: IGI Global. doi:10.4018/978-1-5225-3940-7.ch006

Ayish, M., & Dahdal, S. (2019). Using Mobile Devices by Media Students as a Tool for Digital Storytelling. In A. Darshan Singh, S. Raghunathan, E. Robeck, & B. Sharma (Eds.), *Cases on Smart Learning Environments* (pp. 34–44). Hershey, PA: IGI Global. doi:10.4018/978-1-5225-6136-1.ch003

Baporikar, N. (2019). E-Learning Strategies for Emerging Economies in the Knowledge Era. In J. Pelet (Ed.), *Advanced Web Applications and Progressing E-Learning 2.0 Technologies in Higher Education* (pp. 150–171). Hershey, PA: IGI Global. doi:10.4018/978-1-5225-7435-4.ch008

Barth, I., Spector-Cohen, E., Sitman, R., Jiang, G., Liu, F., & Xu, Y. (2019). Beyond Small Chunks: Designing Vocabulary OERs for Mobile Learning. *International Journal of Computer-Assisted Language Learning and Teaching*, 9(2), 79–97. doi:10.4018/IJCALLT.2019040105

Berg, C. W., Shaw, M., Contento, A. L., & Burrus, S. W. (2019). A Qualitative Study of Student Expectations of Online Faculty Engagement. In K. Walters & P. Henry (Eds.), *Fostering Multiple Levels of Engagement in Higher Education Environments* (pp. 220–236). Hershey, PA: IGI Global. doi:10.4018/978-1-5225-7470-5.ch010

Berry, S. (2019). The Role of Video and Text Chat in a Virtual Classroom: How Technology Impacts Community. In J. Yoon & P. Semingson (Eds.), *Educational Technology and Resources for Synchronous Learning in Higher Education* (pp. 173–187). Hershey, PA: IGI Global. doi:10.4018/978-1-5225-7567-2.ch009

Bezboruah, K. C. (2019). Live Sessions and Accelerated Online Project-Based Courses. In J. Yoon & P. Semingson (Eds.), *Educational Technology and Resources for Synchronous Learning in Higher Education* (pp. 23–55). Hershey, PA: IGI Global. doi:10.4018/978-1-5225-7567-2.ch002

Brautlacht, R., Poppi, F., Martins, M. L., & Ducrocq, C. (2017). European Dialogue Project: Collaborating to Improve on the Quality of Learning Environments. In P. Vu, S. Fredrickson, & C. Moore (Eds.), *Handbook of Research on Innovative Pedagogies and Technologies for Online Learning in Higher Education* (pp. 393–426). Hershey, PA: IGI Global. doi:10.4018/978-1-5225-1851-8.ch017

Bugawa, A. M., & Mirzal, A. (2018). The Impact of Web 2.0 Technologies on the Learning Experience of Students in Higher Education: A Review. *International Journal of Web-Based Learning and Teaching Technologies*, *13*(3), 1–17. doi:10.4018/IJWLTT.2018070101

Calonge, D. S., Riggs, K. M., Shah, M. A., & Cavanagh, T. A. (2019). Using Learning Analytics to Improve Engagement, Learning, and Design of Massive Open Online Courses. In K. Walters & P. Henry (Eds.), *Fostering Multiple Levels of Engagement in Higher Education Environments* (pp. 76–107). Hershey, PA: IGI Global. doi:10.4018/978-1-5225-7470-5.ch004

Chadha, A. (2019). Graduate Online Pedagogy: A Framework for Collaborative Communities of Learning. In K. Walters & P. Henry (Eds.), *Fostering Multiple Levels of Engagement in Higher Education Environments* (pp. 108–131). Hershey, PA: IGI Global. doi:10.4018/978-1-5225-7470-5.ch005

Chigwada, J. P. (2019). Supporting Information Literacy Skills of Students for a Successful Transition to Higher Education: Opportunities and Challenges for Libraries in the Digital Era. *International Journal of Library and Information Services*, *8*(1), 24–30. doi:10.4018/IJLIS.2019010102

Daunert, A. L., & Price, L. (2019). Do I Know My Learners…?: The Conditions and Factors to Consider in Embedding Ubiquitous Technologies Into the Plan and Design of the Learning Process. In J. Pelet (Ed.), *Advanced Web Applications and Progressing E-Learning 2.0 Technologies in Higher Education* (pp. 77–102). Hershey, PA: IGI Global. doi:10.4018/978-1-5225-7435-4.ch005

Delello, J. A., & Consalvo, A. L. (2019). "I Found Myself Retweeting": Using Twitter Chats to Build Professional Learning Networks. In J. Yoon & P. Semingson (Eds.), *Educational Technology and Resources for Synchronous Learning in Higher Education* (pp. 88–108). Hershey, PA: IGI Global. doi:10.4018/978-1-5225-7567-2.ch005

Related Readings

Delello, J. A., Hawley, H., McWhorter, R. R., Gipson, C. S., & Deal, B. (2018). Gamifying Education: Motivation and the Implementation of Digital Badges for Use in Higher Education. *International Journal of Web-Based Learning and Teaching Technologies*, *13*(4), 17–33. doi:10.4018/IJWLTT.2018100102

Durnalı, M., Orakcı, Ş., & Aktan, O. (2019). The Smart Learning Potential of Turkey's Education System in the Context of FATIH Project. In A. Darshan Singh, S. Raghunathan, E. Robeck, & B. Sharma (Eds.), *Cases on Smart Learning Environments* (pp. 227–243). Hershey, PA: IGI Global. doi:10.4018/978-1-5225-6136-1.ch013

Eakins, A. (2019). Developing a Sense of Community Through Engaging Platforms in Support of Online Graduate Students Socialization. In K. Walters & P. Henry (Eds.), *Fostering Multiple Levels of Engagement in Higher Education Environments* (pp. 156–175). Hershey, PA: IGI Global. doi:10.4018/978-1-5225-7470-5.ch007

El Mhouti, A., & Erradi, M. (2019). Harnessing Cloud Computing Services for E-Learning Systems in Higher Education: Impact and Effects. *International Journal of Information and Communication Technology Education*, *15*(2), 18–30. doi:10.4018/IJICTE.2019040102

Elharakany, R. A., Moscardini, A., Khalifa, N. M., & Elghany, M. M. (2018). Modelling the Effect on Quality of Information and Communications Technology (ICT) facilities in Higher Education: Case Study—Egyptian Universities. *International Journal of System Dynamics Applications*, *7*(3), 1–30. doi:10.4018/IJSDA.2018070101

Francisco, D. (2019). Beyond Instructional Engagement: Rethinking the Role of Online Faculty in Higher Education. In K. Walters & P. Henry (Eds.), *Fostering Multiple Levels of Engagement in Higher Education Environments* (pp. 192–219). Hershey, PA: IGI Global. doi:10.4018/978-1-5225-7470-5.ch009

Ganendran, L. (2019). Disrupting Learning of Statistics: Using an Appreciative Inquiry Approach to Create Smart Learning Designs. In A. Darshan Singh, S. Raghunathan, E. Robeck, & B. Sharma (Eds.), *Cases on Smart Learning Environments* (pp. 45–62). Hershey, PA: IGI Global. doi:10.4018/978-1-5225-6136-1.ch004

Gierl, M., Bulut, O., & Zhang, X. (2018). Using Computerized Formative Testing to Support Personalized Learning in Higher Education: An Application of Two Assessment Technologies. In R. Zheng (Ed.), *Digital Technologies and Instructional Design for Personalized Learning* (pp. 99–119). Hershey, PA: IGI Global. doi:10.4018/978-1-5225-3940-7.ch005

Gutierrez, J. A., & Bursztyn, N. (2019). The Story of Ice: Design of a Virtual and Augmented Reality Field Trip Through Yosemite National Park. In A. Darshan Singh, S. Raghunathan, E. Robeck, & B. Sharma (Eds.), *Cases on Smart Learning Environments* (pp. 1–16). Hershey, PA: IGI Global. doi:10.4018/978-1-5225-6136-1.ch001

Hamilton, E., & Owens, A. M. (2018). Computational Thinking and Participatory Teaching as Pathways to Personalized Learning. In R. Zheng (Ed.), *Digital Technologies and Instructional Design for Personalized Learning* (pp. 212–228). Hershey, PA: IGI Global. doi:10.4018/978-1-5225-3940-7.ch010

Harrati, N., Bouchrika, I., Mahfouf, Z., & Ladjailia, A. (2017). Evaluation Methods for E-Learning Applications in Terms of User Satisfaction and Interface Usability. In P. Vu, S. Fredrickson, & C. Moore (Eds.), *Handbook of Research on Innovative Pedagogies and Technologies for Online Learning in Higher Education* (pp. 427–448). Hershey, PA: IGI Global. doi:10.4018/978-1-5225-1851-8.ch018

Hastie, M. (2019). Building Futures: Using Educational Robots to Teach STEM in a Smart Learning System in Abu Dhabi. In A. Darshan Singh, S. Raghunathan, E. Robeck, & B. Sharma (Eds.), *Cases on Smart Learning Environments* (pp. 17–33). Hershey, PA: IGI Global. doi:10.4018/978-1-5225-6136-1.ch002

Helfaya, A., & O'Neill, J. (2018). Using Computer-Based Assessment and Feedback: Meeting the Needs of Digital Natives in the Digital Age. *International Journal of Teacher Education and Professional Development*, *1*(2), 46–71. doi:10.4018/IJTEPD.2018070104

Hiasat, L., & Pollitt, A. J. (2019). Educators' Roles in Creating Smart Learning Environments for Emiratis in Tertiary Education. In A. Darshan Singh, S. Raghunathan, E. Robeck, & B. Sharma (Eds.), *Cases on Smart Learning Environments* (pp. 256–282). Hershey, PA: IGI Global. doi:10.4018/978-1-5225-6136-1.ch015

Holcomb, J. (2019). Creating an Environment That Supports Online Faculty Engagement at All Levels. In K. Walters & P. Henry (Eds.), *Fostering Multiple Levels of Engagement in Higher Education Environments* (pp. 237–259). Hershey, PA: IGI Global. doi:10.4018/978-1-5225-7470-5.ch011

Huang, J., & Vedantham, A. (2019). Cabot Science Library: Creating Transformative Learning Environments in Library Spaces. In A. Darshan Singh, S. Raghunathan, E. Robeck, & B. Sharma (Eds.), *Cases on Smart Learning Environments* (pp. 284–298). Hershey, PA: IGI Global. doi:10.4018/978-1-5225-6136-1.ch016

Related Readings

Hunaiti, Z. (2017). Digital Learning Technologies: Subjective and Objective Effectiveness Evaluation in Higher Education Settings. *International Journal of Handheld Computing Research*, 8(2), 41–50. doi:10.4018/IJHCR.2017040103

Hwang, G., Chen, B., & Huang, S. (2018). Development and Analysis of an Enhanced Multi-Expert Knowledge Integration System for Designing Context-Aware Ubiquitous Learning Contents. *International Journal of Distance Education Technologies*, 16(4), 31–53. doi:10.4018/IJDET.2018100103

Inghilterra, X. (2019). Temporal Asynchrony of Socio-Technical Devices in Distance Learning?: Origins of Cleavage Between Academics and Learning Communities. In J. Pelet (Ed.), *Advanced Web Applications and Progressing E-Learning 2.0 Technologies in Higher Education* (pp. 57–76). Hershey, PA: IGI Global. doi:10.4018/978-1-5225-7435-4.ch004

Isaias, P., Miranda, P., & Pífano, S. (2019). Higher Education and Web 2.0: Barriers and Best Practices From the Standpoint of Practitioners. In J. Pelet (Ed.), *Advanced Web Applications and Progressing E-Learning 2.0 Technologies in Higher Education* (pp. 103–127). Hershey, PA: IGI Global. doi:10.4018/978-1-5225-7435-4.ch006

Jiang, Y., Clarke-Midura, J., Baker, R. S., Paquette, L., & Keller, B. (2018). How Immersive Virtual Environments Foster Self-Regulated Learning. In R. Zheng (Ed.), *Digital Technologies and Instructional Design for Personalized Learning* (pp. 28–54). Hershey, PA: IGI Global. doi:10.4018/978-1-5225-3940-7.ch002

Johnson, C., & Altowairiki, N. (2017). Developing Teaching Presence in Online Learning Through Shared Stakeholder Responsibility. In P. Vu, S. Fredrickson, & C. Moore (Eds.), *Handbook of Research on Innovative Pedagogies and Technologies for Online Learning in Higher Education* (pp. 151–177). Hershey, PA: IGI Global. doi:10.4018/978-1-5225-1851-8.ch008

Kehus, M. J. (2019). Best Practices for Engaging Graduate Students in Problem-Based Learning. In K. Walters & P. Henry (Eds.), *Fostering Multiple Levels of Engagement in Higher Education Environments* (pp. 21–48). Hershey, PA: IGI Global. doi:10.4018/978-1-5225-7470-5.ch002

Kerns, W. A. (2019). Quality Assurance Within Synchronous Sessions of Online Instruction. In J. Yoon & P. Semingson (Eds.), *Educational Technology and Resources for Synchronous Learning in Higher Education* (pp. 211–228). Hershey, PA: IGI Global. doi:10.4018/978-1-5225-7567-2.ch011

Khouja, M., Rodriguez, I. B., Ben Halima, Y., & Moalla, S. (2018). IT Governance in Higher Education Institutions: A Systematic Literature Review. *International Journal of Human Capital and Information Technology Professionals*, 9(2), 52–67. doi:10.4018/IJHCITP.2018040104

Kilpatrick, C. D. (2019). Faces or Fingers: Building Community With Synchronous Chat. In J. Yoon & P. Semingson (Eds.), *Educational Technology and Resources for Synchronous Learning in Higher Education* (pp. 1–22). Hershey, PA: IGI Global. doi:10.4018/978-1-5225-7567-2.ch001

Koo, K. (2019). Is It Real or Not?: Experiences of Synchronous Learning and Training for Counseling Graduate Students. In J. Yoon & P. Semingson (Eds.), *Educational Technology and Resources for Synchronous Learning in Higher Education* (pp. 129–150). Hershey, PA: IGI Global. doi:10.4018/978-1-5225-7567-2.ch007

Korucu, A. T., & Atun, H. (2017). Use of Social Media in Online Learning. In P. Vu, S. Fredrickson, & C. Moore (Eds.), *Handbook of Research on Innovative Pedagogies and Technologies for Online Learning in Higher Education* (pp. 1–18). Hershey, PA: IGI Global. doi:10.4018/978-1-5225-1851-8.ch001

Koskey, K. L., & Benson, S. N. (2017). A Review of Literature and a Model for Scaffolding Asynchronous Student-Student Interaction in Online Discussion Forums. In P. Vu, S. Fredrickson, & C. Moore (Eds.), *Handbook of Research on Innovative Pedagogies and Technologies for Online Learning in Higher Education* (pp. 263–280). Hershey, PA: IGI Global. doi:10.4018/978-1-5225-1851-8.ch012

Kumar, T. S. (2019). A Private Cloud-Based Smart Learning Environment Using Moodle for Universities. In A. Darshan Singh, S. Raghunathan, E. Robeck, & B. Sharma (Eds.), *Cases on Smart Learning Environments* (pp. 188–202). Hershey, PA: IGI Global. doi:10.4018/978-1-5225-6136-1.ch011

Lee, V. R. (2018). Personal Analytics Explorations to Support Youth Learning. In R. Zheng (Ed.), *Digital Technologies and Instructional Design for Personalized Learning* (pp. 145–163). Hershey, PA: IGI Global. doi:10.4018/978-1-5225-3940-7.ch007

Lemanski, L., & Van Deventer, M. M. (2019). A Framework for the Redesign Principles That Improved Engagement in an Online Graduate Class. In K. Walters & P. Henry (Eds.), *Fostering Multiple Levels of Engagement in Higher Education Environments* (pp. 49–75). Hershey, PA: IGI Global. doi:10.4018/978-1-5225-7470-5.ch003

Related Readings

Leonardou, A., Rigou, M., & Garofalakis, J. D. (2019). Open Learner Models in Smart Learning Environments. In A. Darshan Singh, S. Raghunathan, E. Robeck, & B. Sharma (Eds.), *Cases on Smart Learning Environments* (pp. 346–368). Hershey, PA: IGI Global. doi:10.4018/978-1-5225-6136-1.ch019

MacCallum, K., Day, S., Skelton, D., & Verhaart, M. (2017). Mobile Affordances and Learning Theories in Supporting and Enhancing Learning. *International Journal of Mobile and Blended Learning*, *9*(2), 61–73. doi:10.4018/IJMBL.2017040104

MacLeod, J., & Yang, H. H. (2018). Intercultural Computer-Supported Collaborative Learning: Theory and Practice. In R. Zheng (Ed.), *Digital Technologies and Instructional Design for Personalized Learning* (pp. 80–97). Hershey, PA: IGI Global. doi:10.4018/978-1-5225-3940-7.ch004

Mata, L. (2019). Current Studies Based on the Investigation of the Attitudes Towards the Internet in Higher Education. In J. Pelet (Ed.), *Advanced Web Applications and Progressing E-Learning 2.0 Technologies in Higher Education* (pp. 1–19). Hershey, PA: IGI Global. doi:10.4018/978-1-5225-7435-4.ch001

Mata, L., Panisoara, G., Fat, S., Panisoara, I., & Lazar, I. (2019). Exploring the Adoptions by Students of Web 2.0 Tools for E-Learning in Higher Education: Web 2.0 Tools for E-Learning in Higher Education. In J. Pelet (Ed.), *Advanced Web Applications and Progressing E-Learning 2.0 Technologies in Higher Education* (pp. 128–149). Hershey, PA: IGI Global. doi:10.4018/978-1-5225-7435-4.ch007

McGinn, A. L. (2019). Synchronous Online Learning: The Experiences of Graduate Students in an Educational Technology Program. In J. Yoon & P. Semingson (Eds.), *Educational Technology and Resources for Synchronous Learning in Higher Education* (pp. 279–302). Hershey, PA: IGI Global. doi:10.4018/978-1-5225-7567-2.ch014

Merzon, E., Galimullina, E., & Ljubimova, E. (2019). A Smart Trajectory Model for Teacher Training. In A. Darshan Singh, S. Raghunathan, E. Robeck, & B. Sharma (Eds.), *Cases on Smart Learning Environments* (pp. 164–187). Hershey, PA: IGI Global. doi:10.4018/978-1-5225-6136-1.ch010

Moos van Wyk, M. (2018). Flipping the Class for Students to Learn to Teach Economics. In R. Zheng (Ed.), *Digital Technologies and Instructional Design for Personalized Learning* (pp. 287–306). Hershey, PA: IGI Global. doi:10.4018/978-1-5225-3940-7.ch014

Mouri, K., Ren, Z., Uosaki, N., & Yin, C. (2019). Analyzing Learning Patterns Based on Log Data from Digital Textbooks. *International Journal of Distance Education Technologies*, *17*(1), 1–14. doi:10.4018/IJDET.2019010101

Mukherjee, A., Goyal, P., Singh, A., Khosla, A. K., Ahuja, K., & Chand, K. (2019). Pursuit of Research: A Gamified Approach Promoting Research Engagement Among Undergraduate Students. In K. Walters & P. Henry (Eds.), *Fostering Multiple Levels of Engagement in Higher Education Environments* (pp. 132–155). Hershey, PA: IGI Global. doi:10.4018/978-1-5225-7470-5.ch006

Munawar, S., Toor, S. K., & Hamid, M. (2019). Designing an Intelligent Virtual Laboratory Using Intelligent Agent Technology. In A. Darshan Singh, S. Raghunathan, E. Robeck, & B. Sharma (Eds.), *Cases on Smart Learning Environments* (pp. 330–345). Hershey, PA: IGI Global. doi:10.4018/978-1-5225-6136-1.ch018

Nuninger, W. (2017). Common Scenario for an Efficient Use of Online Learning: Some Guidelines for Pedagogical Digital Device Development. In P. Vu, S. Fredrickson, & C. Moore (Eds.), *Handbook of Research on Innovative Pedagogies and Technologies for Online Learning in Higher Education* (pp. 331–366). Hershey, PA: IGI Global. doi:10.4018/978-1-5225-1851-8.ch015

Ogden, L., & Shambaugh, N. (2017). Best Teaching and Technology Practices for the Hybrid Flipped College Classroom. In P. Vu, S. Fredrickson, & C. Moore (Eds.), *Handbook of Research on Innovative Pedagogies and Technologies for Online Learning in Higher Education* (pp. 281–303). Hershey, PA: IGI Global. doi:10.4018/978-1-5225-1851-8.ch013

Olesova, L., & Lim, J. (2017). The Impact of Role Assignment on Cognitive Presence in Asynchronous Online Discussion. In P. Vu, S. Fredrickson, & C. Moore (Eds.), *Handbook of Research on Innovative Pedagogies and Technologies for Online Learning in Higher Education* (pp. 19–39). Hershey, PA: IGI Global. doi:10.4018/978-1-5225-1851-8.ch002

Oliveira, A., & Pombo, L. (2018). EduLabs: Promoting a Smart and Personalized Learning. In R. Zheng (Ed.), *Digital Technologies and Instructional Design for Personalized Learning* (pp. 191–210). Hershey, PA: IGI Global. doi:10.4018/978-1-5225-3940-7.ch009

Ongoro, C. A., & Mwangoka, J. W. (2019). Smart Interactive Game-Based System for Preschools in Tanzania. In A. Darshan Singh, S. Raghunathan, E. Robeck, & B. Sharma (Eds.), *Cases on Smart Learning Environments* (pp. 81–98). Hershey, PA: IGI Global. doi:10.4018/978-1-5225-6136-1.ch006

Related Readings

Ostrowski, C. P., Lock, J. V., Hill, S. L., da Rosa dos Santos, L., Altowairiki, N. F., & Johnson, C. (2017). A Journey Through the Development of Online Environments: Putting UDL Theory into Practice. In P. Vu, S. Fredrickson, & C. Moore (Eds.), *Handbook of Research on Innovative Pedagogies and Technologies for Online Learning in Higher Education* (pp. 218–235). Hershey, PA: IGI Global. doi:10.4018/978-1-5225-1851-8.ch010

Ouyang, F., & Scharber, C. (2018). Adapting the TPACK Framework for Online Teaching Within Higher Education. *International Journal of Online Pedagogy and Course Design*, 8(1), 42–59. doi:10.4018/IJOPCD.2018010104

Oyarzun, B. A., Conklin, S. A., & Barreto, D. (2017). Instructor Presence. In P. Vu, S. Fredrickson, & C. Moore (Eds.), *Handbook of Research on Innovative Pedagogies and Technologies for Online Learning in Higher Education* (pp. 106–126). Hershey, PA: IGI Global. doi:10.4018/978-1-5225-1851-8.ch006

Pima, J. M., Odetayo, M., Iqbal, R., & Sedoyeka, E. (2018). A Thematic Review of Blended Learning in Higher Education. *International Journal of Mobile and Blended Learning*, 10(1), 1–11. doi:10.4018/IJMBL.2018010101

Poole, F. J., Franco, J., & Clarke-Midura, J. (2018). Developing a Personalized, Educational Gaming Experience for Young Chinese DLI Learners: A Design-Based Approach. In R. Zheng (Ed.), *Digital Technologies and Instructional Design for Personalized Learning* (pp. 253–274). Hershey, PA: IGI Global. doi:10.4018/978-1-5225-3940-7.ch012

Psaltis, A., & Mourlas, C. (2018). Realtime BioSensing System Assessing Subconscious Responses of Engagement: An Evaluation Study. In R. Zheng (Ed.), *Digital Technologies and Instructional Design for Personalized Learning* (pp. 307–333). Hershey, PA: IGI Global. doi:10.4018/978-1-5225-3940-7.ch015

Pulla, S. (2017). Mobile Learning and Indigenous Education in Canada: A Synthesis of New Ways of Learning. *International Journal of Mobile and Blended Learning*, 9(2), 39–60. doi:10.4018/IJMBL.2017040103

Qian, Y. (2017). Computer Simulation in Higher Education: Affordances, Opportunities, and Outcomes. In P. Vu, S. Fredrickson, & C. Moore (Eds.), *Handbook of Research on Innovative Pedagogies and Technologies for Online Learning in Higher Education* (pp. 236–262). Hershey, PA: IGI Global. doi:10.4018/978-1-5225-1851-8.ch011

Rao, T. V., Sankoju, C., & Sultana, S. T. (2018). Enabling and Integrating Technology With Personalized Learning. In R. Zheng (Ed.), *Digital Technologies and Instructional Design for Personalized Learning* (pp. 275–286). Hershey, PA: IGI Global. doi:10.4018/978-1-5225-3940-7.ch013

Robeck, E., Raghunathan, S., Singh, A. D., & Sharma, B. (2019). Diverse Applications of the Elements of Smart Learning Environments. In A. Darshan Singh, S. Raghunathan, E. Robeck, & B. Sharma (Eds.), *Cases on Smart Learning Environments* (pp. 118–141). Hershey, PA: IGI Global. doi:10.4018/978-1-5225-6136-1.ch008

Robertson, M. K., & Piotrowski, A. (2019). Authentic Inquiry With Undergraduate Preservice Teachers in Synchronous Interactive Video Conferencing Courses. In J. Yoon & P. Semingson (Eds.), *Educational Technology and Resources for Synchronous Learning in Higher Education* (pp. 109–128). Hershey, PA: IGI Global. doi:10.4018/978-1-5225-7567-2.ch006

Romero-Hall, E., & Vicentini, C. R. (2017). Multimodal Interactive Tools for Online Discussions and Assessment. In P. Vu, S. Fredrickson, & C. Moore (Eds.), *Handbook of Research on Innovative Pedagogies and Technologies for Online Learning in Higher Education* (pp. 85–105). Hershey, PA: IGI Global. doi:10.4018/978-1-5225-1851-8.ch005

Roye, J., & Cauble, D. M. (2019). Online Synchronous Activities to Promote Community of Inquiry in Two Nursing Courses. In J. Yoon & P. Semingson (Eds.), *Educational Technology and Resources for Synchronous Learning in Higher Education* (pp. 56–70). Hershey, PA: IGI Global. doi:10.4018/978-1-5225-7567-2.ch003

Sánchez-Acevedo, M. A. (2019). Indigenous Languages Learning Through Serious Games Based on Second Language Acquisition Theories. In J. Pelet (Ed.), *Advanced Web Applications and Progressing E-Learning 2.0 Technologies in Higher Education* (pp. 35–56). Hershey, PA: IGI Global. doi:10.4018/978-1-5225-7435-4.ch003

Santoianni, F., & Ciasullo, A. (2018). Digital and Spatial Education Intertwining in The Evolution of Technology Resources for Educational Curriculum Reshaping and Skills Enhancement. *International Journal of Digital Literacy and Digital Competence*, 9(2), 34–49. doi:10.4018/IJDLDC.2018040103

Related Readings

Scott, J. D. (2017). Promoting Learner Interaction and Personalized Learning Experiences with a Google+ Social Media Model: How to Replace the Traditional Discussion Forum. In P. Vu, S. Fredrickson, & C. Moore (Eds.), *Handbook of Research on Innovative Pedagogies and Technologies for Online Learning in Higher Education* (pp. 40–59). Hershey, PA: IGI Global. doi:10.4018/978-1-5225-1851-8.ch003

Seifert, T. (2019). Improving Involvement Through Interaction in Synchronous Teaching/Learning in Higher Education. In J. Yoon & P. Semingson (Eds.), *Educational Technology and Resources for Synchronous Learning in Higher Education* (pp. 229–254). Hershey, PA: IGI Global. doi:10.4018/978-1-5225-7567-2.ch012

Sharma, B. N., Fonolahi, A. V., Bali, A., & Narayan, S. S. (2019). The Online Mathematics Diagnostic Tool for Transformative Learning in the Pacific. In A. Darshan Singh, S. Raghunathan, E. Robeck, & B. Sharma (Eds.), *Cases on Smart Learning Environments* (pp. 63–80). Hershey, PA: IGI Global. doi:10.4018/978-1-5225-6136-1.ch005

Stirtz, G. E. (2017). Online Professional Development in Academic Service-Learning: Promoting Community Engagement in Public Education. In P. Vu, S. Fredrickson, & C. Moore (Eds.), *Handbook of Research on Innovative Pedagogies and Technologies for Online Learning in Higher Education* (pp. 60–84). Hershey, PA: IGI Global. doi:10.4018/978-1-5225-1851-8.ch004

Sural, I., & Yazici, M. (2018). Learner Performance and Satisfaction Level in Personalized Learning Environments. In R. Zheng (Ed.), *Digital Technologies and Instructional Design for Personalized Learning* (pp. 55–79). Hershey, PA: IGI Global. doi:10.4018/978-1-5225-3940-7.ch003

Svenningsen, L., Bottomley, S., & Pear, J. J. (2018). Personalized Learning and Online Instruction. In R. Zheng (Ed.), *Digital Technologies and Instructional Design for Personalized Learning* (pp. 164–190). Hershey, PA: IGI Global. doi:10.4018/978-1-5225-3940-7.ch008

Thomas, M., Harris, R., & King-Berry, A. (2017). Creating Inclusive Online Learning Environments That Build Community and Enhance Learning. In P. Vu, S. Fredrickson, & C. Moore (Eds.), *Handbook of Research on Innovative Pedagogies and Technologies for Online Learning in Higher Education* (pp. 304–330). Hershey, PA: IGI Global. doi:10.4018/978-1-5225-1851-8.ch014

Throne, R., & Bourke, B. (2019). Online Research Supervisor Engagement: Fostering Graduate Student Researcher Positionality. In K. Walters & P. Henry (Eds.), *Fostering Multiple Levels of Engagement in Higher Education Environments* (pp. 1–20). Hershey, PA: IGI Global. doi:10.4018/978-1-5225-7470-5.ch001

Tobin, T. J., & Honeycutt, B. (2017). Improve the Flipped Classroom with Universal Design for Learning. In P. Vu, S. Fredrickson, & C. Moore (Eds.), *Handbook of Research on Innovative Pedagogies and Technologies for Online Learning in Higher Education* (pp. 449–471). Hershey, PA: IGI Global. doi:10.4018/978-1-5225-1851-8.ch019

Tsvetkova, N., Antonova, A., & Hristova, P. (2017). Developing a Pedagogical Framework for Simulated Practice Learning: How to Improve Simulated Training of Social Workers who Interact with Vulnerable People. In P. Vu, S. Fredrickson, & C. Moore (Eds.), *Handbook of Research on Innovative Pedagogies and Technologies for Online Learning in Higher Education* (pp. 127–150). Hershey, PA: IGI Global. doi:10.4018/978-1-5225-1851-8.ch007

Varney, J. (2019). Effective Student-Advisor Engagement and Relationship Building in Online Graduate Programs. In K. Walters & P. Henry (Eds.), *Fostering Multiple Levels of Engagement in Higher Education Environments* (pp. 176–191). Hershey, PA: IGI Global. doi:10.4018/978-1-5225-7470-5.ch008

Veerabathina, N. (2019). Synchronous Learning in an Asynchronous Environment for Orientation, Intervention, Interaction, and Students Retention. In J. Yoon & P. Semingson (Eds.), *Educational Technology and Resources for Synchronous Learning in Higher Education* (pp. 71–87). Hershey, PA: IGI Global. doi:10.4018/978-1-5225-7567-2.ch004

Venkataraman, S., & Sharma, S. K. (2019). Educational Robotics in Smart Learning. In A. Darshan Singh, S. Raghunathan, E. Robeck, & B. Sharma (Eds.), *Cases on Smart Learning Environments* (pp. 244–255). Hershey, PA: IGI Global. doi:10.4018/978-1-5225-6136-1.ch014

Vu, L. (2017). A Case Study of Peer Assessment in a Composition MOOC: Students' Perceptions and Peer-grading Scores versus Instructor-grading Scores. In P. Vu, S. Fredrickson, & C. Moore (Eds.), *Handbook of Research on Innovative Pedagogies and Technologies for Online Learning in Higher Education* (pp. 178–217). Hershey, PA: IGI Global. doi:10.4018/978-1-5225-1851-8.ch009

Related Readings

Wang, S., & Hartsell, T. (2017). Perceived Factors Influencing Instructors' Use of E-Textbooks in Higher Education. *International Journal of Information and Communication Technology Education*, *13*(4), 87–97. doi:10.4018/IJICTE.2017100107

Warner, S. C. (2019). Infusing 21st Century Skills in a Smart Learning Environment for Secondary Mathematics Classrooms. In A. Darshan Singh, S. Raghunathan, E. Robeck, & B. Sharma (Eds.), *Cases on Smart Learning Environments* (pp. 99–116). Hershey, PA: IGI Global. doi:10.4018/978-1-5225-6136-1.ch007

Yi, S. (2019). Beyond Button Smashing: Utilizing Minecraft and Other Video Games as Synchronous Learning Tools for Science Learning. In J. Yoon & P. Semingson (Eds.), *Educational Technology and Resources for Synchronous Learning in Higher Education* (pp. 188–210). Hershey, PA: IGI Global. doi:10.4018/978-1-5225-7567-2.ch010

Young, C., DeMarco, C., Nyysti, K., Harpool, A., & Mendez, T. (2019). The Role of Faculty Development in Online Universities. In K. Walters & P. Henry (Eds.), *Fostering Multiple Levels of Engagement in Higher Education Environments* (pp. 260–275). Hershey, PA: IGI Global. doi:10.4018/978-1-5225-7470-5.ch012

Zheng, R. Z. (2018). Personalization With Digital Technology: A Deep Cognitive Processing Perspective. In R. Zheng (Ed.), *Digital Technologies and Instructional Design for Personalized Learning* (pp. 1–27). Hershey, PA: IGI Global. doi:10.4018/978-1-5225-3940-7.ch001

Zheng, R. Z., Dreon, O., Wang, Y., & Wang, S. (2018). College Students' Perceptions on the Role of Digital Technology and Personalized Learning: An International Perspective. In R. Zheng (Ed.), *Digital Technologies and Instructional Design for Personalized Learning* (pp. 229–252). Hershey, PA: IGI Global. doi:10.4018/978-1-5225-3940-7.ch011

Zukowska, J. J., & Sroczyński, Z. (2019). Advanced Human-Computer Interaction in E-Learning Systems for Handicapped People. In J. Pelet (Ed.), *Advanced Web Applications and Progressing E-Learning 2.0 Technologies in Higher Education* (pp. 172–202). Hershey, PA: IGI Global. doi:10.4018/978-1-5225-7435-4.ch009

About the Contributors

Shalin Hai-Jew works as an instructional designer at Kansas State University (K-State). She has taught at the university and college levels for many years (including four years in the People's Republic of China) and was tenured at Shoreline Community College but left tenure to pursue instructional design work. She has Bachelor's degrees in English and psychology, a Master's degree in Creative Writing from the University of Washington (Hugh Paradise Scholar), and an Ed.D in Educational Leadership with a focus on public administration from Seattle University (where she was a Morford Scholar). She tested into the University of Washington at 14. She reviews for several publishers and publications. She has worked on a number of instructional design projects, including public health, biosecurity, one health, mental health, PTSD, grain science, turfgrass management, social justice, and others. She has authored and edited a number of books. Hai-Jew was born in Huntsville, Alabama, in the U.S. Currently, she is working on multiple projects. Her instructional design and research work require a complex mix of knowledge, skills, methods, and technologies.

* * *

Ouhao Chen is currently a Lecturer/Research Scientist in National Institute of Education, Nanyang Technological University, Singapore. After completing his PhD in Educational Psychology, from the School of Education, University of New South Wales, Australia, he worked as a Post-doctoral Research Associate on MOOC project, in the School of Education, Southern Cross University, Australia. His main research interests are instructional design, cognitive load, math education and technology-based learning. Ouhao Chen has authored over 10 papers in the top journals of Educational Psychology.

Rebecca Curnalia is an Associate Professor in the Department of Communication at Youngstown State University.

About the Contributors

Amber Ferris (Ph.D., Kent State University) is an Associate Professor in the School of Communication at the University of Akron. Her research interests focus primarily on the uses and effects related to media and new technologies.

Slava Kalyuga is Professor of Educational Psychology at the School of Education, the University of New South Wales, where he received a Ph.D. His research interests are in cognitive processes in learning, cognitive load theory, and evidence-based instructional design principles. His specific contributions include detailed experimental studies of the role of learner prior knowledge in learning (expertise reversal effect); the redundancy effect in multimedia learning; the development of rapid online diagnostic assessment methods; and studies of the effectiveness of different adaptive procedures for tailoring instruction to levels of learner expertise. He is the author of four books and more than 130 research articles and chapters in these research areas.

Renee Kaufmann (Ph.D., University of Kentucky, 2014) is an assistant professor in the College of Communication and Information, School of Information Science at the University of Kentucky. Her research lines examine online learning in higher education and the use communication technologies for educational and relational outcomes.

Michael Strawser (PhD, University of Kentucky) is Assistant Professor and the Director of Graduate Programs in the School of Communication at Bellarmine University.

Index

2D Diagram 150
3D Diagram 150
4D Diagram 150

A

Alpha Testing 171, 182
atmospherics 66, 160

B

backwards curriculum design 68, 75, 77, 91-93, 103
beta testing 64, 171, 182
boutique 151-158, 160-163, 166
Boutique instructional design 152, 154, 161-162
Broad research 171

C

cognitive load theory 1-2, 5, 7-8, 10-11, 13-14, 16-18, 25
complex-skill capabilities 68, 75
content experts 123, 154-155
Continuance 66
curricular infusions 105-110, 112, 114-116, 118-119, 122-123
curriculum design 68-70, 72-75, 77, 91-93, 97, 103

D

deep research 168-169, 171
design/development 108, 116

differentiated instruction 59

F

formal/structured learning 68, 75, 92, 94, 103-104, 160
FUTURE PROJECTIONS 134, 140

G

Game Tree 134, 150
generational differences 47-49

H

human cognitive architecture 1-2, 8, 13, 18, 25

I

informal learning 68-70, 74-75, 77, 91, 94, 103
INITIAL SETUP 53, 59
instructional design 1-2, 4, 6-9, 27-28, 40-47, 49, 53, 61, 64, 72, 108, 119, 134-136, 140, 148, 151-155, 157-158, 161-163, 166, 168-177, 180-182
integrated learning paths 68, 76

L

learning preferences 42-43, 46, 49, 97, 169
learning styles 40, 42-43, 46-49
long-term memory 1-2, 13, 25, 57-58
Lossiness 66

Index

M

Millennials 40-45, 47-48
Monotemporal 137, 150

N

nonformal learning 69, 94, 104

P

Pluritemporal 137, 150
project post-mortem 172

R

Redundancy Effect 10, 25
resources depletion effect 2, 14, 17

S

Self-Directed Learning 28, 104
serialized 53-55, 57, 59-61, 64-65, 67
serialized online learning 53-55, 57, 59-61, 64-65
Spaced Practice Design (Spacing Effect) 1-2, 15-18, 25

Spatiality 150
Split-Attention Effect 25
subject matter experts 154, 168, 171, 178

T

timeline 134, 137-138, 141-142, 150

U

USES AND GRATIFICATIONS 27, 29

V

Visual Transitions 150

W

Worked Example Effect 8, 17, 25
working memory 1-2, 4-18, 25-26, 55, 57-58
working memory resources depletion 1-2, 14, 16-18, 26

Purchase Print, E-Book, or Print + E-Book

IGI Global's reference books can now be purchased from three unique pricing formats:
Print Only, E-Book Only, or Print + E-Book.
Shipping fees may apply.

www.igi-global.com

Recommended Reference Books

Preparing the Higher Education Space for Gen Z

ISBN: 978-1-5225-7763-8
© 2019; 253 pp.
List Price: $175

Assessment Practices and Pedagogical Models for Immigrant Students

ISBN: 978-1-5225-9348-5
© 2019; 454 pp.
List Price: $255

Prevention and Detection of Academic Misconduct in Higher Education

ISBN: 978-1-5225-7531-3
© 2019; 324 pp.
List Price: $185

Care and Culturally Responsive Pedagogy in Online Settings

ISBN: 978-1-5225-7802-4
© 2019; 423 pp.
List Price: $195

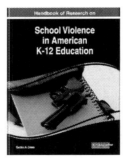

School Violence in American K-12 Education

ISBN: 978-1-5225-6246-7
© 2019; 610 pp.
List Price: $275

Critical Assessment and Strategies for Increased Student Retention

ISBN: 978-1-5225-2998-9
© 2018; 352 pp.
List Price: $195

Looking for free content, product updates, news, and special offers?
Join IGI Global's mailing list today and start enjoying exclusive perks sent only to IGI Global members.
Add your name to the list at **www.igi-global.com/newsletters**.

Publisher of Peer-Reviewed, Timely, and Innovative Academic Research

IGI Global
DISSEMINATOR of KNOWLEDGE

www.igi-global.com | Sign up at www.igi-global.com/newsletters | facebook.com/igiglobal | twitter.com/igiglobal

Ensure Quality Research is Introduced to the Academic Community

Become an IGI Global Reviewer for Authored Book Projects

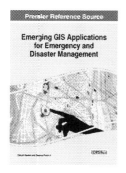
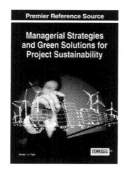

The overall success of an authored book project is dependent on quality and timely reviews.

In this competitive age of scholarly publishing, constructive and timely feedback significantly expedites the turnaround time of manuscripts from submission to acceptance, allowing the publication and discovery of forward-thinking research at a much more expeditious rate. Several IGI Global authored book projects are currently seeking highly-qualified experts in the field to fill vacancies on their respective editorial review boards:

Applications and Inquiries may be sent to:
development@igi-global.com

Applicants must have a doctorate (or an equivalent degree) as well as publishing and reviewing experience. Reviewers are asked to complete the open-ended evaluation questions with as much detail as possible in a timely, collegial, and constructive manner. All reviewers' tenures run for one-year terms on the editorial review boards and are expected to complete at least three reviews per term. Upon successful completion of this term, reviewers can be considered for an additional term.

If you have a colleague that may be interested in this opportunity, we encourage you to share this information with them.

IGI Global Proudly Partners With eContent Pro International

Receive a 25% Discount on all Editorial Services

Editorial Services

IGI Global expects all final manuscripts submitted for publication to be in their final form. This means they must be reviewed, revised, and professionally copy edited prior to their final submission. Not only does this support with accelerating the publication process, but it also ensures that the highest quality scholarly work can be disseminated.

English Language Copy Editing

Let eContent Pro International's expert copy editors perform edits on your manuscript to resolve spelling, punctuaion, grammar, syntax, flow, formatting issues and more.

Scientific and Scholarly Editing

Allow colleagues in your research area to examine the content of your manuscript and provide you with valuable feedback and suggestions before submission.

Figure, Table, Chart & Equation Conversions

Do you have poor quality figures? Do you need visual elements in your manuscript created or converted? A design expert can help!

Translation

Need your documjent translated into English? eContent Pro International's expert translators are fluent in English and more than 40 different languages.

Hear What Your Colleagues are Saying About Editorial Services Supported by IGI Global

"The service was very fast, very thorough, and very helpful in ensuring our chapter meets the criteria and requirements of the book's editors. I was quite impressed and happy with your service."

– Prof. Tom Brinthaupt,
Middle Tennessee State University, USA

"I found the work actually spectacular. The editing, formatting, and other checks were very thorough. The turnaround time was great as well. I will definitely use eContent Pro in the future."

– Nickanor Amwata, Lecturer,
University of Kurdistan Hawler, Iraq

"I was impressed that it was done timely, and wherever the content was not clear for the reader, the paper was improved with better readability for the audience."

– Prof. James Chilembwe,
Mzuzu University, Malawi

Email: customerservice@econtentpro.com   www.igi-global.com/editorial-service-partners

www.igi-global.com

Celebrating Over 30 Years of Scholarly Knowledge Creation & Dissemination

InfoSci®-Books

A Database of Over 5,300+ Reference Books Containing Over 100,000+ Chapters Focusing on Emerging Research

GAIN ACCESS TO **THOUSANDS** OF REFERENCE BOOKS AT **A FRACTION** OF THEIR INDIVIDUAL LIST **PRICE**.

InfoSci®-Books Database

The **InfoSci®-Books** database is a collection of over 5,300+ IGI Global single and multi-volume reference books, handbooks of research, and encyclopedias, encompassing groundbreaking research from prominent experts worldwide that span over 350+ topics in 11 core subject areas including business, computer science, education, science and engineering, social sciences and more.

Open Access Fee Waiver (Offset Model) Initiative

For any library that invests in IGI Global's InfoSci-Journals and/or InfoSci-Books databases, IGI Global will match the library's investment with a fund of equal value to go toward **subsidizing the OA article processing charges (APCs) for their students, faculty, and staff** at that institution when their work is submitted and accepted under OA into an IGI Global journal.*

INFOSCI® PLATFORM FEATURES

- No DRM
- No Set-Up or Maintenance Fees
- A Guarantee of No More Than a 5% Annual Increase
- Full-Text HTML and PDF Viewing Options
- Downloadable MARC Records
- Unlimited Simultaneous Access
- COUNTER 5 Compliant Reports
- Formatted Citations With Ability to Export to RefWorks and EasyBib
- No Embargo of Content (Research is Available Months in Advance of the Print Release)

*The fund will be offered on an annual basis and expire at the end of the subscription period. The fund would renew as the subscription is renewed for each year thereafter. The open access fees will be waived after the student, faculty, or staff's paper has been vetted and accepted into an IGI Global journal and the fund can only be used toward publishing OA in an IGI Global journal. Libraries in developing countries will have the match on their investment doubled.

To Learn More or To Purchase This Database:
www.igi-global.com/infosci-books

eresources@igi-global.com • Toll Free: 1-866-342-6657 ext. 100 • Phone: 717-533-8845 x100

www.igi-global.com